T0028758

RISING
FROM THE
ASHES

PAULA YOO

RISING
FROM THE
ASHES

**LOS ANGELES, 1992.
Edward Jae Song Lee,
Latasha Harlins, Rodney King,
and a City on Fire.**

NORTON YOUNG READERS
AN IMPRINT OF W. W. NORTON & COMPANY
INDEPENDENT PUBLISHERS SINCE 1923

For information about permission to reproduce selections from this book, write to
Permissions, W. W. Norton & Company, Inc., 500 Fifth Avenue, New York, NY 10110

For information about special discounts for bulk purchases, please contact
W. W. Norton Special Sales at specialsales@wwnorton.com or 800-233-4830

Manufacturing by Versa Press
Book design by Hana Anouk Nakamura
Production manager: Delaney Adams

ISBN 978-1-324-03090-4

W. W. Norton & Company, Inc., 500 Fifth Avenue, New York, N.Y. 10110
www.wwnorton.com

W. W. Norton & Company Ltd., 15 Carlisle Street, London W1D 3BS

1 2 3 4 5 6 7 8 9 0

CONTENTS

1   Intersection of Florence and Normandie Avenues, considered the flashpoint of the 1992 Los Angeles uprising

2   Empire Liquor Market and Deli, where Soon Ja Du shot and killed Latasha Harlins

3   Central Avenue, site of the first fatality of the Los Angeles uprising

4   Radio Korea

5   Parker Center, headquarters of the LAPD

6   Hannam Chain Market World, where security guard Patrick Bettan was shot and killed

7   Rodeo Galleria, site of a gun battle broadcast on live television

8   Pizza Go, site of Eddie Jae Song Lee's death

9   Intersection of 116th Street and Avalon Boulevard, flashpoint of the 1965 Watts rebellion

10   Lakeview Terrace, site of the beating of Rodney Glen King by LAPD officers

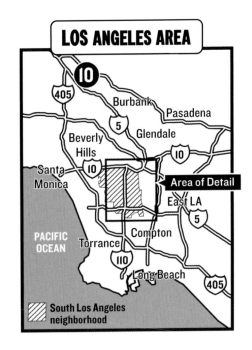

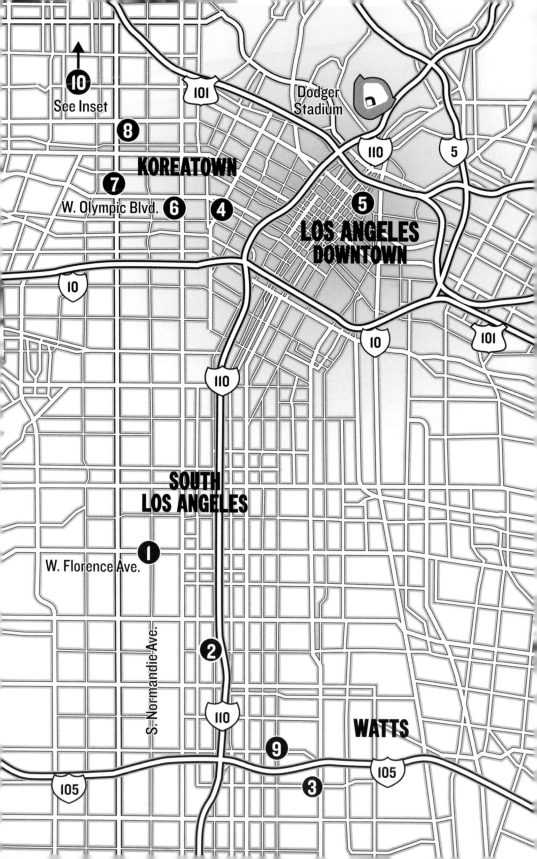

RISING FROM THE ASHES

Graffiti tags remind Los Angeles of its past, including references to the 1965 Watts uprising alongside the year 1992 and the names of Rodney King and Latasha Harlins.

An out-of-control fire destroys a Koreatown shopping mall on the corner of 6th Street and Western Avenue, leaving nothing but a skeletal frame.

"LOS ANGELES IS STILL ON EDGE"

"How can you sit there and not do anything?"

Edward "Eddie" Jae Song Lee was furious.

It was Thursday, April 30, 1992, and Los Angeles was on fire.

Especially Koreatown, where the Lee family lived. Los Angeles County boasted the largest Korean American population in the country, and this 2.9-square-mile neighborhood was its shining jewel.

The Lee family listened as Korean immigrant store owners, many of whom could not speak fluent English, begged Radio Korea 1540 AM reporters to call 911.

Oh my God, that's my store! It's burning.

I run a small sewing business. The shoe store right beneath us is completely destroyed.

Can someone come and help guard our store? We're being broken into.

Twenty-four hours earlier, a jury had acquitted all four Los Angeles Police Department officers in the previous year's beating of Rodney Glen King. On March 3, 1991, police pulled King over for speeding and suspected drunk driving. Under the orders of Sergeant Stacey Koon, LAPD officers Laurence Powell, Timothy Wind, and Theodore Briseno beat King with their batons, claiming he was resisting arrest, even though he was unarmed and lying on the ground. King suffered multiple injuries, including eleven fractures at the base of his skull, broken bones, shattered teeth, and temporary memory loss.

A bystander across the street recorded everything on his camcorder, later seen by millions all over the world.

It wasn't just the brutal violence of the video that shocked people. It was also the brutal image of an unarmed Black man being beaten by four police officers.

After the verdicts were announced, angry protesters gathered. The first fire broke out about 7:30 p.m.

By the next morning, eight people had been killed and hundreds injured. Police blocked off major freeways. Mail service was suspended. Concerts, sports games, and other events were canceled. A citywide curfew was imposed. The Los Angeles Unified School District closed its schools, including Fairfax High School, where Eddie's younger sister, Jenny Lee, seventeen, attended.

Mayor Tom Bradley declared a state of emergency. Governor Pete Wilson activated two thousand National Guard troops.

But the fires kept burning.

"And the agony continued long after the sun came up," declared one TV news reporter. "A full twenty-four hours after the stunning verdicts, Los Angeles is still on edge."

"Everything we have worked for is now in flames," a frustrated

Eddie told his family, who owned a luggage store in Koreatown. "How can we sit here and watch it happen? We Koreans should go out and protect our own."

Despite his mother's protests, Eddie stormed out.

• • •

But the verdict in the Rodney King case was not the only spark that lit the city on fire. Protesters who destroyed Korean-owned stores also shouted, "This is for Latasha!"

On March 16, 1991, just two weeks after the beating of Rodney King, store owner Soon Ja Du accused Latasha Harlins of shoplifting a bottle of orange juice. Du shot Latasha as she turned to leave the store. The fifteen-year-old girl died instantly, holding money in her hand.

Du was found guilty of manslaughter, not murder, and Judge Joyce Karlin shocked the city by sentencing Du to only five years' probation and a $500 fine.

Judge Joyce Karlin was white. Soon Ja Du was Korean American. Latasha Harlins was Black.

Latasha's death was still fresh in people's minds when the jury announced their "not guilty" verdicts in the LAPD–Rodney King trial.

• • •

The 1992 Los Angeles uprising lasted five days, causing 63 deaths and $1 billion in damages, including 2,300 Korean-owned stores destroyed.

But behind the vast numbers were the stories of people with much in common—and much to live for.

Especially those of three young people at the heart of this civil unrest:

Rodney Glen King, twenty-five, grew up fishing along the Sacramento River with his father, had a passion for music, and was a devoted L.A. Dodgers baseball fan.

Latasha Lavon Harlins, fifteen, was a high school honor roll student who wrote poetry, ran track, and dreamed of becoming a lawyer.

Edward Jae Song Lee, eighteen, was a college freshman who loved cars, rock 'n' roll oldies, and camping under the stars with his family.

Although they never met each other, their lives would forever be connected after the fires cooled.

On Friday, May 1, 1992, a heartbroken King came out of seclusion to issue a public statement.

"Can we all get along?" he asked.

It was a simple question that didn't have a simple answer.

Chapter 1

EDDIE

A Long Life

On May 24, 1974, Edward Jae Song Lee faced the biggest decision in his life so far.

Which object would he pick up?

It was Eddie's 돌 dol—his first birthday. Established around the eighteenth century when surviving one's first year was considered a milestone, Korean custom celebrated a baby's first birthday with an elaborate feast and a fortune-telling ceremony called the 돌잡이 doljabi.

Several objects were laid out before him, each one symbolizing his possible future. If Eddie picked up a book, he would become a scholar. A paintbrush? An artist. Money? Rich. And so on.

Eddie wore a traditional 한복 hanbok outfit of pink silk trousers and a green jacket with wide, rainbow-striped sleeves. His grandmother prepared sweet rice cakes and 미역국 miyeok guk,

A portrait of the Lee family in happier days. (Clockwise from the top left) Jenny, Eddie, Jung Hui, and Young Hi.

a Korean seaweed soup traditionally eaten on birthdays or after giving birth. Piles of fresh oranges, apples, pears, and persimmons symbolized prosperity.

To his parents' delight, Eddie grabbed a handful of 쌀국수 ssalguksu, rice noodles, from a bowl. His grandmother, who was visiting from Korea, had cooked them specially.

Eddie's mother, Jung Hui Lee, laughed as her son waved the noodles in the air. "I think he grabbed it because it was edible," she said, smiling.

Eddie Lee, wearing his traditional Korean dol first-birthday hanbok, with his father.

Noodles symbolized a long life.

Eddie's future was looking bright.

"We Came Here with Dreams"

Eddie was suspicious.

Where was his mom?

Once again, Jung Hui Lee had left for her nightly "meeting." Eddie had no idea where she had gone.

Eddie was now twelve years old. Ever since his father, Young Hi Lee, had moved temporarily back to Korea to start a new business venture, Eddie noticed 엄마 Umma, his mom, went out every night.

It was Eddie's duty to take care of his younger sister, Jenny, when their mother was gone. Even though they were only a year apart, Korean culture placed a huge emphasis on age hierarchy. It was customary for Koreans to address people slightly older than them as "Older Brother" and "Older Sister," even if they weren't related. Men referred to an "Older Brother" in Korean as 형 Hyung, and women referred to him as 오빠 Oppa.

Eddie took his role as Jenny's oppa very seriously. He made sure his sister did her homework. He cleaned the house and washed the laundry. Whenever their parents worked nights, he grilled hamburgers and microwaved Swanson's TV meals and frozen Stouffer's pizzas for dinner. Jenny, who had been diagnosed with the autoimmune disease lupus three years earlier, often lost her appetite during flare-ups. Eddie would playfully chase her around the house, making sure she at least ate some Korean dried-seaweed snacks.

"We knew how to fend for ourselves," said Jenny.

Like many Korean immigrants who moved to Los Angeles in the 1970s, the Lees opened a store. They worked twelve-hour days at a warehouse on Berendo Street selling suitcases, wallets, purses, and other travel items. They named their luggage import-export business ED Trading Company after Eddie. They drove to weekend swap meets to sell more wares. Jung Hui also worked part-time at a sewing factory.

"Mornings I worked in the sewing factory and came home by four in the afternoon," Jung Hui said. "My husband left for the night shift at six in the evening. So we raised our son as if we were passing a marathon baton. We did not want to put our son in the hands of strangers."

Eddie still found time to play games with his friends, many of them also Korean American. An active Cub Scout and popular student, Eddie loved roller skating, skateboarding, and playing tag and 다방구 dabanggu, a Korean childhood game that combined hide-and-seek with tag. On Saturdays he attended Korean school, and every year he showed off his taekwondo black-belt skills at the Los Angeles Korean Festival. He was so proud of his Korean heritage that he shared kimchi with his classmates at lunch in elementary school.

"We all loved him," remembered childhood friend James Kang. "He was a happy guy. If you were in a sad mood, he would be there to cheer you up."

"He was a take-charge kind of person," Jenny said. "He knew how to do a lot of things. When we went camping, he was the one to set up the tent. He knew how to fix cars. He was more hands-on, practical, and street smart."

Jenny admitted she was her oppa's opposite. "I was painfully shy, very timid," she said. But eventually, Eddie's outgoing personality inspired her to come out of her shell. "With my brother, I wasn't shy. I could speak up."

When Eddie finally asked his mother where she went every night, she told him, "You don't have to know."

But he was determined to find out Umma's secret. He snuck out one night and followed her on his bike. To his surprise, his mother entered a nearby bank. It was after hours.

"I wanted to save money for the future," Jung Hui explained. "So I cleaned the bank at night." But she kept this second job a secret from her family.

Eddie watched his mother empty a black leather bag filled with cleaning supplies. She dusted the windowsills, sanitized the counters, wiped down the desks. As she struggled to push the heavy vacuum cleaner, he rushed over, startling her.

"Mom, I'll do the vacuuming," he said, "so you can empty the trash cans and clean the desks."

Jung Hui's heart broke. Her son had discovered her secret. But their family needed the money from this job. She handed over the vacuum cleaner.

"He had a strong body," she said. "He vacuumed for me. We went from one place to another with that heavy vacuum cleaner."

Eventually, Eddie brought his sister along for these janitorial night shifts. "I just remember running around," she said. "My brother was, of course, more helpful than I was at emptying the trash, cleaning up, picking up stuff, tidying up."

When Jenny grew restless, Eddie entertained her by playing games with her. "We would do like hide-and-seek or tag, swing around in a swivel chair, stuff like that," she remembered.

Cleaning commercial buildings at night with her two young children was not part of Jung Hui's American dream. "I still feel pain in my chest when I think of those times," she said. "It hurts."

Her husband was also heartbroken when he returned from Korea to find his family doing night janitorial work. "It didn't make me feel good," he said quietly.

"We came to America to spread our young dreams," Jung Hui said, "to raise our future children. We were young and our dreams small, but we came here with dreams."

The Three Waves

Working around the clock, seven days a week, and even having their children help with the labor was the reality for many Korean immigrant families in America.

Korean immigration was divided into what is known as the Three Waves.

The First Wave was from 1903 to 1949. Until 1903, Koreans only visited America for education and diplomacy. In 1890, the first Korean to become an American citizen was Seo Jae-pil, who

(*Left*) Dosan Ahn Chang Ho, the prominent Korean politician–turned–migrant worker who established the first Korean American immigrant community in Riverside, California, in the early 1900s. Two of his sons, Philip and Ralph Ahn, became actors in Hollywood and his oldest daughter, Lieutenant Susan Ahn Cuddy, was the first female gunnery officer in the U.S. Navy.

(*Below*) Members of the Riverside Koreatown community.

sought political exile in Norristown, Pennsylvania, and changed his name to Dr. Philip Jaisohn. On January 13, 1903, the S.S. *Gaelic* arrived in Honolulu, Hawaii, with 102 Koreans (56 men, 21 women, and 25 children) to work on the islands' sugarcane plantations and establish permanent roots in America. January 13 is now known as Korean American Day to commemorate the arrival of these first families.

Other Korean immigrants entered the United States through places like Alaska, San Francisco's Angel Island, and the East Coast. In 1905, activist Dosan Ahn Chang Ho and his wife, Lee Hye-Ryeon (later known as Helen Ahn), established the first Korean American community in Riverside, California. The Ahns and hundreds of other Korean laborers worked in the orange groves. They settled by the railroad tracks in downtown Riverside in a place called Pachappa Camp. Records of this settlement were discovered in 2014 by University of California, Riverside, professor Edward Taehan Chang and his students, who confirmed that Pachappa Camp was the "first Koreatown in America."

The Ahns' oldest daughter, Susan Ahn Cuddy, joined the U.S. Navy and became the first female Asian American naval officer and its first female gunnery officer. Her younger sister, Soorah Ahn Buffum, was a successful restaurateur. All three sons, Philip, Ralph, and Philson, worked as actors in Hollywood, with Philson eventually becoming an engineer. Philip was the most prolific, playing more than 270 characters, including his most famous role as Master Kan in the popular 1970s *Kung Fu* TV series. Philip Ahn was the first Asian American actor to receive a star on the Hollywood Walk of Fame.

The Second Wave of six thousand Korean immigrants swept into America between 1950 and 1964, mostly students and teachers, doctors, lawyers, politicians, and entrepreneurs.

In 1945, shortly after gaining its independence from being

a Japanese colony, Korea was divided at the 38th parallel. The United States military occupied the southern part of the country until the formation of the Republic of Korea under the leadership of President Syngman Rhee on August 15, 1948. The Soviet Union backed Kim Il Sung, who formed the Democratic People's Republic of Korea in the north on September 9, 1948. But tensions between the countries flared, resulting in war on June 25, 1950, when North Korean troops invaded South Korea.

Eddie's mother vividly remembers when the bombing began. She and her six brothers fled to a friend's house.

"My brothers and I were in the middle of the mountains waiting for my parents to come back," she recalled. "They went down to the village to get our belongings. But we saw the bombs fall and the village was burning. We were terrified and thought that my friends had died. We all cried and just stood there and watched." To this day, Jung Hui still has vivid flashbacks of the war. "Even now, when I hear the sound of rebar pounding the ground at an apartment building construction, I feel my whole body shrinking and collapsing."

Jung Hui's family soon reunited and hid in the mountains for the next six months. On December 31, 1950, the Chinese army, allies of North Korea, attacked Seoul. Three days later, the U.S. Army evacuated the city.

On January 4, 1951, Jung Hui and her family were among the thousands who fled by boat to the Chungcheong province south of Seoul in a massive evacuation known as 일사후퇴 Il Sa Hoo Tae, the January 4th Retreat.

"It was so cold since it was wintertime," Jung Hui remembered. "I was wearing a coat made out of a thick blanket. I had terrible seasickness."

The fighting stopped with a bitter truce on July 27, 1953, when both countries, neither one admitting defeat, signed the Korean Armistice Agreement. More than 36,000 American soldiers were killed and 100,000 wounded, along with 100,000 casualties for United Nations forces and 900,000 Chinese soldiers killed. Two to three million Korean civilians are estimated to have been killed. These numbers mark the Korean War as one of the deadliest conflicts of the Cold War era.

Although there have been intermittent talks about reunification, for over seventy years the two countries, South Korea and North Korea, have remained technically at war and divided at the 38th parallel. Known as the Demilitarized Zone, or DMZ, it is considered one of the most heavily fortified borders in the world.

After the war, Jung Hui's father developed a chronic illness. While her mother worked to support the family, all the house chores fell on Jung Hui's shoulders as the only daughter in the family. Her back ached and her hands cracked and bled from constantly cleaning, starching, and ironing her brother's school uniforms, along with sweeping and mopping the house and cooking meals for the whole family. "I could not hang out with friends after school," she said. "I had no freedom." After her father died and her grandmother was diagnosed with stomach cancer, Jung Hui put aside her dreams of college. She stayed home as the caregiver.

In 1971, after her grandmother died, Jung Hui, by then twenty-seven, met her future husband, Young Hi Lee, thirty-five, a salesman at a musical instrument store. They married and moved to America the following year, two among the 299,000 Koreans who immigrated to the United States between 1965 and 1980, after President Lyndon B. Johnson signed the Immigration and Nationality Act of 1965. This group was known as the Third Wave.

In 1960, 84 percent of immigrants to the United States were

born in Europe or Canada. Only 3.8 percent were from Asia, and this low percentage was similar for non-white immigrants from Mexico, Latin America, Africa, and other parts of the world. The Immigration and Nationality Act of 1965 overhauled the restrictive and racist federal quota system for non-white immigrants outside of Europe. After it was signed into law, annual immigration increased dramatically to almost a half million people per year, with only 20 percent from Europe.

By 1970, 63 percent of the Third Wave Korean immigrants—including Eddie Lee's family—had settled in Southern California and would create one of the largest Korean American communities in America. A decade later, "Koreatown" was designated as an official neighborhood in Los Angeles County, with its own Koreatown sign installed in 1982 at the Normandie exit off the Santa Monica 10 freeway.

"The Happiest Time"

Growing up, Eddie's life wasn't always hard work. The Lee family loved camping at Kings Canyon National Park, 250 miles north of Los Angeles, hiking under the canopy of the giant Sequoia trees and swimming in nearby streams. Eddie, an avid outdoorsman, helped set up the tent and grilled 갈비 galbi short ribs marinated in soy sauce, and roasted marshmallows by the campfire.

"He loved fishing too," Jung Hui remembered. "When we planned family camping, he prepared everything, including food, so my husband and I just went alongside. He was a born leader."

Jung Hui had high hopes for her ambitious son. After all, anything was possible in America. She believed that from the first day she arrived in America.

As Jung Hui and her husband's flight landed at the Los Angeles International Airport on April 14, 1972, she stared in awe at the

Eddie was a protective and loving 오빠 Oppa (big brother) to his younger sister, Jenny. "We were very close when we were younger," Jenny remembered. "So we're like either cuddling each other or we're right next to each other with our arms around each other. I was always very proud of him being my brother. We were close."

massive sprawl of freeways below. You could drive anywhere in Southern California on these endless roads, from the beaches to the mountains to the vast desert in between.

Even more impressive?

"Trees," Jung Hui said, smiling at the memory. "I arrived in April. Flowers were all over. When I was picked up from the airport, going on the freeway, I saw the trees on the side of the road."

Jung Hui marveled at the trim, green, manicured lawns outside rows of single-story houses with Spanish-tiled rooftops. "One more cool thing was the water sprinklers," she exclaimed. "That was so cool. It was fantastic."

What most Americans took for granted, from lawn sprinklers to massive, tree-lined freeways, was a miracle for Jung Hui.

"When I left Korea, everything was destroyed after the war," she explained. "So the highways in America were very impressive to me. It was amazing. What was most beautiful to me was the clean and orderly cities because Korea was still in shambles. Everything there was still a mess. America was very different. When I look back, this was probably the happiest time."

But Jung Hui and other Korean immigrants would soon learn that like the Demilitarized Zone that divided Korea, the L.A. freeways were their own borders, separating the city into separate—and unequal—worlds.

Rodney Glen King, at his home in Rialto, California, gazes at two milestones in his life: childhood, and the May 1, 1992, press conference during the Los Angeles uprising when he asked for peace.

Chapter 2
GLEN

Saturday, March 2, 1991:
"We Had No Definite Destination in Mind"

Rodney Glen King was in a good mood.

The twenty-five-year-old Glen, as his family and friends called him, was hanging out with his friends Bryant "Pooh" Allen, also twenty-five, and Freddie Helms, twenty-one, in Altadena, a Los Angeles suburb. They cheered and raised their beers as the Clippers, a local basketball team, beat the Minnesota Timberwolves 104 to 102 on TV.

Afterward, they hung outside, drinking and listening to music on the radio. Glen, who dreamed of starting his own music company one day, freestyle rapped along with some original beats.

The music reminded Glen of how he used to sing with his friends from high school at one of his favorite parks. Glen loved nature. As a child, he swam at the local watering hole near the

Devil's Gate Dam in Pasadena with his brothers. He fished with his dad, Ronald King, in the Sacramento River and at the Hansen Dam in Lakeview Terrace. He played baseball in high school and loved skiing on nearby Mt. Baldy.

Glen suggested they go out for a drive. "We had no definite destination in mind but talked about checking out a park where my father and I used to hang out."

Helms sat in the front seat of Glen's five-door, white 1987 Hyundai Excel, Allen in the back. They drove west on Interstate 210, the Foothill Freeway, passing by Glen's childhood hangout, the Devil's Gate Dam.

It was just before midnight on a Saturday, and traffic was light. The speed limit was seventy miles per hour, but Glen didn't keep track of his speedometer. "Trouble is, after a few miles at that speed, ninety starts to feel like eighty," he later said.

He pressed down on the gas pedal.

Redlining

Los Angeles County is a seemingly endless maze of more than 515 miles of freeway. But many Los Angeles residents did not know about their insidious history.

If you looked at a map of Los Angeles from the 1940s, chances are you could accurately predict where most Black and other communities of color resided.

They lived in the red zones.

These colorful maps, splashed with green, blue, yellow, and red hues, revealed an ugly picture. Each colored grid reflected a certain rating of safety and "desirability." The green, blue, and yellow zones were considered the "best" areas, with green representing the most desirable neighborhoods. The red areas were considered the least desirable. The zones were drawn following

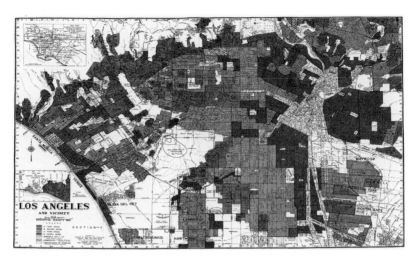

A typical "redlining" map of Los Angeles from 1939. Colored grids signified a neighborhood's "desirability" and led to racial segregation.

the passage of the National Housing Act of 1934. The availability of mortgage loans to buy houses depended on the zone, with few loans available in the red zones, and racist real estate rules called "covenants" prohibited Black people from buying houses in the desired green, blue, and yellow zones.

Like the Three Waves of Korean immigration, the Black exodus to California came in a wave known as the Great Migration. From 1910 to 1970, six million Black people left the American South to escape Jim Crow segregation laws, all-white "sundown towns" that prohibited the presence of Blacks and other people of color at night, and the threat of lynching for the promise of a better—and equal—life elsewhere. Due to a shortage of workers during World War II, California's steel and iron works plants hired Black workers for the first time. L.A.'s Black population boomed from 63,000 in 1940 to 350,000 by 1965, making up 14 percent of the city's population.

But Black residents soon discovered the Ku Klux Klan existed even in sunny California. During the 1920s, the state was home to the second largest number of KKK chapters in the country, with many members in law enforcement, including police chiefs and judges.

Redlining and the existence of housing covenants also forced many new Black residents to the city's "red" zones. As Black families moved in, white families moved out. This "white flight" turned Watts, Compton, and other areas in South Los Angeles (originally called South Central L.A.) into mostly Black neighborhoods. At first, some of these neighborhoods prospered, especially the West Adams district. In fact, one street there was even nicknamed Sugar Hill after the famous New York City neighborhood that flourished during the Harlem Renaissance of the 1920s. Three thousand miles away, legendary Black Hollywood stars like Academy Award winner Hattie McDaniel and entertainer Bill "Bojangles" Robinson moved into West Adams's stately mansions and held lavish parties.

In 1945, housing covenants were ruled unconstitutional after civil rights attorney Loren Miller successfully argued that they violated the Fourteenth Amendment, which granted citizenship to all people born or naturalized in the United States—including formerly enslaved people and their descendants. Racist housing covenants and Whites Only property signs were now illegal in California. But city planners soon discovered it was easier and more cost-effective to build a giant freeway through a red zone instead of the more expensive green, blue, and yellow zones. And it was legal.

Thousands of houses in the red zones were bulldozed to make way for massive freeways so mostly white motorists had easier access to stores and parks instead of having to drive through the red zones.

Even Sugar Hill and West Adams did not survive. City planners split the affluent neighborhood in half with the construction of Interstate 10, the Santa Monica Freeway, which led to the ocean. Despite the area's Black Hollywood movie-star residents, officials claimed this decision was for "slum clearance."

California's freeways kept segregation alive by dividing Los Angeles County along racial lines. Like the demilitarized zone separating North and South Korea at the 38th parallel after the Korean War, Los Angeles now had its own versions of the DMZ.

The 10. The 405. The 110.

And the 210. Built in 1964, the Foothill Freeway snaked past the Devil's Gate Dam, splitting white and Black neighborhoods in Pasadena where Glen grew up.

And on Sunday, March 3, 1991, Rodney Glen King ended up on the "wrong" side of this border.

"Pull Over!"

It was now after midnight. Glen and his friends flew down the 210 freeway.

Glen also felt like he was flying in life. He was due to start a new construction job on Monday, the perfect gift for his twenty-sixth birthday, just one month away.

Up ahead, California Highway Patrol officer Melanie Singer and her husband, CHP partner Timothy "Tim" Singer, were also on the 210.

Officer Melanie Singer spotted a white Hyundai Excel race by, swerving erratically. Three Black men sat in the car. Only the driver was wearing his seatbelt.

The Singers, who were white, chased the car down the 210.

But Glen and Allen were singing along to De La Soul blasting from the radio, while Helms had fallen asleep in the back. None of them heard the sirens.

Glen finally glanced up at the rearview mirror and saw the flashing red lights. He instinctively pressed his foot down on the gas pedal.

Allen stopped singing. "Rodney, why don't you pull over?" he asked, alarmed.

Glen had recently been released from the California Correctional Center on good behavior after serving the first year of a two-year sentence for second-degree robbery at a grocery store in Monterey. His parole agent, Tim Fowler, said King was remorseful for his actions and that the store owner had forgiven him. "He was unemployed and untrained," Fowler said. "It was spur of the moment. The opportunity was there. He recognizes it was stupid."

Glen had been on parole for two months. He had recently remarried and had a loving relationship with his two young daughters and two stepsons from previous relationships. His new job started tomorrow.

Instead of slowing down, Glen hit a hundred miles per hour.

"Pull over!" Allen shouted.

Helms woke up, startled by the red flashing lights and wailing sirens. "They seen three Black guys in the car," Helms said, wondering if the police might pull them over and "beat the mess out of them. I was scared."

So was Glen. "I was scared of going back to prison," he said. "I just kind of thought the problem would just go away."

Glen tried to outrun the police. The Los Angeles police had a bad reputation—especially with young Black men.

The Thin Blue Line

In April 1952, *The Thin Blue Line* debuted on KNBH, L.A.'s NBC affiliate TV station. The show's creator, LAPD chief William

LAPD chief William H. Parker (left) and Mayor Sam Yorty (center) at the 1962 Los Angeles Police Academy graduation ceremony.

H. Parker III, and a panel of experts answered questions about law enforcement in an attempt to increase the public's faith in its police department.

At the time, the LAPD had a reputation as one of the most corrupt police departments in the country. Parker had vowed he would rid the city of the "crooked rats who would change the City of Angels into the City of Diablos."

Parker wanted to change the image of the LAPD: they were no longer corrupt and racist; they were your friendly neighborhood cops, risking their lives every day to stop crime and keep L.A. safe. He believed the police represented a "thin blue line" protecting a civilized society from crime and chaos.

The U.S. Commission on Civil Rights disagreed. In January 1960, they held hearings in L.A. to investigate multiple accusations of racial bias and abuse by the LAPD against the city's communities of color. Black suspects in Los Angeles were disproportionately arrested at a much higher rate than white suspects. For example, in 1959, a judge challenged the LAPD for arresting 12,000 Black suspects on gambling charges versus only 1,200 white suspects in a two-year period.

The department's biggest race scandal took place on December 25, 1951, when several police officers, drunk at an office Christmas party, brutally beat five Mexican American men and two white men who were in jail for alleged underage drinking and resisting arrest. It was so violent that the blood of these young men, all of them in their early twenties, covered the walls. They suffered broken bones and ruptured organs.

For the first time in the LAPD's history, multiple officers were criminally convicted for excessive force. Eight were indicted on state charges, but only five were ultimately convicted. Chief Parker suspended forty officers without pay.

But during the 1960 civil rights commission hearings, Chief Parker, then fifty-five, bristled at charges of racism in the LAPD, especially on his watch.

He reminded the commission that the LAPD was the first police department in the country to hire a Black officer, in 1886, followed by the first Black firefighter and the first Black policewoman. The LAPD had also appointed the country's first Asian American police officer in 1913—Chinese American Lung Yep—prompted by L.A.'s growing Chinatown population. In 1943 the LAPD promoted its first Mexican American captain and started Spanish-language classes for all officers.

"There is no segregation or integration problem in this community," Parker testified. He wondered why no one was speaking up for the police. More than two thousand officers were injured in the line of duty in 1958. "There is no one concerned about the civil rights of the policeman. And that is a real problem."

Chief Parker was proud of modernizing the LAPD with its state-of-the-art crime laboratory. He was ahead of his time with promotion, creating clever advertising campaigns to win back the public's confidence. Dull LAPD annual statistics reports were revamped into colorful brochures. Fashion shows promoted the LAPD's female officers. He invited the press to do "ride-alongs" with patrol officers. He even started a "public information division" where officers brainstormed positive story ideas and sent press releases to the media.

But Parker's biggest influence in rehabilitating the LAPD's public image was creating two TV shows in the early 1950s—*The Thin Blue Line* and *Dragnet*—with his speechwriter Gene Roddenberry, who had joined the police force in 1949. *Dragnet* reenacted real-life LAPD cases, each episode opening with the LAPD sergeant's badge on-screen as a narrator announced, "Ladies and gentlemen, the story you are about to see is true. The names have been changed to protect the innocent."

In 1957, Roddenberry retired from the LAPD and created the now-classic science fiction TV series *Star Trek*. Roddenberry modeled the character of Mr. Spock, the pointy-eared Vulcan alien character known for his logic and suppressed emotion, after Chief Parker. But all this positive publicity about Parker's "thin blue line" protecting the public did not seem to match up to what Black and other residents of color were experiencing in real life.

William Bratton, LAPD chief of police from 2002 to 2009, believed Parker's "legendary 'thin blue line' comment" did not only mean separating an orderly society from disorder.

"Most people think he was referring to the thin blue line between anarchy and chaos," Bratton said. "But what Parker was talking about was keeping them—the minorities—away from everybody else."

The War on Drugs

"Just Say No!"

"This is your brain on drugs."

In the 1980s the administration of President Ronald Reagan declared a "War on Drugs" that included the "Just Say No" educational campaign in schools, anti-drug advertising campaigns, and legislation such as the Anti-Drug Abuse Act of 1986 with its much harsher mandatory minimum sentences for drug offenses.

This wasn't the first time the government had waged a war against drugs. President Richard Nixon had first coined the "war on drugs" phrase after signing the Comprehensive Drug Abuse Prevention and Control Act of 1970 to provide more drug addiction rehabilitation programs and stricter drug enforcement laws. Nixon condemned drug abuse as "America's public enemy number one."

This war, however, disproportionately impacted Black communities during the 1970s. Black suspects were arrested at twice the rate of white suspects for drug-related offenses. By 1991, Black suspects made up 41 percent of all drug arrests, even though 84 percent of drug users were white while only 15 percent were Black.

And then a new drug emerged. Crack cocaine.

Although no one knows its exact origins, crack cocaine's roots go as deep as 1976, when a group of chemistry students at the University of California, Berkeley, developed a simple recipe to dissolve cocaine powder with water and baking soda, then boil it down into pebble-sized "rocks." Instead of inhaling powdered cocaine, users lit these "rocks" in a glass pipe, smoking it for an immediate rush.

Crack turned out to be more potent and addictive, producing an immediate euphoria. This powerful addiction made users willing to risk another hit despite crack's dangerous side effects of anxiety, convulsions, and even heart attacks and respiratory failure.

And crack was cheap. This drug sold for only $10 to $20 per ounce compared to prices as high as $5,000 per ounce of powdered cocaine, making crack more accessible to a larger population.

"It is as though McDonald's had invented the opium den," said one neuroscientist at Yale Medical School.

Drug traffickers and gangs could barely keep up with the demand. Competition to sell crack tripled the number of gangs in L.A. from 45 in 1978 to 151 in 1982. By 1984, five "cookhouses" existed in South Central L.A. to manufacture crack cocaine, making millions of dollars in profit. One Los Angeles–based drug trafficker, Rickey Donnell "Freeway Rick" Ross, made $900 million in less than ten years.

Los Angeles became known as the "crack capital of the world."

To combat what was being called a "crack epidemic," President Reagan signed the 1986 Anti-Drug Abuse Act into law, creating new federal mandatory minimum prison sentences for illegal drug use. But the punishment for the selling or buying of crack cocaine was a hundred times harsher than for powder cocaine. Possession of 5 grams of crack cocaine resulted in a minimum of five years in prison without parole compared to 500 grams of powder cocaine. As a result, the average federal drug sentence for Black offenders in 1986 was 11 percent higher than for white offenders. Within four years, that gap increased to 49 percent.

By 1989, President George H. W. Bush addressed the nation on live television about America's "gravest domestic threat," holding up a bag of crack cocaine that had just been seized by authorities from a park across from the White House. "It's as innocent looking as candy," he said. "But it's turning our cities into battle zones."

For Police Chief Daryl F. Gates, this truly was a war. He established Operation Hammer to round up gang members suspected of dealing drugs. The LAPD used six-ton armored tanks with fourteen-foot-long steel battering rams to smash down doors of suspected crack cookhouses. LAPD helicopters hovered over mostly Black neighborhoods. When police pulled over Black youth for minor driving infractions, they also frisked them for drugs.

The LAPD also offered incentive rewards for officers to bust up drug trafficking. Police often profiled young Black men for minor, nonviolent crimes in order to find out if they were also in possession of crack cocaine. Black celebrities were also harassed by the police, including Los Angeles Laker basketball player and former Rookie of the Year, Jamaal Wilkes, who later filed a complaint after being briefly pulled over and handcuffed "because I was an African American driving a Trans Am."

Operation Hammer fostered more resentment and distrust between the Black community and the LAPD. Even though 66 percent of crack users were white or Latino, more than 80 percent of those arrested and sentenced for crack offenses were Black. "People ask why Black people don't trust (public) institutions," explained Roland G. Fryer, an economics professor at Harvard University who studied crack cocaine's impact on the Black community. "It's because we have watched how we've treated opioids—it's a public health concern. But crack (cocaine) was, 'lock them up and throw away the key, what we need is tougher sentencing.'"

The Watch Commander

On Saturday, March 2, 1991, Sergeant Stacey C. Koon arrived early for his 11:00 p.m. night shift as the watch commander for the

LAPD Foothill Station. His schedule included leading a training session for his officers.

For that night's session, Koon was supposed to teach rookies how to use the PR 24 baton effectively on suspects resisting arrest by using "power strokes" to incapacitate but not permanently injure a suspect. Rookies practiced by hitting a wooden post wrapped in rubber tires.

Instead, Koon, forty-one, postponed roll call and training to catch up on some routine paperwork. He was eager to hit the streets. Unlike other officers who wanted to move up the ladder, the fourteen-year veteran Koon preferred walking the beat in "the war zone." "My real love was working the streets, especially during the morning watch from 11 PM to 7 AM," he said. "That's when you get the opportunity to put bad guys in jail. And that's what I liked doing."

Koon graduated with degrees in criminal justice and public administration from California State University, Los Angeles, and the University of Southern California. He originally wanted to become an economist, so he worked at a bank before joining the Air Force in 1971. He entered the LAPD Police Academy in August 1976, graduating twelfth in his class.

"Ninety-five percent of the people in this world are wholesome, contributing members of society," Koon believed, and the other five percent needed to be in jail "so they can't do harm to themselves" or others.

As Koon finished his paperwork, Highway Patrol officers Melanie and Tim Singer were in hot pursuit of the runaway Hyundai, which had reached speeds up to 115 miles per hour, according to their radar. Two more squad cars joined them, along with an LAPD helicopter spotlighting the white car from the sky. They were now two miles from the Foothill Station.

Officer Tim Singer's voice crackled across the radio. "We're southbound on Foothill from Van Nuys . . ."

Koon knew by their confused directions that the cop couple was lost.

He rushed to his squad car to assist them.

"You Won't Get Hurt"

A panicked Glen ignored his friends' shouts to pull over. He couldn't afford to be caught breaking his parole so soon after he had gotten his life back together.

He spotted the exit sign for Paxton Avenue. He made a sharp right across three lanes of traffic.

The Singers immediately followed the Hyundai down the off-ramp.

"By now the chase was in the Foothill Division of the LAPD," Koon said. "It was my territory." The Hyundai was near the Hansen Dam Recreation Park, which Koon considered a "very bad area" because of the many drug deals and violent encounters that had taken place there over the years.

Glen raced through the dimly lit suburban streets of Lakeview Terrace, tailed by several squad cars, including those driven by the Singers and now Koon. As he approached the intersection of Foothill Boulevard and Osborne Street near the Hansen Dam, a red truck pulled out, blocking the road.

Glen slammed on his brakes just in time, mere inches away from the truck.

The Singers reached Glen's car first.

Officers Laurence Powell, twenty-eight, and his partner, rookie cop Timothy Wind, thirty, soon arrived, followed by veteran Theodore Briseno, thirty-eight, and his probationary partner.

Koon's was the third squad car to arrive. He glanced around the "very bad area" by the Hansen Dam Park entrance across from a gas station and liquor store. Just down the street stood the Corral, a popular saloon that had recently been used as a location for the filming of the 1991 blockbuster movie *Terminator 2: Judgment Day*.

It was now 12:50 a.m. on Sunday, March 3, 1991. The fifteen-minute chase had finally ended.

What happened next would set Los Angeles on fire.

But it was not the first time.

August 11, 1965: "Burn, Baby, Burn!"

Marquette Frye swerved to avoid a pothole.

It was August 11, 1965, four months after Rodney Glen King was born.

Around 7:00 p.m., Marquette, twenty-one, and his stepbrother Ronald Frye, twenty-two, flew down Avalon Boulevard in their mother's 1955 Buick Special after hanging out at a nearby bar. They were heading back home to Watts for a family dinner.

But California Highway Patrol officer Lee W. Minikus pulled them over on the corner of South Avalon and 116th Street on suspicion of drunk driving. Marquette failed a sobriety test.

"I was just doing my job," Minikus said. "That's why we got paid: to arrest people breaking the law. Marquette was breaking the law."

The traffic stop started out peacefully. Marquette, still in a good mood, cracked a few jokes about drinking and trying to avoid that pothole. Officer Minikus laughed. He allowed Ronald to get their mother, Rena Price, because they lived just two blocks away.

A small crowd of curious onlookers gathered.

Demonstrators swarm a police car in Watts on August 12, 1965, during six days of civil unrest after a confrontational traffic stop of a young Black motorist by white police officers.

When Rena and Ronald returned, Rena berated her son for drunk driving. The two argued. His good mood gone, Marquette suddenly refused to comply with the police.

More police arrived as backup. As the crowd doubled in size, Marquette tried to escape, but another officer hit him with his baton. Marquette ducked, so the officer's baton struck him in the head instead, drawing blood.

Ronald rushed over to defend his brother. Witnesses later claimed some of the cops called Rena a "bitch" and shouted racist slurs at them. When another cop accidentally pushed Rena down, her sons attacked him. Rena jumped on top of the officer's back.

At this point, the crowd had swelled to over two hundred witnesses.

The police handcuffed Marquette, Roland, and Rena and put them in the patrol car. The crowd booed.

It was only 7:45 p.m. when someone threw a bottle at the patrol cars as the police left with the Frye family. More bottles and rocks followed. As the night progressed, some demonstrators pulled civilian motorists out of their cars and beat them. Others smashed store windows and set the buildings on fire. Firefighters arriving at the scene ducked bullets as they tried to control the fires.

In a desperate attempt to save their businesses, Black store owners placed handwritten signs in their windows that said "Negro-Owned," "Spare Us," and "Pass Me By."

Marquette's arrest was the match that had ignited a long-simmering anger over decades of police brutality and systemic racism against the Black community.

"Burn, baby, burn!" protesters shouted.

Meanwhile, Minikus had no idea what had erupted. He booked Marquette Frye for drunk driving and put him in jail overnight. Marquette was later found guilty of drunk driving, battery, and property damage. Despite their argument of self-defense, Ronald and Rena were found guilty of interfering with a police officer. Both brothers each received three years' probation, and Rena had to pay a $250 fine.

As Minikus headed to the parking lot after work that night, a group of reporters surrounded him.

"Did you know you started a riot?" a reporter asked.

Minikus realized he was not going home. He ended up working for the next five days straight, trying to stop the civil unrest that some people felt was partially his fault.

. . .

The civil unrest in Watts, later referred to as the Watts rebellion or uprising, lasted from August 11 to 16, 1965. The governor ordered an 8:00 p.m. curfew, and 13,900 National Guard troops with almost 2,000 law enforcement officers were called in. There was more than $40 million in damage, with 1,032 people injured and 3,438 arrested.

Thirty-four people were killed.

On August 17, 1965, civil rights activist Dr. Martin Luther King Jr. visited Watts. He declared that the "economic deprivation, racial isolation, inadequate housing, and general despair" forced upon the Black community had planted the seeds of this protest.

Although Dr. King believed "violence is not the answer to social conflict," he called out for everyone to take personal responsibility and accountability for the civil unrest sweeping the nation. He vowed to work with community leaders to create resources to end racism and prevent the need for future uprisings.

"I humbly request that all of us accept our share of responsibility for these [past] days of anguish," he said.

• • •

Marquette Frye never fully recovered from the Watts rebellion. He struggled with pressure over the years from both the Black and white communities to be a role model. He claimed police harassed him because of his past, arresting him more than thirty times for minor offenses and saying to him, "You're the guy who started the Watts Riots."

Seeking privacy and peace, Marquette switched back to his birth name of Marquette Price. When he died of pneumonia on December 20, 1986, the coroner could not identify him because of that name change. It took four days until officials realized he was *the* Marquette Frye. He was only forty-two years old.

"I'm no villain, I'm no hero," Marquette insisted. "I was just another brother on the street."

On August 12, 1965, when a friend bailed him out of jail, Marquette had no idea that protests had broken out after his arrest. As they drove home, he looked in horror at the destruction as people shouted, "Viva Marquette!"

"I could see the smoke from the freeway," Marquette remembered. "It looked like somebody had dropped a bomb. I heard on the radio about how many people had died and then I started to cry."

March 3, 1991:
"I Didn't Know Why They Were So Mad"

On March 3, 1991, twenty-six years after Officer Lee Minikus arrested Marquette Frye, CHP officers Melanie and Tim Singer had no idea their traffic stop with Rodney Glen King would become just as historic.

"Get out of the vehicle!" Officer Tim Singer shouted through the loudspeaker. "Hands up. Get on your stomach. Put your hands behind your back. Now!"

But Glen and his friends couldn't hear anything. Not with the shrill feedback and static from the loudspeaker, the nonstop police sirens, and the roar of the helicopter.

Tim Singer approached the white Hyundai on foot. He shouted his commands again.

Allen and Helms immediately got out of the car.

Two officers ordered Allen and Helms to lie face down on the ground and handcuffed their hands behind their backs.

But Glen was still in the car.

The police grew suspicious. *What was he up to?*

It turned out Glen was struggling to take off his seatbelt. He finally yanked it off and emerged from the driver's side to face what looked like an army.

Eleven additional LAPD units had joined the chase. Almost fifty cops now surrounded Glen.

"Put your hands up where we can see them!" Officer Melanie Singer shouted. "Take three steps back and lay down. Spread your arms and legs apart."

King later admitted he was surprised to see the "police lady." Distracted by the noise and chaos, a confused Glen instead knelt down on all fours.

But the "police lady" was not amused. A high school track star who had won a four-year athletic college scholarship, Singer had a reputation for her "good sense of right and wrong" after joining the California Highway Patrol in 1989. Later in court, she testified that Glen looked "almost happy, jovial, smiling," as if he did not understand the gravity of the situation. "He was dancing around. . . . He was smiling at me as he got down on all fours and paraded around."

"Knock it off!" Melanie pulled out her gun. So did the other cops.

Sergeant Koon stepped forward to deescalate the confrontation. "By drawing her gun, [she] was unnecessarily raising the level of force," he explained. "That's when I got involved. I had to. It was a dangerous situation."

"Put your guns away!" Koon shouted.

At first, Glen was relieved when he saw Sergeant Koon. "When I seen the stripes on the guy's arm, I thought everything was going to be under control," he said.

Instead, Koon also yelled at Glen. "Spread your legs apart and lay down! I mean it! I mean it!"

It dawned on Glen that he might be in danger. "I didn't know why they were so mad. I thought, they want to blow my fucking brains out, man."

But Koon claimed he thought Glen, at 6 feet, 3 inches, and 225 pounds, was the danger, not the other way around. Glen appeared to be disobeying orders, making Koon suspect he might be a "dusted suspect," meaning high on PCP (phencyclidine), a powerful and illegal hallucinogen.

But Glen had no PCP or other hard drugs in his system. Blood and urine tests taken five hours after his arrest revealed traces of marijuana and that his blood-alcohol level was 0.079 percent, just below the legal limit of 0.08 percent in California.

Koon ordered Powell to subdue the suspect. Although both men were around the same age and size, Powell was at a disadvantage. He had recently switched shifts to the morning watch and had not yet adjusted to his new sleep schedule. Minutes before

A still from the March 31, 1991, video shot by George Holliday from the balcony of his apartment showing LAPD officers beating an unarmed Rodney Glen King with batons while other officers stand and watch.

joining the chase, Powell had complained to another officer, "I can't sleep, that's the problem."

Glen easily pushed the exhausted Powell away.

Koon claimed he saw Glen reach into his pockets. "An exceptionally dangerous action since he hadn't been cuffed and searched and the officers on the scene had no idea whether he was armed," he said.

The sergeant ordered his officers to "swarm" Glen. It was an LAPD tactic to force an unwilling suspect into a prone position by having each officer grab the suspect's arms and legs, rendering him helpless.

"I felt a blow to my head," King said. "It was a real hard kick from the boot. It was enough to make me feel my jawbone move. My face got rearranged."

• • •

On the other side of the Hyundai, Glen's friends lay face down in the dirt, surrounded by officers with their guns drawn. Freddie Helms later told attorneys that an unidentified officer kicked him in the side and hit his head with a baton, drawing blood and requiring a hospital visit afterward.

"I just heard Rodney scream," Helms remembered. "I know that they was beating him up, doing real bad. . . . I was scared."

• • •

Before the officers could subdue and handcuff Glen, he staggered back on his feet. Sergeant Koon held up his taser, a device used by police departments as a "less lethal" weapon to incapacitate resisting suspects.

"Get down!" Koon shouted. "Do it now or I'll tase you!"

But Glen didn't hear Koon. He looked around for an escape.

Glen's sudden movements scared Koon. He pulled the trigger, which fired two wired, dart-shaped, barbed probes into Glen's back. Electricity traveled along the attached copper wires, shocking him with 50,000 volts of electricity.

Glen screamed. He fell and shook for several seconds. "I felt a little string going in my body. And then I heard ZZZZZZZ!" Temporarily paralyzed, he couldn't pull the wire from his back. "It was a weird feeling, man. My brain was working but my body wasn't."

But Glen managed to stand up again, shocking Koon who was accustomed to suspects remaining incapacitated after being tased. He tased Glen again, this time in the chest. Another 50,000 volts.

Glen went numb. "No pain," he told himself. "No pain. No pain. No pain." He stumbled forward, the taser wires trailing from his back.

Koon commanded his officers to use their PR 24 batons. "Hit the joints!" he shouted. "Hit the wrists! Hit his elbows! Hit his ankles! Hit his knees!"

These were the same "power stroke" baton commands Koon was supposed to have taught earlier that evening.

Officers Powell, Briseno, and Wind struck Glen multiple times in the shoulder, arms, chest, and back. Glen fell. As he rose to his knees, another officer hit his left arm. Glen fell again. The police continued to strike their batons against his body. His knee. His thighs. His shoulder. His back.

As one cop reached for his handcuffs, Glen began to rise. Another officer stomped his shoulder. Glen propped himself up on his hands and knees. The officers kept striking. Three blows against his back. Three kicks to his shoulder and back area. Another strike to his left arm.

In the end, the officers struck Glen with their batons fifty-six times.

"I looked around for a safe place to run, to get out of there, but they were all around me," Glen said. "There was nothing I could do."

He collapsed, soaked in his own blood and urine, too weak to fight back. "Everything after that was really nerves, my nerves holding me together."

But as he glanced at the nearby entrance to the Hansen Dam Recreation Park, Glen remembered all the good times he had there as a child. "My dad and I used to fish there all night long," he said.

As he flashed back to those days, it was no longer his nerves keeping Glen together.

"Live Through This"

"Who wants to go fishing?"

Glen loved whenever his father, Ronald King, asked that question. "Those were just the sweetest words to my seven-year-old

An avid fisherman since childhood, Rodney Glen King loved to fish near his home whenever he had a free moment.

ears, and had me out in Daddy's car with my rod and tackle before he was finished asking," he said.

Catching pickerel, carp, and trout along the Sacramento River and at the Hansen Dam "was pure heaven." Glen's father was often called by his nickname, Kingfish.

But life wasn't always heaven between Glen and his father. Ronald King grew up in Sacramento. After high school, he married and moved his family to Altadena for the promise of work. But construction jobs were few and far between.

Ronald was also an alcoholic. As unemployment exacerbated his drinking, Glen's mother, Odessa King, found solace in religion, joining the Jehovah's Witnesses.

Like Edward Jae Song Lee's mother, Jung Hui, Roland King finally found work as a night janitor. He started his own business, King's Maintenance. He brought his children along on his night shifts at a medical center in Pasadena until 2:00 a.m. And just like Eddie and Jenny, seven-year-old Glen and his brothers helped their father clean the building. Roland blasted his favorite country music, from Johnny Cash to Buck Owens to Willie Nelson, on a portable radio to keep everyone awake. "Daddy would have us cleaning and waxing them floors every damn night," Glen said.

Glen's fatigue and inability to concentrate the next day in class led to his elementary school teachers misdiagnosing him and sending him to special education classes. Several students began bullying Glen, who cried, saying at the time he felt "broken."

Growing up, Glen found peace outdoors, from fishing to playing outfield and third base on the school baseball team. "Baseball saved me."

But baseball couldn't save Glen from following in his father's footsteps. "The first time I drank alcohol at age eleven, it felt like someone threw a switch in the back of my head," he said. "I loved it right from the start. . . . I was immediately hooked."

Glen drank to cope with his father's physical abuse. From sunny mornings fishing together by the water to being whipped with a belt or extension cord, Glen grew up both loving and hating his father.

And now, as the LAPD officers beat Glen, the pain suddenly felt familiar to him.

"Every baton blow was a terrible shock of the most horrible pain, kind of like Daddy being at his drunkest extension-cord-swinging worst," he said.

As the pain faded, Glen grew frightened. Was he dying?

"I began to think about all the Blacks down South who were slaves and had been beaten and lynched," he later wrote in his memoir, *The Riot Within: My Journey from Rebellion to Redemption*. "I felt a strange power at that moment, as if their spirits were all coming together to help me through this."

Although he lay immobile on the ground, Glen was determined not to let his ancestors down.

"Glen, you got to live through this," he told himself. "Do not let them down. Make them proud of what you can take."

As the beating continued, it wasn't just the ancestors looking after Glen.

Someone else was watching.

Chapter 3
THE VIDEOTAPE

"What Did We Just See?"

George Holliday was obsessed with his new video camera.

The thirty-one-year-old plumber had just bought the Sony Video8 Handycam as a Valentine's Day gift for his wife, Maria. It was a rare splurge: the young couple was saving up to buy a house and start a family. They lived in a modest apartment in Lakeview Terrace just ninety feet across from a gas station and the Corral bar.

Back then, these small and portable camcorders were becoming more popular with the general public. "When you have the new camera, new toy, you're filming everything—whatever's happening around you," Holliday said. He had recently videotaped a scene from the movie *Terminator 2: Judgment Day* being shot outside the Corral bar. "I actually have footage on the original tape of [Arnold] Schwarzenegger getting on the bike and riding off," he said.

That Saturday night, Holliday and his wife went to bed early. Tomorrow would be busy: they had promised to videotape a friend running in the Los Angeles Marathon before attending a wedding.

At 12:45 a.m., a helicopter roared overhead, rattling the windows. Police sirens woke them up. They went to the balcony to see several police cars surrounding a white Hyundai parked near the Corral.

Holliday ran to the living room to get his camcorder.

"Oh, my God!" Maria shouted.

By the time Holliday returned, the beating had begun. He fumbled with his camcorder, finally figuring out how to turn the autofocus off. He hit "record."

"The rest is history," he said. "What you see on the video, on the tape, is what I captured there."

• • •

Holliday's video is seven minutes and fifty-eight seconds long.

The brutal violence happens in the first two minutes. LAPD officers beat Rodney King into submission with their batons. They handcuff and hogtie him. The remaining footage shows police placing King in a patrol car and driving off while his friends Allen and Helms are released.

"What did we just see?" Holliday asked his wife. "What happened? Why did we witness this?"

But it was late, and they had to wake up at 6:00 a.m. for the marathon and wedding.

Holliday couldn't forget the violent images, especially because he had grown up in Argentina under the dictatorship of military leader Jorge Rafael Videla and his Argentine police force, who

George Holliday, at a press conference on March 28, 1991, holds the camcorder he used to film the LAPD beating of Rodney Glen King. This photo, published in newspapers across the country, was taken by Craig Fujii, the Associated Press photographer who would be beaten himself during the 1992 uprising.

would "take matters into their own hands and take care of business right there and then," he said.

Holliday moved to Los Angeles in 1980, eventually starting his own plumbing company. Given his new life in America, Holliday couldn't understand what he had witnessed outside his apartment. "There must be something that this guy did to deserve what's happening to him right now," he thought. "In the United States, police, they're all good, they all do the right thing. They don't do anything wrong."

"Finally It Was on Camera!"

On Monday, March 4, Holliday called the local police station and asked about what had happened in the early hours of Sunday morning.

"We don't give out any information," the switchboard operator said.

Holliday made another call, this time to the KTLA Channel 5 news station. KTLA news director Warren Cereghino was shocked by the videotape. "We realized from the first that it was important." He immediately sent a copy to LAPD headquarters. But Police Chief Daryl F. Gates was out of town. His assistant chief Robert Vernon started an investigation.

An interview with KTLA reporter Stan Chambers and the Hollidays aired at 10:00 p.m. that same night, featuring sixty-eight seconds of Holliday's videotape.

"That's when everything blew up," Holliday remembered.

The next morning, dozens of reporters swarmed the Hollidays' apartment. The couple received over a hundred phone calls a day, forcing them to change their phone number three times.

By Wednesday, Holliday's video had aired on CNN and across the country. His video had gone "viral" decades before that social media slang term was invented.

The video disturbed many police officers. "When the officers saw the tape, there wasn't a word said," recalled one LAPD captain. "They were in shock."

But few were shocked in the Black community.

"Many of us who had been trying to convince the public that these kinds of incidences were happening were almost relieved," said Karen Bass, a social worker–turned–congresswoman who would become the first Black female mayor of Los Angeles in 2022. "It was like, finally! Finally it was on camera! And the world was gonna be able to see and we would finally be able to hold police officers accountable."

"This was a lynching on tape," said filmmaker John Singleton, the first Academy Award–nominated Black director for his groundbreaking movie *Boyz n the Hood*, about police brutality and anti-Black racism. "I was like, 'Whoa, they finally got them on tape doing this.'"

Many rap and hip-hop artists who had been expressing their anger over police brutality in their music finally felt vindicated. "It ain't nothing to me," said rapper MC Ren of N.W.A. "It's just nobody ever captured it on the videotape like homeboy did." Rapper Nas agreed. "It's like, 'We got you! We got you.'"

Civil rights attorney Constance L. Rice, a relative of former U.S. Secretary of State Condoleezza Rice, wondered if this videotape would be the tipping point for the LAPD's history of excessive force against the Black community. "Is this gonna be enough to finally blow the LAPD open? Will it finally be enough for them to see what every day African Americans have been talking about for twenty years and have been ignored?"

• • •

On March 7, Police Chief Daryl F. Gates announced the four officers involved in the Rodney King beating would be investigated. Fifteen other officers were suspended.

Four days later, a grand jury watched the video and heard testimony from witnesses. Deputy District Attorney Terry White asked George Holliday why he videotaped the beating instead of just calling the police.

"They were there," Holliday answered.

• • •

On March 14, a grand jury indicted LAPD officers Stacey Koon, Laurence Powell, Timothy Wind, and Theodore Briseno for assault and use of excessive force on Rodney Glen King.

The LAPD's Internal Affairs Division also conducted a

massive investigation of the incident, interviewing seventy-four people, including King, witnesses, and other police officers on duty that night.

Rodney King claimed he heard racist slurs during the beating, which other witnesses and officers denied. But some police bystanders, including CHP officer Melanie Singer, testified King was trying to obey Koon and his men. "King did not aggressively kick or punch the officers," she told investigators. "He was merely trying to get away."

A 314-page report was released in May 1991, recommending that the four officers be fired.

The FBI confiscated Holliday's camcorder and videotape. They would hold onto it for the next thirty years.

Meanwhile, the media, law enforcement, and the general public were not the only ones shocked by Holliday's video.

"That's My Dad?"

"Wait, what? That's my dad?"

On Monday, March 4, Glen's seven-year-old daughter, Lora Dene King, and her mother, Dennetta Lyles King, were visiting Lora's grandmother. The TV was on in the background, set to KTLA Channel 5. The phone rang. It was Lora's aunt.

"Is that Rodney on the TV?" she asked.

Dennetta glanced over at the TV. "As soon as I looked, I knew it was him."

Lora cried. Why did the police hurt her father? A self-described "super daddy's girl," the shy Lora lit up whenever she was with her father. "I was extremely shy," she said. "Like severely, extremely shy. I didn't like talking at all."

Lora expressed herself through art, drawing, and painting. She had recently fallen in love with folding paper origami birds.

Glen encouraged Lora and all his children to step outside their comfort zones by taking them on spontaneous adventures. He once woke the children up at 7:00 a.m. to take them on a skiing trip, even though they had never skied before.

"It was so funny, we weren't prepared at all." Lora laughed. "The next day, I had bruises everywhere because we were falling. I was like, this is hard, how do people do this for a sport?"

Unlike her father, Lora was not a fan of fishing. "I didn't have any patience. I was like, 'This is stupid, we're sitting here forever.'" But she treasured spending time with her father, especially after they finally caught some trout.

"He can season and fry fish really good," she said. Her father also made the best fried peanut butter and jelly sandwiches as an after-school snack. She remembered when he introduced her to sushi. "He would get so upset because we couldn't eat with chopsticks. I'm a lefty, so I never learned. He'd be like, 'This is embarrassing!' And I was like, 'Are you serious? I'm eight!'"

But Glen also had a serious side and expected his children to do well in school. "He was very active when it came to schooling, back-to-school nights. He would literally sit in the front row and take notes, engage in conversation with the teacher."

As Lora watched the TV in horror, she had no idea that the beating had happened right outside the Hansen Dam Recreation Park where she and her father used to fish.

"That's My Friend at the End of the Day"

Dennetta Lyles King hid in the bathroom to cry.

"I cried because one of the news reporters said he might have died," said Dennetta. "And that just brought back memories of my father dying when I was six years old, so I was like, oh, my God, how am I gonna tell Lora? But then it wasn't true."

Rodney King and former wife, Dennetta Lyles King, share a laugh in 1995 after attending their daughter Lora King's fifth-grade graduation ceremony. Although they divorced, the two remained friends and were committed to raising Lora together.

Dennetta and Glen attended John Muir High School in Pasadena. But they didn't meet until after Dennetta graduated in 1981. She was hanging out with a friend at the park when she spotted Glen across the way. It was love at first sight.

"He was gorgeous . . . tall, beautiful." She laughed. "He was a *fine* man!"

Dennetta also fell in love with Glen's positive spirit. "He was always happy. He was smiling, he was upbeat. He was always, 'Yeah! Let's move!' He never sat still. He reminded me of my father."

The two teenagers spent weekends driving through the hills surrounding the Rose Bowl, singing along to their favorite songs by the Temptations. "We used to go there and park and look at the moon. We talked about our plans and what we wanted to do in life. And we just loved to be outside. It was beautiful."

Their daughter, Lora, was born in 1984. They wed at a small

chapel in Las Vegas the following year with Glen's brother Paul as their witness. Glen, who had dropped out of high school, had just been accepted into construction school. He was excited to find steady work in construction because he would be able to work in his favorite place—the outdoors.

In between construction school and working freelance labor jobs, Glen was an "amazing dad," Dennetta said. "He loved Lora!"

But after five years of marriage, Dennetta and Glen grew apart. "We were young and didn't know better," she said. They divorced in 1990.

Determined to be present for Lora, Glen and Dennetta remained friends and co-parents.

"We were better when we were divorced," Dennetta said. "Because we grew up together. That's my friend at the end of the day. No matter whether we didn't work out or not. He loved me and I loved him. And we loved her. It was the kids come first. Period."

"God Bless the Child"

Rodney Glen King was released from the Los Angeles County Jail three days after the beating. No criminal charges were filed against him due to lack of evidence, according to the district attorney's office.

He wore a blue hospital smock and sat in a wheelchair, his leg in a cast, as he addressed the media.

"I was scared for my life. So I laid down real calmly and took it like a man." He raised his shirt to show a giant bruise on his chest and arm. "It hurts real bad."

Glen insisted that he obeyed the police. "No, no, no. I wouldn't strike back. I don't think no one would strike back against four or five guns aimed at him."

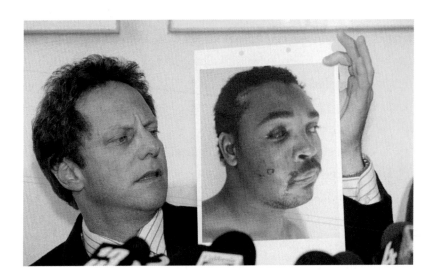

(Above) Rodney King's attorney Steven Lerman holds up a photo of King taken shortly after the beating. At this March 8, 1991, press conference, doctors detailed King's extensive injuries.

(Right) King, who underwent five hours of reconstructive surgery, shows reporters his many bruises and injuries at a press conference after being released from the hospital. "I was struck all over," he said. "In my back. All in my arms. My legs. Every bone in my body was hit that night. I laid down. I kept telling myself it would be over soon."

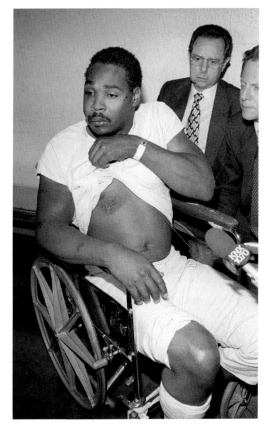

When Lora visited her father, she cried, barely able to recognize him—his swollen face, the bruises and cuts, the twenty stitches in his mouth, his bloody eye. "I didn't go near him because I was terrified. He didn't look the same."

Glen motioned for his daughter. Despite the pain, he managed to smile and say her name.

Hearing his voice reminded Lora of how her father always sang the Billie Holliday song "God Bless the Child" to her. She was no longer scared. "The only reason I knew it was him was because of his voice and his smile and then his laugh."

She ran over and hugged her father.

* * *

Glen had trouble sleeping. He suffered from constant headaches and partial numbness on the right side of his face. He used a wheelchair and cane to move about. He was restless, stuck inside the house. He couldn't even watch TV because some channel was always showing *that* video.

"He's depressed," Dennetta said. "He's scared. Because they beat him up like that and he feels that his manhood has been taken, and he's scared because he doesn't know if they're going to try to beat him up again or kill him or what."

During the beating, several tooth fillings fell out, forcing Glen to eat a soft food and liquid diet. Dennetta remembered how Glen was always brushing his teeth and "used to get on the girls all the time about brushing their teeth. He believed in pretty teeth."

Five doctors tended to King's injuries—a broken leg, shattered cheekbone, and a fractured eye socket. The base of his skull was broken in eleven places. He had a severe concussion and burns from where Sergeant Koon had tased him twice. He underwent five hours of reconstructive surgery to repair facial nerve damage. Even more concerning was Glen's slurred speech and memory loss. His days were filled with appointments and consultations with a neurologist, eye surgeon, physical therapist, and psychiatrist.

These injuries did not match the initial police report and Stacey Koon's sergeant's log, filed after the March 3, 1991, arrest. Those reports stated Rodney King had allegedly resisted arrest and attacked first and that his injuries were "of a minor nature"—contusions, abrasions, a split upper lip, and facial cuts.

"It is a horrible, horrible, brutal beating," said one of his doctors at a press conference, concerned that some injuries might be permanent.

Dennetta felt betrayed. "I have cops in my family. My mother is married to a retired vice sheriff. My uncle was a lieutenant in the LAPD at Carson Station. Back in the day, our police knew my grandma, knew our kids, knew everybody! They had a good relationship with our neighborhood. But now . . . they shoot first and that's why I'm scared of the police." She refused to watch the video again after it first aired on KTLA. "I can't even watch the video to this day."

And Glen wasn't the only one having trouble sleeping. "I had nightmares all the time," Lora said. "I peed in the bed. I had rashes on my face."

One night when Lora was staying at her father's house, she woke up to his cries. "From time to time, he would have nightmares. I didn't know what to do. So I hugged him." Later in school, she drew a pink car with orange wheels. Her father sat in the driver's seat, frowning. Several faces hovered around the car. Some wore police caps. Others held sticks. They were all smiling.

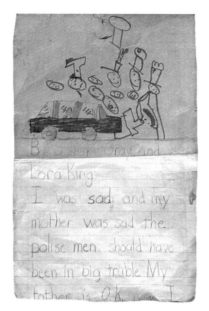

Seven-year-old Lora King did a school report on what happened to her father, Rodney King, on the night of March 3, 1991. She ended her report on a happy note, writing, "My father is O.K. now. My dad Rodne King is bringing me to open house! I think that's wonderful. Thank you. The End."

"I was sad and my mother was sad," Lora wrote. "The polise men should have been in big truble."

Looking back, Lora realized how their roles had switched that night. It was her turn to comfort her father. "When I was a little girl, he used to always sing 'God bless the child that has his own, he just don't worry 'bout nothing 'cause he's got his own' all the time when I was little," she said. "Now that I'm older, I definitely can relate to that song. The words are very true."

Page B-11

On Sunday, March 17, the *Los Angeles Times* ran a front-page story about Rodney King: "The Man Swept Up in the Furor: Friends, Family Say King Was Sometimes Lost but Never Violent."

Girl, 15, Shot to Death Over Orange Juice

A 15-year-old girl was shot to death Saturday morning by the owner of a liquor store in South Los Angeles who said she struggled with the juvenile after she allegedly tried to steal a bottle of orange juice, authorities reported.

Police Detective Jeff Alvarado said authorities were considering seeking charges against the owner in the killing of the unidentified girl, who was shot at about 9:45 a.m. at Empire Liquor-Market at 9127 S. Figueroa St.

Details surrounding the incident were sketchy Saturday evening, but Alvarado said the girl and the owner of the store, who authorities declined to identify, got into a dispute over a bottle of orange juice that the girl allegedly had in her hand as she was leaving the store.

Alvarado said the woman pulled a pistol from under the store's counter and confronted the girl, who gave back the orange juice.

A struggle apparently ensued but as the girl tried to walk away, the store owner shot the teen-ager in the back of the head, killing her, Alvarado said.

The owner later complained of a head injury suffered during the brief struggle with the girl, Alvarado said. The woman was taken to Martin Luther King Jr./Drew Medical Center for treatment but was not taken into custody.

Buried at the bottom of page B-11 in the *Los Angeles Times*, next to a March 17, 1991, front-page story about Rodney King, is a small item about a teenaged girl killed by a store owner in a dispute over a bottle of orange juice. The names of the two were later revealed to be Latasha Harlins and Soon Ja Du. This shooting happened just two weeks after the LAPD beating of Rodney King.

The story continued on page B-11.

For those who looked closely, there was also a six-paragraph story buried on the bottom of the same page with the headline "Girl, 15, Shot to Death over Orange Juice."

"A 15-year-old girl was shot to death Saturday morning by the owner of a liquor store in South Los Angeles who said she struggled with the juvenile after she allegedly tried to steal a bottle of orange juice, authorities reported."

The article did not identify the girl or the store owner.

But two days later, everyone would know their names.

Chapter 4
TASHA

Tasha, Tee, Nookie, and Trell

Latasha Lavon Harlins never left the house without her notebook. She loved to write—anything from poetry to her ideas for the future.

"I would see her always just writing," said her younger sister, Christina. "In her room on the bed, at the dinner table, in the living room, even outside at the park, with her little notepad. She was just writing. Sometimes she would just look at the sky. She was processing, she was thinking. She would go to a peaceful place to think and write."

"Tasha," as her family and friends called her, had big plans. She would become a lawyer, run her own business, and still have time to write her poetry. Until then, fifteen-year-old Tasha helped her grandmother take care of her cousin and two younger siblings—Tee, Nookie, and Trell.

Tasha's sister, Christina, eight, went by Nookie. Their brother,

Slaying of Black in Korean Market

■ The killing of an innocent 15-year-old black patron by a Korean market owner (Metro, March 19) who thought the teenager was shoplifting should trigger in-depth soul-searching on the part of African-American leaders. This incident, the well-publicized beating of Rodney King by members of the Los Angeles Police Department, the recent racist remarks of Japanese officials about African-Americans and the report of the National Opinion Research Center that white stereotypes of blacks are still widely held are symptomatic of a serious problem that African-American leaders must address.

Racism is not inherent. It is learned. The national and international attitude of non-blacks toward African-Americans is largely shaped by misconceptions gleaned from the mass media. No matter how law-abiding, churchgoing and patriotic the masses of black people are, if others view us in great measure through "Soul Man," "In Living Color," crime reports on the 6 o'clock news and other media stereotypes, these non-black people—who generally have only minimal contact with African-Americans—will subconsciously disrespect us as individuals and as a collective.

Hence, a market owner *assumes* that a black girl is shoplifting, police *assume* that every black male driver is violent, Japanese leaders *assume* that African-Americans are the bane of this society and white Americans *assume* that most of us are drug addicts, criminals and welfare recipients.

One of the main reasons that black leaders have failed their constituency is that they have not mustered the fortitude to confront the racist image makers in Hollywood. Until black stereotypes are eliminated, African-Americans will continue to suffer a negative reflex from others, and the resignation of 10,000 police chiefs will not solve this problem.
LEGRAND H. CLEGG II, Chairman
Coalition Against Black Exploitation
Compton

■ Another teen-ager was senselessly murdered in Los Angeles. This time it was one of our classmates, Latasha Harlins. Latasha was in the 9th grade at Westchester High School; she was one of us. It could have been any one of us who was shot, but this time it was Latasha. We would like to know why.

Was Latasha shot and killed because of racial intolerance? Was Latasha shot and killed because there is too little gun control? Was Latasha shot and killed because we don't get upset enough about murders that happen in South-Central Los Angeles? Why is there an empty desk in her classes? Who can answer our questions?

We, Latasha's classmates, want her family to know that our thoughts and sympathy are with them. We're sure that they would like to know why, too. When will this stop?
DAVID GUERRERO
MALORA GUERRERO
Los Angeles

The letter included signatures of 234 of Latasha Harlins' classmates.

■ I am deeply disturbed by the death of young Latasha Harlins. However, I am equally disturbed by the attempts to make this seem like yet another racially motivated incident. In the wake of the Rodney King incident it seems that this would be the easy thing to do.

I am a police officer who works in the area where the Empire Market is located. I have spoken with Joseph Du and his family on numerous occasions. They have been terrorized by local gang members, shot at and threatened. Things got so bad that they even closed down the store for two weeks last month. I arrested one of the gang members who was wanted for these acts of terrorism and he and two other gang members are being held on bail of over $200,000. Yet others connected in these crimes are still outstanding and continue to threaten the Dus, who are currently going to court on this matter. The family is extremely frightened and shook up over the incident. Soon Ja Du in particular has become very jittery, afraid these gang members are going to kill her and her family.

Obviously, Soon Ja Du was in no mental state to have been working at the store after all that had happened. Although this mental anguish does not excuse what she did to Latasha, I think it will help the public understand why this tragic event happened. Let's not incite another public outcry, this time against Korean-Americans. Rather, let's reveal what this is really about. It is not just a case of a store clerk overreacting and acting negligent. It is in a growing number of innocent people

How to Write Us

Latasha Harlins

being affected by the terrorism and violence of the street gangs in L.A.
G. HOLMSTROM
Los Angeles

■ The shooting of 15-year-old Latasha Harlins in a South-Central Los Angeles market was, indeed, tragic. But can someone explain just why she put the orange juice in her knapsack before paying for it?
CHRISTY M. HAYS
Canoga Park

■ It's no wonder that the police beat up and maim a black man for no apparent reason. It's no wonder that a headline in The Times read "Slain Girl Was Not Stealing Juice, Police Say" (March 19). And it's no wonder that the top moneymaking films of the week are "Silence of the Lambs," "New Jack City" and "Sleeping With the Enemy." Does art mirror life, or is it vice versa? In either event it doesn't say much for society in the '90s. And it makes me very sad.
MARJORIE L. SCHWARTZ
Los Angeles

Gulf Victory

■ This euphoria about the victory in the Persian Gulf only shows how serious America's inferiority complex is today. How else could we think that this was such a great success? We launched a war

Two weeks after Latasha Harlins was shot and killed, the *Los Angeles Times* published her school yearbook photo. She was a track star and an aspiring poet and dreamed of becoming a lawyer. Next to her photo was a letter written and signed by 234 of Latasha's classmates and teachers, demanding answers on her death.

Vester, ten, went by Trell. Tasha's fourteen-year-old cousin, Shinese, nicknamed Tee, was practically like another sister because she lived with them.

Growing up, Tasha, Tee, Nookie, and Trell loved playing Double Dutch jump rope and hide-and-seek. They raced each other on their roller skates and bikes. The athletic Tasha often took them to the nearby park to play basketball and softball.

After school, they rushed home to catch their favorite daytime soap opera, *The Young and the Restless*. They also loved 1990s sitcoms like *Martin* and *A Different World*.

Tasha and Shinese had an especially close relationship. Only five months apart, they bonded despite opposite personalities. Tasha loved to dance and lip-sync with her brother and sister to their favorite songs from popular 1990s musicians, including Boyz II Men, Tupac, Lil' Kim, TLC, Chuck D and Public Enemy, Run DMC, and Tevin Campbell.

"I'm the one of the family that don't have no dancing rhythm," Shinese said, smiling. "I got two left feet. No rhythm at all, so they make fun of me when I dance!"

When it came to movie night, Shinese preferred Disney cartoons, including her favorites, *Lady and the Tramp* and *The Fox and the Hound*. Tasha loved scary movies.

Shinese Harlins (left) and Latasha (right) were cousins, but they felt as close as sisters and were inseparable growing up.

"I don't mess with Freddie and Jason," Shinese said, laughing. "My heart gets to beating fast. Can't do it, so no!" Tasha teased Tee for being a scaredy-cat and gave her an extra nickname—Gizmo, from the movie *Gremlins*.

But Tasha made sure everyone did their chores and homework. "Half of the time, she had her serious hat on," Christina remembered. "Like, 'Okay, fun time is over. Get back to reality.'"

Christina looked up to Tasha. "She was a wonderful big sister," she said, fondly remembering how Tasha braided her hair every morning into two pigtails and made everyone peanut butter, ham, or turkey sandwiches to take to school for lunch.

"She was a caretaker," Vester said. "She cooked. She made sure we did our chores, did our homework."

After dinner, Tasha and the others sat at the kitchen table to study.

Their grandmother, Ruth Harlins, tested the children with spelling bees every week, with two cents as a prize for each word learned.

"And we knew Tasha was going to get it all right!" Christina said, smiling.

• • •

Grandma Ruth Harlins shared Tasha's determination. Born in 1941 in Tuscaloosa, Alabama, Ruth could trace her family's roots back to the 1830s when her great-great grandfather worked as a freed sharecropper in Mississippi.

After her parents separated, Ruth lived in East St. Louis, Illinois, with her mother. She dreamed of college but left high school after becoming pregnant with Crystal, Tasha's mother. She eventually had three daughters and juggled several jobs while earning her GED diploma and taking college courses at night school. An avid bookworm, Ruth loved studying at the library.

Latasha Lavon Harlins was born on January 1, 1976, in East St. Louis, the first child of Crystal Harlins and Sylvester Acoff. Like Los Angeles, East St. Louis had a similar history of racial segregation, civil unrest, and industrial demise in which many iron, coal, and other factories were shuttered. By the 1970s, East St. Louis was wracked with poverty and high crime rates. In 1980, Ruth decided to relocate the family to California. She found a job as a clerk for the Los Angeles County Department of Public Social Services. Tasha's mother waited tables at a neighborhood tavern, while her father worked at a steel foundry.

Ruth's extended family—including Tasha's family, Tasha's aunt Denise Harlins, and her daughter Shinese—all lived in an apartment located in South Central L.A. (known today as South L.A.). The apartment was near the 77th Street Community Police Station, where Sergeant Stacey Koon first worked as a rookie cop.

After Tasha's parents separated in 1983, Ruth moved everyone to a three-bedroom home on West 91st and Figueroa Streets. Shinese stayed with them so she could attend the same school as her cousins.

Ruth put bunkbeds into one room for Tasha, Tee, Nookie, and Trell. The children stayed up late into the night, gossiping about school and fantasizing about their futures.

"We'd been living together all our lives," Shinese remembered. "Up until the day Tasha died, we were still living together. We talked about how we're gonna get out of the ghetto, our dreams, our goals, taking care of our grandmother when she retired."

"She wanted to make our grandmother proud," Christina said. "Tasha would talk to us about how she's going to be successful . . . to get out of this neighborhood to live a better life. She was just like that—she was that person at a young age who knew what she wanted to do and she was gonna go after that, like no matter what. She knew what she wanted to do in life."

"We Queens"

Tasha's drive for success was rooted in tragedy. On the night before Thanksgiving in 1985, her mother was shot to death in an argument at her boss's birthday party at a nearby club. She was twenty-five years old.

The woman who shot Crystal Harlins was found guilty of manslaughter and sentenced to five years in prison, eligible for parole in two years.

Tasha's family was devastated: they felt justice was not served for Crystal. They believed the killer should have been charged with murder, not manslaughter, and that her sentence was too light. "My daughter was a kind, loving and ambitious person who loved all peoples," said Ruth. "As a result of my daughter's death, it has brought agony, pain, and hurt to me and my family."

Tasha missed her mother. There was now an empty seat at the kitchen table where Crystal used to sit with her children after dinner, making sure they finished their homework.

"Tasha had a special relationship with her mom," Shinese said. "Her mom took her places. They would get their nails done." Shinese remembered how for fun, Crystal sometimes turned their living room into a home salon. "She would polish Tasha's nails and toes, and if I was there, she would do mine as well."

"Our mother wanted to go into real estate," Christina said. "She wanted to just be this awesome, phenomenal woman to her kids and to her family, to show like, 'Hey, if I can do it, anybody can do it.' So I think that's where I get the ambition, the hard-working strength that I have through my mother and through Latasha."

Tasha channeled her grief by studying hard. She wanted to become a criminal attorney and find justice for others. She blossomed at Bret Harte Junior High School, making the honor roll and becoming a star athlete, winning first place in sprints and long jump at track meets.

In the fall of 1990, Tasha and Shinese attended Westchester High School. Although it took an hour to get there by bus, the family chose the school for its rigorous academics.

"We had to leave our house by 6:30 in the morning," Shinese said. Both girls were often still sleepy when homeroom started.

Every morning, Ruth gave two dollars each for her grand-daughters to spend for lunch. They hoarded their leftover change to buy French fries at their favorite diner, Tam's Burger on Figueroa Street, and always made sure they had at least one quarter to play songs on the table-side jukebox. "Our favorite song was 'Stand by Me,'" Shinese said. "That was our song every day."

As a teenager, Tasha was growing aware of how being Black sometimes made her a target. "She just didn't want to end up a statistic," Shinese said. She never forgot when Tasha told her, "We queens. The only way we gonna get treated like we're queens is if we carry ourselves that way. There's nothing that I can't do once I put my mind to it."

"The most important thing to me is my family is always protected by a shield, so that they won't be harmed by dangerous, ruthless, uncaring people," Tasha wrote in a poem for a school assignment in the spring semester of 1991.

The Food Desert

Shinese loved her clock backpack. It was lime green with a round, battery-operated clock in the center. In the early 1990s, clock backpacks were all the rage at school, inspired by Flavor Flav (William Jonathan Drayton Jr.), cofounder of the Grammy-nominated rap group Public Enemy, who always wore a giant, round clock timepiece around his neck. "Time is the most important element," he once said of his trademark look. "And when we stop, time keeps going."

On Friday, March 15, Tasha spent the night at a friend's slumber party. She packed her clothes in Shinese's beloved backpack, promising to take care of it.

The next morning, Shinese waited impatiently for Tasha to return so they could go to the movies.

While they were waiting, Ruth realized they had run out of orange juice for breakfast. Vester and Christina had already left to play basketball at the park. She asked Shinese to pick up some orange juice at the store.

But Shinese didn't want to go. The Harlins lived just a block from the Empire Liquor Market Deli store on Figueroa Street.

"Empire Liquor was more of a convenience store that sold eggs, milk, cheese, and the basic necessities," Shinese said. "I didn't want to go because I hated going down there. They had a perception that we were stealing. So when my grandmother asked me to go there, I refused because I don't like the store."

A Korean immigrant family owned the store, but for Shinese, this was a personal matter, not based on race. She did not believe in any of the racist stereotypes of Korean American store owners.

"We wasn't raised to be a racist or to hate people or to do evil to people," she said. "We was raised to respect our elders, say, 'Yes ma'am, no ma'am,' 'Yes sir, no sir.' We was raised to say 'thank you' and 'you're welcome.' So we wasn't raised to be racist against anyone."

Coincidentally, Tasha's Uncle Richard had worked briefly at Empire Liquor in 1990, bagging groceries before quitting after a few months when asked to work overtime for free. Shinese and her siblings preferred going to another Korean-owned store called Irene Liquor. "They were more friendlier," she said. "They knew us by name, they would give us quarters to play the video games they had. We used to write little notes saying 'IOU. Can you send this home?'"

• • •

Meanwhile, as Tasha walked home from the sleepover, she impulsively popped into Empire Liquor because she was thirsty.

"It's a coincidence that Tasha stopped at the store coming home to get that orange juice," Shinese said.

Empire Liquor Market Deli was one of the few mom-and-pop stores providing food and basic supplies in Latasha Harlins's neighborhood, known as a "food desert" because residents lacked access to larger chain supermarkets like Vons and Ralphs.

Empire Liquor Market Deli was one of the few places that sold orange juice and other basic necessities in Tasha's neighborhood. The area was considered a "food desert," a place where a majority of residents lacked access to affordable and healthy food and lived over a mile away from a proper grocery store.

The food deserts of South L.A. were the result of redlining and the freeways that separated red-zoned Black neighborhoods from wealthier suburban neighborhoods. In 1963, there were seventeen "big box" Vons and Safeway grocery stores in South L.A. By 1991, both companies had relocated over 80 percent of their stores to the suburbs. Other chain supermarkets refused to fill in those gaps, claiming the investment was too risky.

Meanwhile, Korean immigrants bought liquor stores, gas stations, and other small businesses in South L.A., many purchased from middle-class Black and white families whose property values had deteriorated after the 1965 Watts uprising and who were desperate to sell so they could relocate elsewhere.

Some Black residents wondered if majority white-owned banks gave Koreans preferential treatment over Black customers. Black applicants historically had been denied loans at much higher rates than white applicants. Even in 2020, it was reported at one major bank that Black applicants still ranked last to be approved for a home loan: at 47 percent compared to 72 percent for white applicants.

But in reality, many Korean immigrants did not qualify for these loans either. So they used a traditional Korean personal loan system known as 계 gye, a "club" where members contributed money to a group pot. One person would be allowed to use that money for a business venture. They rotated every month so that each member had at least one chance to invest the money. Similar versions of this system existed all over the world, including the

Chinese hui, the Japanese tanamoshi, the West African sou-sou, and the Latin American tanda.

Many Korean American store owners also relied on free labor from children and relatives to make ends meet instead of hiring outside help. This gave the impression that Korean immigrants were exploiting Black neighborhoods by refusing to hire Black staff and invest in the community.

Within just fourteen years, the number of Korean-owned stores in Los Angeles increased by 750 percent. By 1991, 80 percent of all retail businesses in South L.A. were Korean-owned—six hundred mom-and-pop convenience stores, twenty swap meets, two hundred gas stations, and one hundred dry cleaners, plus many restaurants, wig shops and beauty salons, auto repair shops, and stores for jewelry, furniture, and electronics.

Because 1.2 million people in South L.A. did not have access to a big box supermarket, Korean-owned stores evolved to include food staples and basic necessities like diapers and formula. Some liquor stores provided check-cashing services.

And because they were small and did not have the same purchasing power, these stores charged much higher prices than the large national grocery chains. Black residents had no choice but to shop at them.

For Tasha's neighborhood, Empire Liquor Market Deli was an oasis in a vast desert.

"She Had to Work to Survive"

Soon Ja Du was late.

It was 8:00 a.m. on Saturday, March 16. Normally her husband, Billy Hongki Du, would already be working the register. But Billy had trouble waking up that morning after a fourteen-hour shift the night before.

Soon Ja Du hadn't planned to be at Empire Liquor on that Saturday. She usually worked at their second store, Bouquet Canyon Liquor, in Santa Clarita, located about fifty miles north. But she wanted to help Billy since he was so exhausted.

"She only came to the store to help us on Saturday," Billy said. "It was so difficult for me, very tiresome for me to open the store, close the store. That's why she was there."

Working fourteen-hour shifts seven days a week was not what Soon Ja and her husband had envisioned when they moved to America. With her fiftieth birthday just around the corner, Soon Ja suffered from constant fatigue, chronic migraines, and depression.

Los Angeles was a world away from her village in the mountainous North Chungcheong Province of Korea, home to rice, barley, and ginseng fields. But Soon Ja Du's family were not farmers. Her father was a doctor, and her mother was a nurse. Du enjoyed a comfortable life until the Korean War broke out.

After the war, she moved to Seoul. While studying literature in college, she met and married Hongki "Billy" Du. The young couple had two sons and a daughter. Soon Ja stayed at home to raise them while her husband taught taekwondo and worked at his father's construction company. He also served as a major in the Korean army.

"She had a good life," their daughter Sandy Du said. "She never had to work outside of the house."

In December 1976, the Du family moved to America because they wanted to provide a better education for their children. Soon Ja worked various factory jobs, from assembling couches at one factory to being a crocheter for a clothing company. Due to the language barrier, Billy could only find work in America as a repairman for Radio Shack. Despite their hardships, the Du family found solace and community at a local Korean church.

In 1981, Billy took a risk and bought a convenience store in the San Fernando Valley, even though he had no experience running a retail business. All that mattered was that he was his own boss again. "It was his," Sandy said. "That was important."

In 1987, the Du family sold their first store and purchased Bouquet Liquor in Santa Clarita. Their oldest son, Joseph, worked at the store with them.

Two years later, Billy Du bought another new property— Empire Liquor Market Deli in South L.A.—as an investment for his children. "As a parent, he always wanted to earn enough to leave something behind for us," Sandy said.

"I Should Go and Try to Help My Son"

The Du's new store, Empire Liquor, was in a high crime area. In 1990, 936 felonies were reported in the 32 blocks surrounding their store, including over a dozen murders and rapes plus 184 robberies and 254 assaults.

Shoplifting was a regular occurrence. "I see it every day," Joseph later testified in court, claiming customers shoplifted "over forty times" per week. But he was unable to stop the shoplifting. "If I tried to stop them, they show me their guns," he said. Joseph and his father were held up at gunpoint in three separate robberies.

Rival gangs trafficking in crack cocaine had become a frequently violent presence on the streets of South L.A., especially after several local manufacturing plants shut down. General Motors, Goodyear, Firestone, Bethlehem Steel, and more than three hundred other companies had closed, costing over fifty thousand jobs. This surge in unemployment and crime led to what many called a "Black tax"—higher insurance and mortgage interest rates for residents.

Because of the history of brutality by the LAPD, many Black

residents did not trust the police for protection, especially against gangs. In 1969, teenagers Raymond Washington and Stanley "Tookie" Williams and their high school classmates started a group called the Crips to keep their families safe. The Crips wore blue to identify themselves. "We started the Crips to protect ourselves and our families from other gangs," Williams later wrote in his book *Gangs and Violence*.

Despite its origins, the Crips ended up becoming part of the problem as well—especially in 1972, when a rival gang, the Bloods, who wore red colors, emerged. Both gangs became involved in the drug trade, trafficking in marijuana, amphetamines, PCP, and eventually crack cocaine. By 1992, membership in the Crips had risen to 15,742, while membership in the Bloods reached 5,213. In 1981, Williams was convicted of four counts of first-degree murder, along with two counts of armed robbery, and sentenced to the death penalty, although he always maintained his innocence. Over the next two decades, Williams became an activist who advocated against gang violence through his books and youth programs. He was the first person on Death Row to be nominated for a Nobel Peace Prize in 2001. He was executed by lethal injection in 2005, just two weeks before his fifty-second birthday.

By 1990, six hundred gangs, totaling seventy thousand members, had formed throughout L.A. County. Two-thirds of these gangs were Latino, and the rest were mostly Black, with some Asian gangs. Ten percent of gang members across the country were women. Korean American gangs included AB (which stood for "American Burger" where the gang hung out), Old Boys, Hollywood Boys, and the Last Generation Korean Killers. Chinese, Cambodian, Filipino, and other Asian American gangs spread out to Long Beach, the San Fernando Valley, and Orange County.

The Dus reported the armed robberies to the police. In

retaliation, a group of alleged Main Street Crips gang members threatened to kill Joseph Du.

For Soon Ja Du, this was not her American dream. She longed to escape the gritty city for quiet mornings fishing with her family by the ocean. "My mother's biggest prayer was to sell the store," said her daughter Sandy.

But no one ever made an offer to buy Empire Liquor. The Dus remained marooned in this food desert. Billy Du realized he would have to meet with the Crips to restore peace. "We made every possible effort to try to resolve the matter by . . . trying to talk to them, but it was unsuccessful," he said. Fearing for their safety, the Dus shut down the store for two weeks in December 1990.

Ten years earlier, Billy Du had bought two guns for self-defense and to use for hunting—an M1 carbine rifle and a .38 model 64 Smith and Wesson revolver. He kept them hidden under the counter at Empire Liquor, just in case. "The gangsters had come into the store before with machine guns, and they had shot some bullets inside," he said. "I felt that it will be more safe if I could at least show off the gun for my protection."

Meanwhile, the family was losing money on their investment in Empire Liquor. Suppliers canceled their contracts because the Dus' checks kept bouncing. The family grew vigilant, eyeing all their customers to make sure no one was shoplifting because every item stolen sunk them further into debt. Their Black customers, unaware of the armed robberies and the confrontation with the Crips, grew angry, wondering if the family was racially profiling them.

When the store reopened in January 1991, Soon Ja feared for her son's safety. She offered to take his Saturday shift. Joseph didn't want her to work alone at the store, but the protective Soon Ja put her foot down. "As a mother, I felt so terrible that I really felt that I should go and try to help my son," she said.

Joseph finally relented when he found out his mother would at least be working with his father on Saturdays. But he advised her to watch out for potential gang members, saying that the Crips wore certain colors like blue, orange, and gold to identify their allegiance. He also suggested she keep an eye on people who carried a backpack into the store just in case they were hiding a stolen item or weapon inside their bag.

Soon Ja followed her son's advice and kept a vigilant lookout. From January to March of 1991, she and Billy worked together on Saturday mornings without any problems.

But on Saturday, March 16, 1991, Billy woke up late. The couple rushed to open the store at about 8:30 a.m. Soon Ja noticed her husband struggling to stay awake. She persuaded him to rest while she worked the register. "Even though my husband resisted, I insisted and pushed him out," she said.

Billy went to their van parked outside the front of their store for a nap. Soon Ja was the only employee working inside. During the first hour of work, about twenty customers stopped by to purchase items from the store.

Around 9:45 a.m., two children entered. Lakeshia Combs, twelve, wanted to buy hair gel for her mother. Her brother, Ismail Ali, eight, played a game on the video arcade machine by the front door. Soon Ja went behind the counter to get the hair gel for Lakeshia.

Billy was still sound asleep in the van. Soon Ja found the hair gel.

And that was when Tasha entered the store.

Soon Ja spotted a girl in a blue and gold cap with a backpack slung over her shoulder. She remembered what her son had said about blue and gold colors and backpacks.

Although the teenager hadn't done anything wrong, Soon Ja kept watching her.

$1.79

Tasha headed for the back of the store where the juice was stocked. She found a small bottle of orange juice priced at $1.79. She still had Grandma Ruth's two dollars for her school lunch in her pocket. She placed the orange juice bottle into the backpack and pulled out the two dollars.

As Lakeshia paid for the hair gel, she glanced up at the mirror above the cash register and saw Tasha's reflection.

So did Soon Ja. She watched as Tasha stuck the bottle in the backpack. She had seen shoplifters do the same thing in the past.

"When I was working there, I noticed that the people who were shoplifting—they would take the merchandise, would place it inside the bra or anyplace where the owner would not notice, and they would come up to the check stand, to the counter, and buy some small items and pay for it and leave," she said.

Tasha approached the counter. Soon Ja, who later testified in court that she was not aware that Tasha had the money in her hand, didn't understand why the girl was not carrying the bottle. "Please pay for the orange juice," she said.

Soon Ja claimed that Tasha replied, "What orange juice?"

Lakeshia and Ismail remembered the conversation differently. "She said, 'Bitch, are you trying to steal my orange juice?'" Lakeshia later testified in court. "And the Black girl said, 'No.' They was calling each other bitches."

Soon Ja denied ever saying the word "bitch," claiming she didn't even know that word in English. She testified that Tasha had never called her a "bitch" either.

As Soon Ja and Tasha argued, Soon Ja tried to take the bottle of orange juice from the backpack.

But because Soon Ja was two inches shorter than the five-foot-six Tasha, she grabbed her sleeve instead, yanking the girl toward the counter.

Lakeshia and Ismail froze, watching in shock as the store owner and teenager tussled over the orange juice. Ismail remembered Soon Ja shouting, "That's my orange juice!"

Tasha tried to pull away. She had promised her cousin that she would protect her backpack. But Soon Ja would not let go. Tasha's sweater stretched between them like a rubber band, threatening to snap.

"Let me go!" Tasha shouted. "Let me go!"

In this tug of war, the backpack slid down Tasha's arm, hitting Soon Ja's head before landing on the counter. A frightened Ismail immediately backed away, followed by his sister.

Soon Ja clutched Tasha's sleeve. Tasha hit the store owner twice.

"All of a sudden . . . she punched me in the eyes with her fist," Soon Ja later testified in court. "The fist felt like an iron."

Soon Ja finally let go of Tasha. They paused, and then they both lunged for Shinese's backpack. They yanked at it. Tasha hit the storeowner again, trying to make her let go. In the struggle, Soon Ja stumbled back behind the counter, still clutching the backpack.

As Tasha backed away, Soon Ja reappeared with a stool. She threw it at the girl. Tasha sidestepped the stool. It flew by her right side, just missing her. Soon Ja ducked behind the counter again.

Tasha adjusted her sweater and took a step forward. She was not leaving without her cousin's backpack.

Soon Ja's right eye swelled. She grew dizzy. "After she hit me, I thought she was a gang member, and I thought she was going to kill me," she later testified. "And I thought that she had some kind of weapons in that satchel."

Soon Ja rummaged through a pile of paper bags until she

found her husband's .38 Smith and Wesson. She grabbed it. She stood up and faced the girl.

Tasha paused, seeing the gun. She placed the bottle on the counter. Soon Ja knocked it over.

Tasha turned around to leave. She headed for the door, her back facing Soon Ja.

Soon Ja fumbled with the gun.

"And as she was walking away, she shot her," said Ismail.

Soon Ja leaned over the counter, looked down, and screamed.

Tasha lay face down on the floor, blood seeping through her blue and gold UCLA Bruins baseball cap. She still clutched two crumpled dollar bills in her left hand.

Shinese's favorite clock backpack lay across from Tasha on the other side of the counter, filled with her overnight items for the sleepover. A pair of blue pants. Her yellow toothbrush and a tube of toothpaste. A pink and white bottle of Revlon's Moon Drops skin lotion. A blue paisley blouse.

And buried deep inside the backpack?

Tasha's notebook.

"Where Is She?"

Billy Du woke up to the sounds of his wife screaming. He burst into the store just as Lakeshia and Ismail raced out.

"Where is she?" Soon Ja asked over and over. "Call the police!"

A horrified Billy saw a young girl lying face down on the floor about three to four feet away.

Billy ran behind the counter and pressed the emergency button located below. He picked up the phone and dialed 911. "We got a holdup!" he shouted, assuming his wife had been involved in an armed robbery.

The first police officer to arrive on the scene saw Soon Ja passed out behind the counter with Billy on the phone. As he approached Tasha, he observed how she had been shot in the head. He checked for her pulse. There was none.

The paramedics arrived fifteen minutes later. Soon Ja Du was taken to the hospital, where doctors treated her black eye and facial injuries. They found no other serious injury and released her.

A few hours later, police arrested Soon Ja Du. They charged her with first-degree murder. She was denied bail and sent to the Sybil Brand Institute for Women. She remained there for the next ten days.

• • •

Meanwhile, Billy remained at the store with the police. He gave them the gun for evidence.

The police noticed the video surveillance cameras in the store. Billy brought them over to the video recording machine. He rewound the tape and hit play.

As everyone watched, they realized the video had been a fifth witness at the store the whole time.

Chapter 5
"BLACK KOREA"

"When Will This Stop?"

On Saturday, March 23, Latasha Lavon Harlins was laid to rest at Paradise Memorial Park Cemetery in a blush pink coffin accented with pearl tips chosen by her grandmother.

On March 29, a letter to the editor was published in the *Los Angeles Times*:

> Another teenager was senselessly murdered in Los Angeles. . . . Latasha was in the 9th grade at Westchester High School; she was one of us. . . . We would like to know why. Was Latasha shot and killed because of racial intolerance? Was Latasha shot and killed because there is too little gun control? Why is there an empty desk in her classes? Who can answer our questions? When will this stop?

The letter was signed by 234 of Latasha Harlins's classmates.

"This Store Will Never Reopen"

Shinese saw Tasha everywhere.

The TV news showed the shooting of Latasha Harlins over and over on-screen. Shinese stopped watching TV, scared she might see Tasha's last moments again.

She also suffered from survivor guilt. What if she hadn't let Tasha borrow her clock backpack? What if she had gone to the store instead? "My grandmother asked me to go get some orange juice," she said. "Told her, 'I don't wanna get no orange juice. Tell Trell or Nookie to get the orange juice.' But I wish I would have went."

Vester withdrew, and Christina couldn't stop crying. "I do remember being sad a lot because it was a void that was missed," Christina said. "It took a few weeks, like wow, we're at the dinner table and she's not present. Yeah, that was hurtful and sad. So we had to get used to the new norm."

Grandma Ruth was still reeling after the police had knocked on their door and showed a photo of Tasha, asking if she knew the girl. She took down all of Tasha's photos in the apartment. She could no longer walk past the Algin Sutton Recreation Center and hear the children's laughter. Instead, all she heard were Shinese's screams after learning Tasha had been killed.

Knowing the road to recovery would be long and difficult, Ruth arranged for all the children to receive professional counseling to cope with their trauma.

"My grandmother made sure that we had counseling throughout the process and after," a grateful Christina said. "So that helped."

But their grief was public. Reporters constantly stalked Tasha's family. "I stopped going to school," Shinese said. "It was just too much. News people coming to the home and to the school. I shut down."

• • •

Shinese's mother, Denise Harlins, became an activist overnight, founding the Latasha Harlins Justice Committee, which was supported by many prominent Black leaders, including California U.S. congresswoman Maxine Waters, Reverend Jesse Jackson, and L.A. city councilman Mark Ridley-Thomas.

On Thursday, March 21, the Latasha Harlins Justice Committee and more than 150 protesters stood outside Empire

RICK MEYER / Los Angeles Times

Danny Bakewell of Brotherhood Crusade speaks outside the Korean-owned store where a 15-year-old girl was killed.

Blacks Vow to Purchase Korean Market

Five days after Latasha Harlins was killed, a crowd of more than 150 protesters held a press conference with activist Danny Bakewell outside Empire Liquor Market Deli, declaring a boycott of the store.

Liquor, which had been closed for the past five days since the shooting. The protest was organized by Danny Joseph Bakewell, founder of the Los Angeles Brotherhood Crusade, an organization created in 1968 to aid Black low-income families. For Bakewell, this protest was also personal. His youngest daughter, Sabriya Ihsan Bakewell, had just celebrated her sixteenth birthday three days before Latasha was killed. The girls had a lot in common: they both loved to dance and write poetry. Like Tasha, Sabriya wanted to become a lawyer. They could have been friends.

"We are declaring here today that this store will never reopen," Bakewell told the press. "We are closing their store because of murder and disrespect on the part of these people toward us and our community."

They placed a large sign on the store's entrance: Closed for Murder and Disrespect of Black People.

The Black-Korean Alliance

Edward Taehan Chang's heart sank after hearing about Latasha Harlins and Soon Ja Du. An ethnic studies professor who had written books about the Korean and Black communities, Chang believed L.A. was a "ticking time bomb" given its volatile history of race relations.

"It's a matter of who is going to ignite the match," he said. "It was a keg of dynamite ready to explode at any time."

Chang was an active member of the Black-Korean Alliance (BKA). This group was created by the Los Angeles County Human Relations Commission in April 1986 after a record four Korean American store owners were shot to death in the same month in the city, along with thirty-eight other Korean American store owners killed across the country since 1975.

The BKA consisted of several activists, educators, business owners, and leaders from both communities, including BKA cofounder Larry Aubry, a senior consultant for the L.A. County commission and a longtime columnist for the *Los Angeles Sentinel*, a Black newspaper founded in 1933. Aubry, dubbed by many as the "godfather of South Central Los Angeles," was known for his blunt honesty. "He was a conscience of Black LA," remembered his daughter, Erin Aubry Kaplan, also a writer. "He did not hold his tongue, but he really expected engagement. It was sometimes a lonely battle but it did not deter him at all."

BKA members held social and educational events, Thanksgiving barbecues, and food fundraisers for families in need and provided student scholarships for both communities. They arranged diplomatic trips to Seoul for Mayor Tom Bradley and members of the Black Business Association. They drafted a code of ethics and served as mediators to resolve conflicts between Korean American store owners and their customers.

Chang wrote an official statement for the BKA about the Latasha Harlins tragedy, signed by several Korean American organizations, including the Korean Federation of Los Angeles, Korean Chamber of Commerce, Korean American Coalition, and Korean American Grocers Association.

> We, Korean American community leaders, would like to express our deepest regret and sympathy to Latasha Harlins' family and friends. . . . Tragic incidents such as this often focus on differences rather than the commonalities between the two communities. Both Korean Americans and African Americans share

a history of oppression. As racial minorities in this country, we have and will continue to work together toward a greater political and economic equality. In order to strengthen our bonds, we will actively join hands with the African American community to promote peace and harmony.

The Godfather of Asian American Journalism

Four days after Latasha Harlins was shot, a *Los Angeles Times* headline declared, "Racial Tensions Blamed in Girl's Death."

It was the first time Latasha Harlins's and Soon Ja Du's names were revealed along with their races.

Veteran journalist K. W. Lee was furious when the *Los Angeles Times* outed their races. He called it a double standard because neither one was white. "See, the lede says 'Korean-born Soon Ja Du,'" he said. "Why does the grocer, Soon Ja Du, have to be 'Korean-born'? She is American citizen. Would the *LA Times* say every time they use Henry Kissinger, 'German-born Henry Kissinger'? No. They are injecting the race card."

As the first Asian American ever to be hired as a reporter for a mainstream American newspaper (Tennessee's *Kingsport Times News*) in 1955, K. W. Lee became known as the "godfather of Asian American journalism." Born Lee Kyung Won in 1928 in Kaesong, Korea, he moved to America by way of Tennessee right before the start of the Korean War. He chose "K. W. Lee" as both his professional byline and personal name, spending the next three decades as an investigative reporter for several daily newspapers. His most famous exposé saved Korean American Chol Soo Lee from Death Row by proving he was wrongfully convicted for a 1973 San Francisco Chinatown gangland murder.

When K. W. Lee worked as a reporter in West Virginia, a bus driver invited him to sit in the front with the other white passengers. He refused, saying he was not white. He sat in solidarity with the Black passengers in the back of the bus.

One year before Latasha Harlins was killed, K. W. Lee created the *Korea Times English Edition* to provide more nuanced, in-depth stories about the Korean American community. His publication was separate from the Korean-language newspaper the *Korea Times*, established in Los Angeles in 1969.

K. W. Lee's *Korea Times English Edition* examined accusations of anti-Blackness in the Korean community with unflinching honesty and accountability. Lee and Larry Aubry of the *Los Angeles Sentinel* sometimes combined their reporting staffs for joint stories rarely covered in mainstream media on the solidarity forming between the two communities. A spokesperson for the Latasha Harlins Justice Committee who subscribed to the *Korea Times English Edition* praised the newspaper for providing the "fairest coverage" of the Soon Ja Du and Latasha Harlins case.

Although both the Harlins and Du families insisted this was a personal tragedy, headlines across the country sensationalized the race card. Latasha Harlins was always the "Black girl" or the "Black teenager," and Soon Ja Du, the "Korean-born grocer" or the "Korean shopkeeper."

A SENSELESS AND TRAGIC KILLING:
NEW TENSION FOR KOREAN AMERICAN AND
AFRICAN AMERICAN COMMUNITIES.

FRICTION, TEMPERS WORSEN
BETWEEN KOREANS, BLACKS IN L.A.:
A KOREAN WOMAN IS CHARGED WITH
MURDERING A BLACK GIRL, WHOM SHE
ACCUSED OF TRYING TO STEAL A $1.79
BOTTLE OF JUICE.

A SAD TALE OF PERSECUTED MINORITIES:
SLAYING OF A SOUTH CENTRAL TEENAGER
UNDERSCORES THE DISTURBING ECONOMICS
OF BEING KOREANS AND AFRICAN AMERICANS.

Many Korean American store owners were incensed by this coverage, especially in the *Los Angeles Times*. Some refused to stock or sell copies of the *Times* at their stores.

K. W. Lee believed it was easy—and lazy—journalism, creating a "media-fanned bogus race war." "They pitted the blacks against the Koreans," he said.

Former *Los Angeles Times* editor Edward J. Boyer, who was one of the few Black staff writers back then, agreed. "When a Black gangster assaults a Korean, when a Black hold-up man robs, what you have is a criminal assaulting a businessman," he said. "But somehow, the ethnic identities would narrow that focus, so that it became Black on Korean crime."

These tensions even made it on-screen in the early 1990s in popular movies like *Do the Right Thing, Menace II Society,* and *Falling Down,* which depicted Korean merchants as angry and suspicious, especially of Black customers. The Korean American store owner became known as the "middleman minority," caught between Black and white and belonging nowhere.

During the media coverage of the Soon Ja Du–Latasha Harlins

case, Korean American store owners reported a dramatic increase in violence—verbal abuse, physical assaults, and armed robberies. Stores were even firebombed with Molotov cocktails in the name of Latasha Harlins. Later that summer, a Black customer pretended to have a gun during an attempted robbery at a Korean-owned store in South L.A. When the owner shot and killed him, there was a hundred-day boycott against his store, even though authorities determined that the shooting had been in self-defense and declined to prosecute.

Korean American store owners felt they were under siege.

"You had a group of individuals that worked so hard to build this dream of theirs and have so much pride in what they're doing, opening a shop that they put their whole life into," said Roy Choi, a Korean American celebrity chef whose parents owned a Korean restaurant. "In their mind, they're kind of in a protection mode, psychologically, protecting their store, but not realizing that they're in a neighborhood that's not theirs."

Black Americans felt they were under scrutiny, profiled by Korean American store owners and suspected because of their race.

"One day I came up to the counter to pay for a bottle of wine and the guy says to me, 'Oh, you didn't steal anything today.' I stopped going in there right then," said one former customer at Empire Liquor.

But the Dus weren't the only ones accused of discrimination. There were similar reports across the country, from the 1990 year-long boycott of the Korean-owned Red Apple store in Brooklyn, New York, where the store owner was charged with third-degree assault over the price of an apple with a Haitian immigrant customer to picketing over accusations of discrimination against Black customers in Korean-owned stores in Chicago.

"There is consistent and persistent rude treatment," noted John W. Mack, president of the Los Angeles chapter of the Urban League.

In October 1991, rapper and actor Ice Cube released his second solo album, *Death Certificate,* in response to the beating of Rodney King and the shooting death of Latasha Harlins. It debuted at number 2 on the U.S. Billboard Top 200 chart, sold over a hundred thousand copies in its first week, and was certified platinum by the end of 1991. One of the album's most controversial songs was "Black Korea," where Ice Cube raps about being shadowed by Korean American store owners.

> *I ain't tryin' to steal none of yo' shit, leave me alone! . . .*
> *So don't follow me up and down your market*
> *Or your little chop suey ass'll be a target*
> *Of the nationwide boycott . . .*
> *So pay respect to the black fist*
> *Or we'll burn your store right down to a crisp . . .*
> *'Cause you can't turn the ghetto into black Korea.*

"The song is meant to be a warning to Koreans—in strong, threatening terms," Ice Cube said. "If things don't get better, we're going to burn their stores down."

When criticized by some for his raps containing potentially racist, antisemitic, and misogynistic language, the rapper said his lyrics were an artistic expression of rage against anti-Blackness. Everyone, according to Ice Cube, was fair game. "Nobody is safe when you listen to 'Death Certificate,'" he said. "Any of us that has any kind of flaws in our character, [the album] was probably going to find it."

The Korean American Grocers Association protested the

album. Many in the Korean American community claimed the perceived rudeness toward Black customers was in part the result of cultural misunderstandings and language barriers.

"So an African American customer walks into a store," explained UC Riverside professor Edward Taehan Chang. "Now you're supposed to make eye contact and greet. 'Hello, how are you? What can I do for you?' However, in Korea . . . if you do make eye contact, it is shown as a sign of disrespect or trying to make a trouble. And of course, many African American customers took it offensively."

For activist Danny Bakewell, it was ultimately about respect and accountability. "The African American community will no longer sit back and accept disrespect, racism and murder and write it off as 'cultural differences,'" he said. "We are not against Koreans as such. We are against Koreans and anybody else doing business who are disrespectful to Black people."

That fall, a nine-year-old Korean American girl named Juri Kang was shot in the chest during an armed robbery of her parents' gas station in South L.A. The shooter was never caught. Juri survived, but the bullet remains lodged in her bones.

Outraged Black and Korean American community leaders immediately joined in solidarity to condemn her shooting. Urban League president John Mack urged everyone to fight back in solidarity for both Latasha Harlins and Juri Kang. "Stand up once and for all and say 'Enough is enough,'" he said. "We're not going to take this anymore."

Danny Bakewell was heartbroken to learn another child had again been caught in the cross fire. His Brotherhood Crusade volunteered to help Juri Kang's family.

"We are here today to say that we also put a premium on

Violence Condemned

AL SEIB / Los Angeles Times

In October 1991, nine-year-old Juri Kang was shot by a robber at her parents' gas station located just ten blocks from the Du family's Empire Liquor store. Korean American Coalition president Gary W. Kim (center) said the shooting was not race related but instead "reflects the kind of vicious assaults that Korean Americans face daily both at home and at work" due to the high crime rates in the area. Juri's heartbroken father had to return to work the next day to keep his gas station from being ransacked. Juri survived the shooting. "It's a miracle," said one of her doctors. "When she came in, she was critical . . . but children are very resilient. She's going to be fine."

Korean American life," Bakewell announced. "It's a terrible tragedy and my heart goes out to the family."

This rare showing in the media of Black-Korean solidarity validated the many Korean American store owners who had formed strong bonds and friendships with their Black customers over the years.

Brother Lee

At the Farm Fresh Dairy store at 98th Street and South Avalon Boulevard in South L.A., Chung Lee's faithful customers called him "Brother Lee."

Brother Lee knew his customers' names. He gave candy to their children, who nicknamed him Homeboy. He provided free soda at local school events and used store profits to provide uniforms for the neighborhood's Little League baseball team. He hired Black employees. Because welfare checks were sometimes late to arrive in the mail, he extended credit. He even shared his lunch with curious customers who had never tried Korean food before.

Chung Lee, forty-nine, had worked as a tailor in Korea before moving to America in 1974 and opening up his first store. Although he was aware of the high crime rate and the deaths of several Korean American store owners, he was not scared. "There are good people and bad people in every race. We have to sit down and learn from each other."

To celebrate the eighth anniversary of his store in 1982, Chung Lee hosted a Korean barbecue. More than five hundred people showed up to enjoy a thousand dollars' worth of Korean barbecued beef, like thinly sliced 불고기 bulgogi and 갈비 galbi short ribs, along with potato salad and fried rice. "It was like a family reunion," said one customer.

For Brother Lee, it was money well spent to thank his customers. "It isn't much when you think of the eight years these people have given me business. We are all human beings."

Mama's Market

"Pay me next time."

Chung-Bok Hong, forty-nine, and her husband, Jong-Pyo Hong, fifty-eight, ran the 54th and Van Ness Market in Los Angeles, otherwise known as Mama's Market. Their customers nicknamed Chung-Bok "Mama" for trusting them when they did not have enough cash on hand to pay for diapers and other necessities right away.

Like "Brother" Chung Lee, Mama knew about her customers' lives. "How's your brother's leg?" she'd ask. "How's your wife's blood pressure?"

"That's why customers loved her," said her son Edward, twenty-five, who worked at the store. "She had a general concern for people."

Born in northern Korea in 1946, Chung-Bok Hong's family moved to Seoul right before the war started. She married her husband in 1971 when they both were working in Germany—Chung-Bok as a nurse and Jong-Pyo as a coal-mine laborer. They moved to Los Angeles the following year and bought the mini-market.

Mama hit it off immediately with her customers, creating a fun atmosphere at the store, "always smiling, playing, joking," Jong-Pyo remembered. Whenever Mama gave store credit or lowered the price of milk by ten cents to help those in need, she worked extra hours to make up for the loss in profit.

"She was always putting other people's needs above her own," her husband said.

The Korean Godfather of Gangsta Rap

When it came to music, Wan Joon Kim loved Beethoven, not Biggie Smalls ("The Notorious B.I.G." rapper).

Yet all the fifty-seven-year-old Korean immigrant record-store owner sold was hip-hop and rap, especially "gangsta rap," a popular new genre of hard-hitting beats with equally hard-hitting lyrics infused with social commentary about racism, poverty, and police brutality.

Wan Joon Kim ran the popular Cycadelic Records in Compton. It wasn't a brick-and-mortar store. Instead, it was Stall Number Z-7, closest to the main entrance of the Compton Swap Meet. It cost $500 a month to rent the space. In 1983, several

Korean American vendors leased an abandoned Sears building in Compton and renamed it the Compton Fashion Center. It became one of the largest Korean-owned indoor swap meets in L.A. County, with more than three hundred vendors.

Wan Joon and his wife, Boo Ja Kim, originally sold barrettes and hair accessories at a local outdoor flea market. He noticed a nearby vendor selling hip-hop and rap CDs. The line for his booth stretched down the parking lot.

"My dad saw an opportunity," said his son, Kirk Kyung Up Kim, now in his mid-forties. "He saw these big lines [and] said, 'I'm gonna try this.'"

The classical music fan in Wan Joon Kim was confused at first when he listened to rap. "What are these guys talking about?" he asked his children. "Why are these guys so angry?"

"My father knew nothing about hip-hop music," Kirk said. "We listened to music together, and I helped translate the lyrics for him."

"Oh, I like this," Wan Joon Kim told his son. "This music I don't like. But I understand where they come from. They're speaking from their hearts and their minds. I understand that."

Although Wan Joon Kim had grown up across the Pacific, the high poverty rates in Compton reminded him of life in North Korea, where his family had struggled to make ends meet. He identified with what these rappers were saying.

Wan Joon Kim was born in what would become the North Korean capital, Pyongyang, in 1934. When the Korean War broke out in 1950, the sixteen-year-old teenager and his family escaped in his father's fishing boat to Seoul. By 1976, Wan Joon Kim, his wife, and their children moved to Los Angeles.

Wan Joon Kim immediately rented Stall Z-7 at the Compton Fashion Center. His children suggested he call his new record store Psychedelic Records, but their father spelled it as "Cycadelic." They drove all over Los Angeles, looking for rap music to sell at the swap meet. As the radio blared, the children identified hit rap songs that their father should purchase in bulk.

As a kid, Kirk fell head over heels in love with hip-hop and rap. "It spoke to me," he said. "Oldies, hip-hop, and funk. I'm this kid trapped in between this gangsta rap culture and my strict parents." Bullied by racist students at school, Kirk found solace at his father's stall. "I would just see people like running up and hugging my mom, my dad, and they're so nice to me. Whereas when I go to school, everyone's so mean to me."

What Wan Joon Kim didn't realize was that West Coast gangsta rap was poised to become one of the biggest—and most controversial—music trends in the country.

Rap music had originated in New York City during the early 1970s when deejays played stretched-out drum breaks in funk and disco hits so musicians could rap rhymes over the instrumental breaks. Three thousand miles away, Los Angeles youth were inspired by the East Coast rap scene. West Coast gangsta rap emerged as a new genre, its lyrics chronicling the hardships of living in "South Central," which had been devastated by crack cocaine, gang violence, and police brutality. But many gangsta rappers, like Eazy-E of N.W.A., originally called this music "reality rap." "We're telling the real story of what it's like living in places like Compton," Eazy-E explained. "We're giving them reality. We're like reporters. We give them the truth." But many major music retailers at the time refused to sell certain gangsta rap albums, like N.W.A's *Straight Outta Compton*, claiming it "glorified violence" with its provocative language and antipolice themes.

So Wan Joon Kim filled that gap as one of the first distributors of early gangsta rap music. In addition to stocking albums by major label artists, he and another vendor also worked together to press and manufacture multiple copies of records, CDs, and cassette tapes by local independent musicians to sell at the stall. He became known as the "Korean godfather of gangsta rap."

"My dad later on got a kind of notoriety because you're not going to be able to get the latest gangsta rap album from an unsigned, up 'n coming artist at a huge major retailer," Kirk said. "So they came to us."

Wan Joon Kim supported struggling musicians looking for a break, many of whom became famous, including Dr. Dre, Ice Cube, Tupac Shakur (known back then as "2Pac")—and even L.A. Laker and NBA basketball champion Shaquille O'Neal, whose 1994 debut rap album was sold at Wan Joon's stall.

Wan Joon Kim showcased their music, along with photos of the Kim family with their most famous clients, on the back wall. Local rappers dreamed of being on that same display one day. "They would bring their cassettes to my dad's store and be like, 'Yo, Mr. Kim, Pops, what do you think? I want to be famous, I want to get on that wall,'" Kirk said.

Cycadelic Records' reputation skyrocketed. More than a hundred customers stopped by every day, often dancing to the music playing out loud.

"Moms" Boo Ja Kim treated future rap stars like family. She occasionally chastised an aspiring local rapper named Eric Lynn Wright to "pull your pants up!" but always made sure to treat him with freshly baked cookies. Wright later became Eazy-E of N.W.A. Their debut album, *Straight Outta Compton*, sold one million copies on its release in 1988.

"My parents were always hugging customers and picking up little babies and stuff," Kirk said. "Every time one of my dad's VIP customers would come, then there was an ice cream shop right

Gangsta rap's Korean godfather

Wan Joon Kim stocked music others wouldn't touch at his Compton swap-meet stall.

BY SAM QUINONES

By the time Bobby Wilson met Wan Joon Kim, he'd been to 15 record stores.

It was 1994, and no one would stock his cassette, "Comin' From Watts," with raps Wilson had written in prison and recorded himself upon his release. Wilson had a daunting résumé: a decade-long membership in the Grape Street Watts Crip gang; five years incarcerated for attempted murder; the prison nickname "Kill Kill."

Just out on parole and desperate for money to support his wife and child, Wilson's last stop was the Compton Fashion Center indoor swap meet.

Kim, the owner of the Cycadelic record stall, was in his 50s, spoke little English and liked classical music. But

[See **Kim,** E10]

WALLY SKALIJ *Los Angeles Times*

WAN JOON KIM, left, and his son, Kirk, work at the Cycadelic stall in the Compton Fashion Center, where the elder Kim sold early recordings by L.A. gangsta rappers.

Kirk Kim (right) works with his father Wan Joon Kim (left) at Cycadelic Records, located in a stall at the Compton Swap Meet. Wan Joon Kim supported struggling musicians, like former Crips member Bobby Wilson, who was released on parole after a five-year prison sentence for attempted murder. The aspiring rapper's debut album *Comin' from Watts*, sold more than fifteen thousand copies at Kim's store when no one else would stock it. "He gave me my shot," Wilson said. "It saved my life."

next door so he would always buy them ice cream. To this day, I have people messaging me saying, 'My son just graduated high school or college and he was talking about your parents and how your dad used to take us to the ice cream shop.'"

And Wan Joon Kim lived up to his "Pops" nickname. Kirk never forgot the day a security guard brought over a twelve-year-old boy who had been caught shoplifting a CD.

"Why did you do it?" Wan Joon asked the young boy.

"I just wanted to have it," he replied.

Wan Joon Kim remembered his own difficult childhood in Korea. He let the boy keep the CD and told the security guard to let him go. Instead of getting angry, Pops patted the boy gently on the back and said, "Next time, you can just tell me."

"The American dream was most important to him," Kirk said. "He was just chasing the American dream."

During his work breaks, Wan Joon Kim enjoyed sitting outside and gazing at the one lone pine tree standing in the back of the swap meet's parking lot. An avid gardener who loved to plant orchids, this pine tree reminded him of the 소나무 sonamu, the red pine tree, which was the national tree of Korea and a symbol of longevity, honor, strength, and wisdom.

"He would park his car right here," Kirk remembered, smiling. "He used to take a one-hour nap every day. He fell asleep watching that tree. He loved that tree."

But after Latasha Harlins was killed, even Pops encountered some hostility. Shortly after the shooting, a customer confronted Wan Joon Kim because he was Korean and spit on him.

"I remember my dad crying," Kirk said. "But he wiped it off and he just fucking went on."

Although Wan Joon Kim believed this was an isolated incident, he was still rattled.

"But we had more moments where it was good, you know," Kirk said, crediting his father's resilience. "I've only just begun to actually realize all that my dad has taught me."

"A Danger to Society"

On March 26, 1991, Soon Ja Du pled not guilty to the charge of first-degree murder at the Compton Municipal Courthouse.

This was the first time the Du and Harlins families had met in person. Soon Ja slumped back in a wheelchair, her right eye still bruised. Grandma Ruth, Aunt Denise, and the Harlins sat in the front row, stoic.

During the hearing, the Dus' defense attorney, Charles E. Lloyd,

KEN LUBAS / Los Angeles Times

Heung Ki Du, left, sits with wife, Soon Ja Du, charged with killing a black teen-ager in a case that has polarized Koreans and blacks.

Billy Hongki Du weeps as he and his wife Soon Ja Du attend a hearing in the summer of 1991, after Soon Ja Du shot and killed Latasha Harlins in a dispute at their store.

argued that this shooting was an accident and that a charge of murder "defies reason. It was a mistake."

Deputy District Attorney Roxane Carvajal and the Harlins's family attorney, Leon Jenkins, strongly disagreed. Jenkins said it didn't matter what had happened right before Latasha was shot. "You can't use deadly force to repel non-deadly force."

Carvajal reminded the judge that the surveillance video showed Latasha turning her back to Soon Ja, making her completely defenseless when the store owner shot her. "It is clear and evident, Mrs. Du is a danger to society."

The judge at the hearing ruled that Soon Ja Du was not a flight risk. He set her bail at $250,000.

Soon Ja Du was free to go home.

Chapter 6

THE PEOPLE OF THE STATE OF CALIFORNIA V. SOON JA DU

"There Has to Be Justice"

On September 30, 1991, *The People of the State of California v. Soon Ja Du*, presided over by Judge Joyce Ann Karlin, began with its first witness—Ismail Ali.

Eight-year-old Ismail and his thirteen-year-old sister, Lakeshia Combs, were among the thirteen witnesses to testify during the three-day trial. Also included were Joseph, Billy, and Soon Ja Du, Denise Harlins, four LAPD officers, a weapons expert, a videotape editor, and the medical examiner.

Emotions ran high during the three days of court testimony.

Supporters for both families shouted at each other. Four plain-clothes sheriff's deputies were hired to protect Judge Karlin, who had received death threats. Soon Ja Du also received death threats, including one letter that read, "Buddha head, we're going to kill you."

Soon Ja's grown children were furious at the press camping outside their house. "I'm not going to talk with any reporters," her daughter Sandy was overheard saying. "They came over to our house in the middle of the night and scared the hell out of us."

Joseph insisted to the media that the shooting was an accident and had nothing to do with race. "My mother is made a scapegoat of Korean-Black tensions. She was merely trying to protect herself. Why is it they never publicize all the Koreans who were killed?"

Many in the Korean American community also felt the racial makeup of the jury was unfair. Out of the 135 prospective jurors considered for the jury, none were of Korean descent. The jury consisted of five Black, four Latino, three white, and zero Asian American members.

But Jerry Yu, executive director of the Korean American Coalition, believed compassion and justice were not mutually exclusive. He said although many Korean Americans felt compassion for the Du family, they also supported the Harlins family and wanted justice for their child.

"We can relate to [Soon Ja Du] as a Korean and we can pray for her that she not suffer," he said. "But, on the other hand, just because we are Korean, that doesn't mean we wanted her to get off. There has to be justice."

"This Is Not the Movies"

The first day of the trial received national coverage as the surveillance video of Soon Ja Du shooting Latasha Harlins was shown several times in the courtroom.

"This is not television," warned Deputy District Attorney Roxane Carvajal. "This is not the movies. This is real life. You will see Latasha being killed. She will die in front of your eyes."

Jurors and spectators gasped audibly as the one-minute videotape played. Aunt Denise, Grandma Ruth, and cousin Shinese wept. Soon Ja Du bowed her head, distraught. Her daughter Sandy handed her some water, caressing her mother's face. The two women cried.

"That's me!" Ismail Ali said on the witness stand, pointing to the TV as he watched the video.

Defense attorney Charles Lloyd argued that the shooting was an accident and an act of self-defense against an angry teenager who had punched the older store owner several times. He said Soon Ja Du did not premeditate the killing of Latasha Harlins: she had only grabbed the gun to protect herself. He reminded the jury of the multiple armed robberies, shoplifting incidents, and gang member death threats against the Dus over the years.

Lloyd and defense attorney Richard Leonard also brought in an LAPD weapons expert who confirmed the gun was defective. It turned out it had been stolen in the past and had been altered incorrectly, resulting in a defective trigger and hammer that responded to very little pressure and movement.

Prosecutor Carvajal said it didn't matter if it was self-defense on Soon Ja Du's part. Why?

Because Latasha Harlins had surrendered.

Carvajal reminded the jury that Latasha had placed the bottle of orange juice on the counter, had turned around, and was heading for the door when she was shot in the back of the head.

This, according to Carvajal, was first-degree murder.

On the third day, Soon Ja Du took the stand to testify.

"Did You Intend to Kill This Young Lady?"

On October 2, Soon Ja Du was the last witness to testify. She spoke in English and Korean. Three different Korean-language interpreters and her husband translated her testimony. She testified that she was afraid of Latasha Harlins and grabbed the gun in self-defense. She had never held a gun before and was trying to hold it in the way she saw guns used in the movies.

"When you grabbed this gun, did you intend to kill this young lady?" Richard Leonard asked.

"No, not at all," Soon Ja said. "I had no such thought at all." She began to cry.

Carvajal handed the gun over to a nervous Soon Ja Du. There were no bullets in it. She asked the store owner to demonstrate how she held the gun. Earlier witnesses testified Soon Ja had taken the gun out of its holster. Carvajal wanted to show that the store owner had purposely pulled the hammer back in anticipation—and premeditation—of shooting it at the girl.

"I want you to take this gun and show us how you learned in the movies to shoot the gun," Carvajal said.

"Do I have to touch this gun again?" Soon Ja asked.

"Yes, Mrs. Du. I want you to pull the trigger, how you learned in the movies to do it."

Soon Ja held the gun, placing her finger on the grip, not the trigger. She shook the gun.

"So this is how you shoot a gun, right?" Carvajal asked.

"Yes."

The store owner testified she had picked up the gun and suddenly "the girl who was just standing there just a moment ago was no longer there."

"And then what happened?"

Denise Harlins holds her devastated daughter Shinese tightly as they and a group of more than 150 protesters attend a demonstration rally outside the Empire Liquor store six days after Denise's niece, Latasha, was shot and killed by store owner Soon Ja Du in a dispute over a bottle of orange juice.

AL.8228 / Los Angeles Times
Relatives of the slain girl gather at the market in south L.A. They are, left to right, Ahneva Harlins, an aunt; Shinese Harlins, a cousin, and Denise Harlins, an aunt.

"And I did not know that the gun had discharged and like, like a scared, like a crazed person I kept yelling out for my husband. And then my husband came into the store, and I, I asked him, 'Where is that person who hit me?' and then I asked my husband to call the police. And I, I was, and I felt like I was going to vomit, and then I had a terrible headache. And, and I didn't have any strength in my legs, and I remember up to the point where I just fell down and at that—at that time I felt like it was—if I was having a seasickness, and after that I don't know too much."

"Thank you," Carvajal said. "Nothing further."

"Do the People rest?" asked Judge Karlin. "Anything further?"

"Not at this time, your Honor," Carvajal said.

"Railroaded by the Justice System"

On Friday, October 4, 1991, Judge Karlin reduced the charge of first-degree murder to second-degree murder for Soon Ja Du. Karlin believed Soon Ja Du had acted on "rash impulse."

First-degree murder had a maximum penalty of twenty-five years to life in prison. Second-degree murder had a shorter sentence of fifteen years to life.

Carvajal argued that Du did have an "intention to kill" because she shot Latasha in the back of her head. "Deliberation and premeditation can occur in a matter of seconds," the prosecutor said.

The Harlins family denounced Judge Karlin's ruling as "outrageous," saying Soon Ja Du had committed "cold-blooded murder."

Danny Bakewell and the Brotherhood Crusade cited Judge Karlin's decision as another example of systemic anti-Black racism. "It's the kind of thing that I feel causes the African American community to feel that it is getting railroaded by the justice system," he said.

The Verdict

On October 7, 1991, *The People of the State of California v. Soon Ja Du* moved the courtroom to a smaller room that had bulletproof glass separating spectators from the witness stand.

In her closing argument, Roxane Carvajal said Soon Ja Du acted with "gross negligence" in the shooting death of Latasha Harlins. The prosecutor dismissed the defense's claim that Soon Ja Du had no idea how to shoot a gun.

"She doesn't know how to use a gun, yet she takes it out of the holster and points it at Latasha," Carvajal said. "She knows that's how it goes off."

The defense maintained that this was not a crime of premeditated murder but an accident. "You have to consider what was happening at that point in time," said Richard Leonard. "Her state of mind is important." He said Soon Ja Du should be charged with involuntary manslaughter.

Soon Ja Du's fate—and the legacy of Latasha Harlins—was now in the hands of the jury.

. . .

Four days later, on October 11, after much debate and multiple viewings of the videotape, the jury announced their verdict.

Guilty.

But instead of being guilty of second-degree murder, the jury found Soon Ja Du guilty of voluntary manslaughter.

In California, the felony of voluntary manslaughter is defined as the unlawful killing of a person during an argument that escalates suddenly, in the "heat of passion," or when a person has an "honest but unreasonable belief in the need to defend oneself."

This crime had a maximum sentence of sixteen years in prison. Soon Ja Du was freed on a $250,000 bond. Sentencing was scheduled for November.

Soon Ja Du lowered her head and wept with her husband.

Denise Harlins was devastated: the verdict of voluntary manslaughter cheapened her niece's life. "She got away with murder," she told the press. "The judicial system let her get away with murder. There is no justice."

"This system of justice is not really justice," Ruth Harlins shouted. "They murdered my granddaughter!"

Several security guards quickly escorted Soon Ja Du and her family out. They did not speak to anyone.

Although defense attorney Charles Lloyd's request for a reduced charge for his client had been granted, he still acknowledged this was not something to celebrate.

"There's no victory for anybody," he said. "This was just a really very sad, heart-wrenching, soul-searching case."

• • •

Later that night, seven young men stopped by Empire Liquor. A For Sale sign was posted outside the now boarded-up store. They placed a giant poster of Latasha Harlins across the front door with the words "Never Again."

"This Is Not a Time for Revenge"

On November 15, Judge Joyce Karlin listened to the final statements by the attorneys and the Harlins family before announcing her decision in the sentencing of Soon Ja Du.

Both families and their supporters, along with dozens of TV news crews and journalists, packed the L.A. Superior Court.

Prosecutor Roxane Carvajal asked for the maximum sentence of sixteen years, also recommended by the official probation report. "If Mrs. Du is not incarcerated in this case, the message we are sending is, 'Yes, you can kill people and we do not put you in jail for that.' "

Judge Karlin criticized the prosecutor's statement as "dangerous rhetoric." "This is not a time for revenge," she said. "And it is not my job as a sentencing court to seek revenge for those who demand it."

But Carvajal didn't want revenge. She wanted justice for an honor roll student, a track star, and a "beautiful 15-year-old girl who was trying to do everything right" who had been killed. "Mrs. Du believed the victim was a gang member and that she was stealing from the store. She feared for her life. . . . She was wrong on all counts. Latasha was not stealing from the store. Latasha was not a gang member. Latasha was not trying to kill her. Latasha was trying to get her backpack and that was all."

Defense attorney Charles Lloyd vented his frustration at the media insinuating that this killing was racially motivated. "People have tried to make this a racial case. . . . It was unfortunately a teenage youngster going into a store where the owners had been threatened, had been robbed, had been burglarized. Threats have been made to burn their store down, to kill them, and a very fragile 49-year-old lady at the time using reasonable force as a shop owner has the right to do, attempted to question the young lady about some orange juice."

Although Lloyd believed Soon Ja Du had reacted in self-defense, he expressed sorrow for the Harlins. He said in his twenty-nine-year career that this was "the most difficult case I've ever had in my life."

"I have nothing but compassion [for] the family of this victim," Lloyd said. "I think this is so unfortunate. I mean this from the bottom of my heart. . . . This is a heart-wrenching case." He insisted that Soon Ja Du was "very remorseful" and presented a letter she wrote on October 25, 1991, to the family, translated by her daughter.

"I feel like I am suffering in a nightmare," Soon Ja Du wrote. "I am sad and overwhelmed by this incident. I would never intentionally harm anyone, let alone kill her. I'm struggling with unbelievable guilt feelings. Through this incident, I empathize with Latasha Harlins' family and friends. Being a mother myself, I full share in the sorrow."

Although Carvajal acknowledged the "great emotional burden" suffered by the Du family, "that does not outweigh the fact that Latasha Harlins was killed, a 15-year-old girl who had no reason to die, who should not have died but for Mrs. Du's actions."

Carvajal said any sentence less than the maximum sixteen years would send a message that Black life—and the life of a Black teenaged girl—was cheap. "Any other sentence, your Honor, would create a perception in the mind of the community that young black children do not receive the full protection of the law. The people strongly urge this court not to treat Latasha's life as if it were worthless because it was not."

Latasha's grandmother Ruth Harlins was the last person to address Judge Karlin. "My family and I have grieved severely. Soon Ja has her daughter with her in court today, but my granddaughter has been murdered and buried. . . . The joy and happiness that my granddaughter Latasha Harlins brought into our lives . . . will be no more."

She requested Soon Ja Du be given the maximum sentence. "I would be very disappointed if Soon Ja Du got away with probation. Thank you, your Honor."

$500

Throughout the three days of witness testimony for *The People of the State of California v. Soon Ja Du*, race was never mentioned.

The witnesses and legal counsel never once suggested that either Soon Ja Du or Latasha Harlins harbored any racist feelings toward each other.

The Du and Harlins families themselves did not express any feelings of anti-Black racism or anti-Asian xenophobia during their testimony.

The Dus insisted their fears were for gang members and not the Black community in general.

Latasha's aunt Denise Harlins dismissed allegations of racial tension between the Black and Korean communities. "There's never been any racial tensions," she said. "To me, it's economic."

Judge Karlin was the only one who brought up race in the courtroom.

She accused supporters of the Du and Harlins families of

demonstrating "intolerance and bigotry toward one another." "Latasha Harlins' death should be remembered as a catalyst that must force members of the African American and Korean communities to confront an intolerable situation by the creating of it solutions, and by creating solutions, hopefully a better understanding and acceptance can result so that similar tragedies will never be repeated."

"It is now a time for healing," Judge Karlin said. She warned both communities to stop "throwing gasoline on a fire that's already burning."

The judge also addressed the moments when Latasha Harlins hit Soon Ja Du. "Although Latasha Harlins was not armed with a weapon at the time of her death, she had used her fists as weapons just seconds before the shooting." Had there been no gun in the first place, the judge theorized Latasha herself could have potentially been charged with assault against the store owner.

Although Judge Karlin agreed Du was guilty of manslaughter, she felt that the store owner's "overreaction" was "understandable," saying that she had acted under "great provocation, coercion, and duress."

"It is my opinion that Mrs. Du is not a danger to the community and that she is not going to reoffend," she said.

The judge then sentenced Soon Ja Du to only five years of probation along with four hundred hours of community service and a $500 fine.

"Is the defendant a danger to society? I think not." Judge Karlin explained that "no matter what sentence this court imposes . . . Mrs. Du will be punished for the rest of her life. This is a crime that she will have to remember and live with every day of her life."

Judge Karlin then addressed the attorneys. "Anything further, counsel?" she asked.

"No, your Honor," Charles Lloyd said.

But prosecutor Roxane Carvajal had one final question.

"Your Honor, just so I'm clear, did you say '$500 fine'?" she asked pointedly.

"Yes."

"Thank you."

"All Hell Broke Loose"

"Murderer!" shouted angry supporters of the Harlins family after the sentencing. "We'll take this to the streets!"

Denise Harlins was so distraught that police officers had to hold her up to keep her from collapsing.

Tempers flared as supporters for both sides screamed and swore at each other in the packed hallway. A dozen sheriffs escorted protesters to the elevators.

"Thank you, God," Soon Ja Du said in Korean before her family and friends quickly escorted her from the courtroom.

Najee Ali, a former Crips gang member–turned–activist, was in tears. He had attended every day of the trial as a member of Danny Bakewell's Brotherhood Crusade. Members of the Harlins family held him back as he accused the Du family's defense attorney Charles Lloyd, who was Black, of being an "Uncle Tom."

"I was stunned that this woman was able to walk out of that courtroom and go home while Latasha's in a graveyard," Ali said later.

"My daughter was around three at the time," he remembered, his voice cracking. "For young Black men, I'm twenty-nine, and Latasha was all of our daughters, all of our baby sisters." For a few moments, he paused and wept, his grief still raw thirty years later. "So when she was murdered, it was like we were all murdered."

"All hell broke loose," Shinese remembered. "The courtroom

erupted. They started tearing that courtroom up. Trash cans, chairs that were sitting out in the hallway, all that was being thrown at the courtroom and everything. And me, I'm like wow, like what is this anger? I didn't understand the verdict of her not getting no jail time."

Outside, Ruth Harlins addressed the media as Shinese wept in the background. "I think it was an injustice. Justice has not been served. This lady has killed my fifteen-year-old granddaughter and she got away with five years' probation? This is an injustice. No. Justice has not been served."

"I'm not mad at any Korean person, I want that clear," emphasized Denise Harlins's friend Gina Rae, cofounder of the Latasha Harlins Justice Committee. "I am angry at the justice system. . . . African Americans don't get justice in the United States today."

While the Du family disappeared immediately from the public eye, the Harlins family and the Black community took to the streets. Danny Bakewell and the Brotherhood Crusade filed complaints against Judge Karlin and held "Karlin must go!" protests outside the Compton Courthouse and the judge's home in Manhattan Beach.

Many in the Korean American community were also disheartened by the sentencing.

Criminal defense attorney Angela Oh, also Korean American, wondered if Soon Ja Du would have received probation if she were not Korean. "I don't believe an African American defendant found guilty of voluntary manslaughter would have got straight probation," she said. Oh also "cringed" whenever people praised Judge Karlin's decision as "just." "It was compassionate, and it was extremely lenient, but I don't agree it was just."

Marcia Choo, the director of the Asian Pacific American Dispute Resolution Center and a member of the Black-Korean

Alliance, predicted Judge Karlin's probation sentencing would set back all of the BKA's progress of reconciliation and bridge-building. "It's going to make things more volatile."

Leon Jenkins, the Harlins's personal attorney, was disillusioned by a system he had spent his whole career championing.

"At one point in my life, I felt that an African American could get justice in this country," he reflected. "But with the Latasha Harlins case, it reinforced the fact that when all things being equal and sides have to be chosen, we were gonna be the ones left out. It's clear that our lives are not as valuable as anyone else in this country."

"I Am Torn between the World of Latasha Harlins and Soon Ja Du"

In a searing editorial for his *Korea Times English Edition* published on November 25, 1991, K. W. Lee condemned Judge Karlin's probation sentencing of Soon Ja Du as a "grievously myopic misjudgment."

"I am torn between the world of Latasha Harlins and Soon Ja Du, each sharing the tragic everyday life in one of the city's most violent and wretched districts—both in pursuit of that elusive American Dream," K. W. Lee wrote. "I, along with every thoughtful Korean . . . share the grief and anger of the Harlins family and friends. Latasha's name is etched deeply in the collective conscience of Korean Americans everywhere in their American passage."

K. W. Lee declared that there was hard work and a lot of soul-searching ahead for the Korean American community. "We New Americans must demonstrate through plain and specific deeds that we are not only good neighbors but participants in helping rebuild the scarred and ravaged neighborhoods. That's the Number One lesson from the Latasha Harlins tragedy. And that's the only way for us to remember and cherish the name of a young soul, who, like so many young African Americans, has died so young."

· · ·

One day after K. W. Lee's editorial was published, someone threw a lit bottle filled with gasoline-soaked rags onto the roof of Ace Liquor. It was the fifth Korean-owned store in South L.A. to be firebombed in the past six months. The bottle burned out quickly, and there was no damage.

"I think Koreans are a target right now," warned Angela Oh. "We have to recognize that Judge Joyce Karlin did not do anything to quell tensions. The easiest targets are individual merchants that are sitting out there."

Her warning would soon become a reality. The fire was already burning.

And another upcoming, high-profile trial would throw gasoline onto this fire.

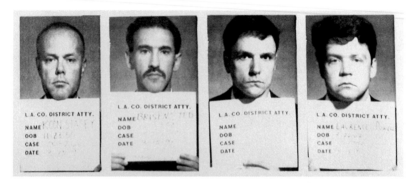

Mug shots from March 14, 1991, of (left to right) LAPD sergeant Stacey Koon and officers Theodore Briseno, Timothy Wind, and Laurence Powell, after they were indicted on excessive force, assault, and other charges in the beating of motorist Rodney King eleven days earlier.

Chapter 7

THE PEOPLE OF THE STATE OF CALIFORNIA V. LAURENCE POWELL, TIMOTHY E. WIND, THEODORE BRISEÑO, AND STACEY KOON

One Story, Two Versions

Not guilty.

That was the plea entered by the four police officers charged in the beating case of Rodney Glen King.

On April 3, 1992, LAPD officer Theodore Briseno testified in court that he was trying to deescalate the situation and stop the other officers' baton blows. "I just thought the whole thing was out of control," he said as George Holliday's video of the LAPD beating of Rodney King was shown to the jury.

On March 5, 1992, *The People of the State of California v. Laurence Powell, Timothy E. Wind, Theodore Briseno, and Stacey Koon* began.

All four police officers were charged with assault and excessive force. Sergeant Koon and Officer Powell were also charged with filing false police reports.

If convicted, they would all face four to eight years behind bars.

There were fifty-four witnesses, most of them LAPD officers, employees, doctors and medical staffers, and experts.

There were 128 pieces of evidence, including police reports, photographs, X-rays of Rodney Glen King's injuries, and the George Holliday videotape.

There were physical demonstrations as both the prosecutor and defense attorneys, along with witnesses, reenacted the baton blows and the beating in the courtroom.

There were tears.

And there was controversy.

Defense attorneys believed the "highly charged political climate" in Los Angeles would prevent their clients from receiving a fair trial there. So the trial was moved from the diverse city of Los Angeles to the East Ventura County Courthouse in Simi Valley.

Only 2 percent of Simi Valley's population was Black, with the majority white.

And Simi Valley was home to almost three hundred LAPD officers and their families. According to an American Civil Liberties Union study, 83 percent of police officers lived outside of Los Angeles back then. Critics said this self-imposed segregation contributed to lack of personal connection between the LAPD and the communities they had vowed "to protect and to serve."

The jury was mostly white—six white men, four white women, one Latina woman, and one Filipina American woman. (In 2012, one of the white male jurors would reveal he had been born to a white mother and Black father but chose to identify as white back at the time of the trial. He later identified as biracial.)

Like the Soon Ja Du trial, the media packed the courthouse. Dozens of sheriff's deputies guarded the area. Everyone had to pass through metal detectors before entering the building.

The opening statements by the prosecutor and defense presented two versions of the same story. Was this a case of self-defense against a "violent felon" on parole resisting arrest? Or was this police brutality against an unarmed man by four "out of control" police officers?

These two arguments mirrored the Soon Ja Du trial, in which the teenager and the store owner were portrayed by opposing sides as both the aggressor and the victim.

"Whatever Rodney King was, or whatever Rodney King did, it did not justify what you saw on this videotape," declared the deputy district attorney and lead prosecutor Terry White. "You have a man who was down, a man who was not resisting, a man who was not aggressive. And yet, those blows from those batons continue and continue and continue for no justifiable reason." He reminded the jury that King had testified in earlier hearings and told the press that he had obeyed the police and he had only risen to his feet in an attempt to run away, not charge at the officers.

But the defense attorneys for the four officers—Darryl Mounger for Koon, Michael Stone for Powell, Paul DePasquale for Wind, and John Barnett for Briseno—had a completely different version of what had happened that night. They argued that their clients did not abuse their power while arresting Rodney King. Instead, their clients were following proper police protocol and training to subdue King's "erratic behavior," alleging that he refused to stay still.

"The only one person who was in charge of this incident was Rodney Glen King," said one of the defense attorneys.

• • •

Although fifty-four witnesses testified over the next two months of the trial, one witness was not present.

Rodney Glen King.

Lead prosecutor Terry White said there was no need for King to testify because George Holliday's video spoke for him. "You have a videotape in this case which shows impartially, without bias, what happened that night."

The People's Exhibit No. 1

On March 5, 1992, the first day of the trial, George Holliday's video, marked as the "People's Exhibit No. 1," was played five times to the jury.

Many of the jurors had trouble watching the violent video.

Dorothy Bailey, sixty-four, was one of the few people who had never seen the video before. "I was as (repulsed) as everybody else in the country was," she said after viewing it for the first time.

But this was not the same video that most people had already seen. Holliday's original video had been edited for TV news broadcasts. The video at the trial included an extra thirteen seconds that the jury—and the world—had never seen before.

In these additional seconds, jurors saw for the first time Rodney King rising from his hands and knees and charging in the direction of Officer Laurence Powell, who hits him in the shoulder with his baton. King falls face down to the ground. The next several seconds were blurry because Holliday was still learning how to operate the focus on his new camera.

"What it shows is . . . that Rodney King charges in the direction of one of the officers, Laurence Powell, who swings the most blows," explained Lou Cannon, a *Washington Post* reporter covering the trial. "The point is, that when you see the abbreviated videotape, what you see is white officers beating a Black man for no reason. So, all of a sudden, there's a reason."

George Holliday was the first witness to testify at the trial. He estimated it took about seventy seconds between the time he heard the commotion outside his window and when he started recording. Because Holliday missed the beginning of the altercation, the defense attorneys claimed the videotape was an unreliable witness because it did not show the full story of Rodney King's actions prior to the beating.

• • •

Once the video came back into focus, jurors saw Powell hitting King numerous times.

By the seventeenth second of Holliday's video, Rodney King was on his stomach. Powell raises his baton, but Officer Briseno stops him, putting his hand out. King rises again. Powell strikes him with his baton. Then Officer Wind steps in, hitting King in the back with his baton. Powell keeps hitting King, who falls down again. As King tries to rise, Powell and Wind hit him again.

By the thirtieth second of the video, King collapses face down. He keeps moving as Powell and Wind hit him continually with their batons. As Powell reaches for his handcuffs, Officer Briseno appears to stomp his foot near King's neck and shoulder.

About ninety seconds into the video, Sergeant Koon approaches King, who is sitting on the ground, his hands on his head. At the end of the video, Officer Briseno handcuffs him.

In addition to being tased twice by Sergeant Koon, Rodney King was hit a total of fifty-six times by Officers Powell, Wind, and Briseno.

Although Rodney King was outnumbered, on the ground, and struck repeatedly, all four officers and their defense attorneys insisted they were the ones who were scared. "I was completely in fear for my life," Officer Powell said on the stand.

In his testimony, Sergeant Koon described Rodney King as "very buffed out" and assumed he was an ex-con. He also repeated his suspicions that King was on PCP, even though toxicology tests later proved he was not. He defended commanding his officers to use their batons because King was an "imminent threat."

"We Hit Quite a Few Home Runs"

As in the Soon Ja Du trial, attorneys for both sides did not want to bring up race. Rodney King was Black. The four LAPD police officers were not—Stacey Koon, Laurence Powell, and Timothy

Wind were white, and Theodore Briseno identified as biracial and Latino (his father was of Mexican descent).

The attorneys believed the topic of race would distract from their job at hand—to determine if four police officers were guilty of assault and the use of excessive force on an unarmed suspect.

But during the two months of testimony and arguments, it became impossible to ignore race. Officers used animal imagery to describe King. "Lizard." "Dog." "Bear." One officer compared King's "staggering" toward them like "a scene from a monster movie." Officer Powell later joked in a patrol-car computer message (an early form of email), "Oops, I haven't beaten anyone this bad in a long time."

Two emergency-room nurses testified Officers Powell and Wind had joked about the beating, comparing it to a baseball game. One nurse said she overheard Powell joke, "We hit quite a few home runs."

The most controversial evidence was the phrase "gorillas in the mist." Earlier that same evening, Officers Powell and Wind had answered a domestic dispute call. Afterward, Powell joked about that call via the patrol-car computer message system, writing, "It was right out of 'Gorillas in the Mist.'"

Gorillas in the Mist was a famous 1988 movie about scientist Dian Fossey, who had spent her life studying mountain gorillas in Congo and Rwanda.

The family involved in that domestic dispute call was Black.

Mayor Tom Bradley, who had fought against racism as the first Black lieutenant to lead an integrated unit at the LAPD in 1958, was disgusted by these "bigoted remarks."

"It is no longer possible for any objective person to regard the King beating as an aberration," Mayor Bradley said. "We must face the fact that there appears to be a dangerous trend of racially motivated incidents running through at least some segments of our Police Department."

Officer Powell testified he was "scared to death" on the night of March 3, 1991, describing Rodney King as a "big man" with "very powerful arms." "I was completely in fear for my life, scared to death that if the guy got up again he was going to take my gun and there would be a shooting and I did everything I could to keep him down on the ground."

"At any time during this evening did it go through your mind that this was not a human being that you were beating?" Deputy District Attorney Terry White asked Powell.

"No."

"He deserves to be treated like a human being, didn't he?"

"Yes, sir."

"He wasn't an animal, was he?"

"No sir," Powell answered. "Just acting like one."

"Enough Is Enough!"

During the closing arguments on April 21 and 22, 1992, *The People of the State of California v. Laurence Powell, Timothy E. Wind, Theodore Briseno, and Stacey Koon* was still one story—but now with three versions.

According to the prosecution, it was four "out of control" police officers committing a horrific act of police brutality against an unarmed man.

According to the defense, it was the "imminent threat" of an allegedly dangerous man resisting arrest and forcing four police officers to resort to lethal force in order to subdue him and protect themselves.

But given the added evidence of racially charged police

communication, a new question had arisen. Did anti-Black racism influence the actions by these police officers against Rodney Glen King?

In his closing arguments, lead prosecutor Terry White condemned the racist language and problematic behavior exhibited by Powell and the other officers after King's arrest. He reminded the jury that the police must not only follow the law but also "treat suspects like human beings."

He accused Sergeant Koon of creating a "managed and controlled cover-up" of the beating scandal. "He knew what the officers were doing, allowed it to go on, and allowed the beating to continue."

White held up Officer Briseno's heavy black boot, the same one he had pressed against Rodney King's neck. Officers Briseno and Wind were both "caught up in the frenzy," White declared.

Despite the dramatic moments and props, White reminded the jury that all they really needed was the videotape. There was no way anyone could misinterpret what was happening on-screen.

"Look at the tape," White said. "What you see is a man feeling the pain of these batons. This was a man in pain. . . . They continued to hit him and hit him and hit him. And you've got to at some point say, 'Enough is enough! Stop it!' "

"You're Going to Have to Stand in Their Shoes"

But the defense team encouraged the jury not to rely completely on the videotape. They said it was an unreliable witness. It was more important, they claimed, to see what happened from the police officers' point of view.

"When you make a decision on whether these officers are guilty or not guilty, you're not going to be able to look through the eye of the camera," said Michael Stone, Laurence Powell's attorney. "You're going to have to stand in their shoes." Stone asked the jury to have compassion for the officers who risked their lives every day to protect and to serve their community. "These are not RoboCops. They hurt [and] they bleed and they die, just like everybody else."

Like prosecutor Terry White, Stone had his own dramatic moment when he dropped a police baton on the floor, the sound clattering through the courtroom. He had jurors hold the baton and imagine what damage it could have done if struck against anyone's head. This demonstration, he told the jury, proved the four officers could not have struck Rodney King in the head because of the baton's heft and weight.

"I want you to handle this baton. I want you to pick it up, and I want you to feel it. And I want you to wonder whether Mr. King would even be alive today."

Attorney John Barnett defended his client, Officer Thomas Briseno, as the only officer who tried to *stop* the beating. He claimed Briseno did not "kick" King in the head but tried to firmly place his foot on King's neck to keep him still in order to stop the three other "out of control" officers from beating him any further. Barnett invoked former chief William H. Parker's famous "thin blue line" phrase, claiming the other three officers "truly believe that it's a jungle and that there is this thin blue line."

Sergeant Koon's attorney, Darryl Mounger, argued Koon was simply trying to protect his officers. "Sgt. Koon was making instantaneous decisions. He didn't have 81 seconds. He had fractions of seconds and he was doing what he had to do when he had to do it."

Timothy Wind was the only police officer who did not testify at the trial. His defender, Paul DePasquale, said Wind did the least amount of beating (fifteen of the fifty-six blows) and behaved professionally the entire time. "All Tim Wind did that night was his job. He didn't make jokes and he didn't have fun and he didn't take any cheap shots."

"When Cops Do Not Follow the Law?"

On April 22, the last day of testimony, prosecutor Terry White gave his final rebuttal to the defense before the case went to the jury. Despite his now hoarse voice and constant coughing, White did not hold back.

Koon's leadership was ineffective and unethical.

Wind was just following orders—but that still was not enough of an excuse.

Briseno "only" kicked King once, but that one kick was still "unreasonable force."

As for the "thin blue line," White asked, "what kind of world would you have without cops? Well, I ask, what kind of world would we have when cops do not follow the law?"

White saved his harshest words for Officer Laurence Powell, calling him a "thug." After more than two months of intense witness testimony and sometimes acrimonious questioning, White was exhausted.

And emotional.

To the shock of those in the courtroom, the prosecutor suddenly rushed from his podium to where Powell was sitting.

"Look at him!" White shouted hoarsely, stabbing his finger in the air, just a few inches away from Powell's face. "This man laughed! This man taunted! And he's denying it!"

Powell was stunned. His attorney, Michael Stone, furious, jumped up and blocked his client.

"Mr. White, get back to the podium," Judge Stanley Weisberg ordered.

White apologized to the jury for his sudden outburst. "That was uncalled for," he said.

But White did not apologize for his fury directed at Powell. "They treated him like an animal, and yet Michael Stone does not . . . want me to call his client a thug," he said.

And then he reminded Powell and everyone in the courtroom of what he had said earlier on the stand.

"You are not a thug but you are acting like one," White said to Powell. "Just like Mr. King wasn't an animal but 'he was acting like one.'"

"The Trial Had Been Stacked against Me from the Start"

Rodney Glen King was upset when he was not asked to testify at the trial. "Those jurors needed to see the person, look into the eyes and hear the voice of the victim in that video."

King also believed the defense team for the police officers had manipulated the facts—and the jury.

"It felt like the trial had been stacked against me from the start," he said. "As if the defense attorneys were saying over and over again, 'What you see is not what happened. You've grown up knowing that the color is blue, but for this trial, we're going to say it's red, and that's what you must agree to believe.'"

"Be Cool"

On April 23, Judge Weisberg told the jurors, "Reach a just verdict, regardless of the consequences."

The jurors were sequestered at a nearby Travelodge. Sheriff's deputies guarded the hotel to keep the jurors safe and to make sure they did not interact with the public or the media. Jurors were forbidden from reading, watching, or listening to the news.

Hotel staff removed all TV sets and radios from their rooms. Even their private phone calls were monitored.

As the jury deliberated, many people in the city assumed the verdicts would be guilty. Public-opinion polls of all races and ethnic groups showed a majority believed the police officers had used excessive force. Even many LAPD officers, including Chief Daryl F. Gates, assumed Officers Powell, Briseno, Wind, and Koon would be convicted.

But not everyone in the Black community was so sure. At the First African Methodist Episcopal (AME) Church of Los Angeles, Reverend Dr. Cecil L. "Chip" Murray urged for calm. The church, founded in 1872, was known for its politically active and socially conscious congregation. So was Reverend Murray: after graduating with a PhD in religion from Claremont College, the now sixty-three-year-old minister was famous for his "faith in action" ministry against racism, poverty, and other social issues.

"Be cool," Murray said. "Even in anger, be cool." He reminded people about the devastation after the 1965 Watts rebellion.

"If you're gonna burn something down, don't burn down the house of the victims, brother!" he said. "Burn down the Legislature! Burn down the courtroom! Burn it down by voting, brother! Burn it down by standing with us at Parker Center, brother! Burn it down by saying to Daryl F. Gates: 'This far, and no farther!'"

After the sixth day of jury deliberations without a verdict, news broke that LAPD chief Daryl F. Gates had put aside $1 million in an overtime fund in case civil unrest occurred after the verdicts.

City councilman Mark Ridley-Thomas criticized Gates, saying this overtime fund made it seem as if the LAPD was "arming itself."

"We should not repeat the errors of the past," Ridley-Thomas said, alluding to the 1965 Watts rebellion. "A massive show of force would be a mistake. These are very tense times."

The councilman and other leaders, along with the First AME Church, set up Operation Cool Response, a group of two hundred volunteers ready to keep the peace in L.A. once the verdicts were announced.

Gates dismissed concerns of potential rioting. "We're not going to overreact to anything," he said. "If we have a problem, we'll be there with enough officers to deal with it, in a proper way," he said confidently.

In less than twenty-four hours, Gates's words would come back to haunt him—and the city.

"Beyond a Reasonable Doubt"

On the night before the seventh day of jury deliberations, juror Virginia Loya hid in her hotel bathroom, crying into her towel so no one could hear her.

Loya called her husband, who comforted her. "Do what you have to do," he advised.

Loya and the other jurors had been debating for days about whether or not the four police officers had actually struck Rodney King in the head with their batons. In addition to the videotape, there was conflicting testimony during the trial. CHP officers Melanie and Timothy Singer testified they saw Powell strike King multiple times on the left side of his head, even though photographs showed no marks there.

"We could not prove to ourselves—beyond a reasonable doubt—based on testimony and looking at the video . . . that there were head shots," said Dorothy Bailey, who had been elected as jury foreperson.

The jury argued the longest about Officer Laurence Powell's innocence or guilt. Loya asked to rewatch the video so many times that the other jurors grew impatient and even made fun of her. She was so conflicted that she fasted for over a day to clear her mind.

Bailey herself had "a vague, nagging feeling that for at least the last ten or eleven seconds of that tape, there was guilt."

But Judge Weisberg had given his instructions: if the jury chose to convict, it had to be "beyond a reasonable doubt."

"You cannot convict a man on a vague, nagging feeling," Bailey said. "You must have an abiding conviction to a moral certainty. . . . It would have been easy to go in and say, 'I have a gut feeling,' and find him guilty. But we couldn't do that."

The next day, the jury finally agreed with each other on all counts except one: they were deadlocked on Powell's fate.

Many people on the jury wept during this final deliberation. "It was highly charged," admitted one juror. "I broke down crying. Several other people did too."

But they were finally done. The jury was ready to announce its verdict.

Wednesday, April 29, 1992, 3:15 p.m.

"We the jury, in the above entitled action, find the defendant Laurence M. Powell not guilty of the crime of assault by force likely to produce great bodily injury, and with a deadly weapon, in violation of Penal Code Section 245A1, a Felony, as charged in Count 1 of the amended indictment, this 29th day of April, 1992, signed by the foreman."

"We the jury, in the above entitled action, find the defendant Timothy E. Wind not guilty."

"Theodore J. Briseno, not guilty."

"Stacey C. Koon, not guilty."

"Not guilty." LAPD officer Laurence Powell (facing the camera) hugs Timothy Wind, with Sergeant Stacey Koon smiling in the background, after hearing the April 29, 1992, jury acquittal of all four officers (including Theodore Briseno) in the beating case of Rodney King.

The jury remained deadlocked eight to four on the charge of "excessive force under the color of authority" by Laurence M. Powell.

In the end, the jury had reached a verdict on all counts except for that one.

And all these verdicts were "not guilty."

"Ladies and gentlemen of the jury, are these your verdicts, so say you one, so say you all?" asked Judge Stanley Weisberg.

"Yes," said the jury.

• • •

It only took a few minutes for the jury to announce all their verdicts.

And it only took a few hours before Los Angeles exploded.

Chapter 8

FLASHPOINT— FLORENCE AND NORMANDIE

"The System Failed Us"

For the past year, Rodney King's children had been to counseling to cope with the trauma of what happened not only to their father but also to them. People stalked them at their elementary schools. Strangers called their homes with death threats, saying their father "had it coming."

Like the Harlins children, Lora and the other King children were scared to leave home. They saw their father everywhere—in the newspaper, on TV, and even on people's T-shirts.

On April 29, 1992, when the not-guilty verdicts were announced, Glen's ex-wife, Dennetta Lyles King, cried even more

April 29, 1992: Demonstrators throw rocks, bottles, and Molotov cocktails at passing cars at the intersection of Florence and Normandie in protest of the not-guilty verdicts in the LAPD beating case of Rodney King. Drivers abandon their cars and escape on foot as several vehicles catch fire.

than when she first saw the Holliday video on the news over a year ago.

"It hurt my heart," she said. "I cried. I really cried. Like, *wow*. It made me see how America really is."

• • •

As the verdicts were announced, Rodney Glen King and his friend Tom Owens were recording each other on their camcorders, just like George Holliday had recorded the LAPD beating. They wanted to capture the moment of justice in Glen's apartment in Studio City.

"Not guilty." "Not guilty." "Not guilty." "Not guilty."

Glen sat "absolutely motionless" as the verdicts were announced. "King's reaction was one of pure disbelief," Owens remembered. "It took him awhile to fully comprehend what had occurred."

As shock and rage flooded his body, Glen wished he could disappear. "I just wanted to close my eyes and open them as another person someplace a thousand miles away," he remembered.

. . .

Mayor Tom Bradley watched the verdicts live on his office TV. The first Black LAPD lieutenant to lead an integrated company of white and Black cops shook with anger at each "not guilty."

He condemned the verdicts, saying at a press conference, "The system failed us."

"Today, the jury told the world that what we all saw with our own eyes was not a crime," he said. "Today that jury said we should tolerate such conduct by those who are sworn to protect and serve. My friends, I am here to tell the jury . . . our eyes did not deceive us. We saw what we saw, and what we saw was a crime. No, we will not tolerate the savage beating of our citizens by a few renegade cops."

Mayor Tom Bradley (himself a retired LAPD officer) looks on at a press conference on April 30, 1992, as LAPD chief Daryl F. Gates (at the microphone) fields questions about the violence and civil unrest sweeping the city of Los Angeles.

Despite his fury, Mayor Bradley pled for calm. He told everyone to channel their "profound rage" to "bring honor to ourselves and our community" and prevent civil unrest like the 1965 Watts rebellion.

"We must not bury the gains we have made in the rubble caused by destructive behavior," he said.

• • •

Reverend Dr. Cecil Murray sat in a meeting room in the basement of the First AME Church, watching the verdicts live on TV.

As the jury kept repeating the words "not guilty," silence and shock reigned through the church.

Reverend Murray remained stoic, but a tear rolled down his face.

"If something in you can die, that something died," he said.

"Now People Won't Say We're All Bad"

When the verdicts were announced, armed sentries stood guard outside the Foothill Station as well as other police stations throughout L.A. County.

Since the 1991 Rodney King beating, the Foothill Station had hired more police officers of color. But as the not-guilty verdicts were announced, several police officers who worked under Sergeant Stacey Koon cheered.

Other police officers at the Foothill Station were just grateful the trial had ended so they could move forward with their jobs. They resented how the public assumed all police officers, no matter how ethical, were "guilty by association."

"Now I can breathe," said one officer. "Now people won't say we're all bad. Now we won't get cursed out all the time."

"Mr. Lee's"

Neighbors had nicknamed the Pay-less Liquor and Deli store on the corner of Florence and Dalton Avenues in South L.A. as "Mr. Lee's" after its Korean American owner Samuel Lee.

After the not-guilty verdicts were announced, five young Black men entered Mr. Lee's. They grabbed several bottles of beer and tried to leave without paying as a protest. Samuel's son David blocked their way out.

The teens grew angry. One smashed his bottle over David's head. The others threw their bottles against the door. As glass shattered, one young man shouted, "This is for Rodney King!"

Samuel Lee, protected behind a bulletproof counter, hit the silent alarm.

"It Got Ugly"

Just a few blocks away from Mr. Lee's liquor store, a growing crowd of protesters gathered under the palm trees at Florence and Halldale. They screamed at several nearby police officers arresting a group of men for breaking car windows and throwing bottles at passing motorists.

But what the crowd saw were cops handcuffing Black men against patrol cars.

"Man, you should be ashamed of yourself!" someone shouted.

"It got ugly," remembered one officer. "We were the friendly neighborhood cops one minute, the next minute we were lunch meat."

"In the Wrong Place at the Right Time"

Like George Holliday, Timothy Goldman had recently bought his first camcorder. He and his brother Terry Ellis had driven around the day before, filming their neighborhood.

When the brothers heard about an irate crowd protesting the cops near where they lived, Goldman grabbed his camcorder, and they headed over.

As they approached the crowd, Goldman hit the "record" button, unaware that he was capturing the first live moments that would erupt into the 1992 Los Angeles uprising.

The crowd began heading east. Goldman and Ellis, who were Black, were also angry about the verdicts. They followed everyone down the block, with Goldman still recording.

But as they reached the corner of Florence and Normandie, Goldman's heart grew heavy at the sight of a crowd throwing rocks and bottles at passing cars and breaking into nearby stores. He had no idea he was now at the flashpoint that would set the entire city on fire.

"All of a sudden, it was transformed into a war zone," he said. "Everything that happened in the riots happened at that intersection. You had the looting, you had the arson, you had the beatings, you had shootings."

It was now 5:25 p.m. Police patrol cars arrived at the corner of Florence and Normandie, responding to calls for backup from the other police officers already in the area.

Goldman and his brother headed for Tom's Liquor, located at the intersection, which was also being ransacked.

Goldman tried to stop the looters. "Be cool, it's not worth it," he shouted at them. But they ignored him. More people rushed into the store. As he kept recording, Goldman suddenly recognized one of the looters on his camcorder.

It was his brother.

Looking back, Terry Ellis regretted his impulsive decision to run into the store. "I might as well get me some beer," he said, describing his feelings at the time. Years later, Ellis would join Reverend Cecil Murray's First AME Church as an usher.

"I didn't scold him for it," Goldman said. "But that's something I wouldn't have done."

The two brothers were close growing up. But after high school, Goldman had gone to serve in the Air Force while his brother served two-and-a-half years in prison for drug offenses. Goldman had moved from Florida back to his old South L.A. neighborhood the previous year. He was living with his mother, a local teacher, while applying for jobs in the airline industry.

Goldman kept recording for three more hours. He captured other pivotal moments that police would later confiscate as evidence. Like the George Holliday video of the LAPD beating of Rodney King, Goldman's Florence and Normandie video would also become a part of history.

"I didn't know it would escalate like it did," Goldman later said. "I was just probably in the wrong place at the right time." But right time or not, Goldman could no longer handle the violence. "I was just too sick to go see anything else," he said. "I turned the camera off, and I just walked home."

"Get Out!"

When the not-guilty verdicts were announced at 3:15 p.m., there were only 838 LAPD police officers on duty.

In a city of over 3.48 million people.

Barely two-and-a-half hours later, about three dozen of those officers found themselves surrounded by more than two hundred demonstrators, some of them armed gang members, at the intersection of Florence and Normandie Avenues in South Los Angeles.

The last LAPD police cruiser leaves Florence and Normandie on April 29, captured by *Los Angeles Times* photographer Hyungwon Kang. "When I heard 'All units, all units, evacuate from Florence and Normandie!' on the police scanner, that's when I knew there was trouble, and that it was going to grow into a bigger problem," Kang said.

People were smashing bricks into windshields of cars passing by, causing terrified drivers to abandon their vehicles. They also threw rocks at nearby LAPD patrol cars.

"Fuck the police!" they screamed.

LAPD lieutenant Mike Moulin knew they were in trouble.

The highest-ranking officer on the scene, the twenty-one-year police force veteran had just driven from the 77th Street police station to the intersection of Florence and Normandie. What he saw was "utter chaos."

"Anarchy was occurring before our very eyes," he said. "The officers were being subjected to bricks, to huge pieces of concrete, to boards, to flying objects."

His officers were completely unprepared. They had no helmets. No face shields. No bulletproof vests. No tear gas.

But they did have guns, and Lieutenant Moulin feared they might have to resort to lethal force if the violence didn't stop. There were only twenty-five to thirty-five cops present among a crowd of hundreds. "We could have a massacre here," he realized.

At 5:43 p.m., Lieutenant Moulin made an announcement through the LAPD patrol-car public address system. "I want everybody out of the area of Florence and Normandie," he said. "Everybody get out of the area."

Moulin's officers were shocked. *Get out?* But they all had sworn to the LAPD oath, "To Protect and to Serve."

"Bullshit," snapped one police officer over the live radio.

Moulin repeated his order over the loudspeaker. "Everybody out of here, Florence and Normandie. Everybody, get out!"

"There was no correct decision to make," Moulin later told reporters, defending his decision to pull out. "We would have had 25 dead police officers and several hundred dead citizens, and you would have been talking about real chaos."

Meanwhile, Police Chief Daryl F. Gates had just left Parker Center for a political fundraiser in Brentwood. As the violence erupted on Florence and Normandie, he was stuck in rush-hour traffic.

Gates later regretted leaving for the fundraiser. There, he confirmed to guests during his speech that the police had been forced to evacuate Florence and Normandie.

"There are going to be situations where people are going to go without assistance," Gates told them. "That's just the facts of life."

Back at Florence and Normandie, the last black-and-white patrol car had left the intersection by 6:25 p.m.

People in the neighborhood were on their own now.

"Get Out of There!"

Carol K. Park's mother was trapped.

The not-guilty verdicts had just been announced.

Son Lye Park was working at the family gas station located just eleven minutes away from Florence and Normandie. A crowd had gathered there, screaming and throwing cans and rocks at cars.

Meanwhile, Carol, twelve, had just come home from school. Carol, along with her two older brothers, had been working at the gas station for the past two years after their father died and they couldn't afford to hire another employee. Many customers were curious about Carol: what was this little girl doing behind the register in a bulletproof cashier's booth? But her mother advised her to say she was sixteen whenever anyone asked her age.

During her all-night shifts after school, Carol took naps in a sleeping bag on the floor. She and her mother rinsed rice in the bathroom sink for dinner.

One of their gas station's most popular sales items was the "love rose," a novelty toy glass pipe containing a cloth rose. Carol later learned their customers replaced the rose with a rock of crack cocaine.

Life was dangerous at the gas station. Bullets from nearby gang shootings nicked their bulletproof window and concrete walls. These bullet holes still exist today.

Carol escaped by reading her favorite *Anne of Green Gables* books during her shifts. "I loved reading old books. Books where there were no such things as gas stations. That's how I left Compton in my brain."

Carol wasn't scheduled to work until the weekend. But after she and her two brothers saw the civil unrest breaking out at Florence and Normandie on TV, they immediately called their mother.

Son Lye told her children that due to the panicked customers, the station pumps had already emptied out. She had sold 9,000 gallons of gas.

"Just leave," Carol's brother shouted. "Just go to the car as fast as you can and get out of there!"

Before she left, Son Lye hid all the cash they had earned that day in a blue water bucket, stuffing rags, paper towels, and empty soda cans on top. She pretended to dump the "trash" into the nearby dumpster as she walked toward her car. It was the longest seventy-five feet she had ever walked in her life.

Son Lye finally arrived home with the blue bucket overflowing with trash and cash. Still in shock, she left it in the living room and proceeded to pull out leftovers from the fridge—some bean sprouts and cold bulgogi.

"She ate like nothing had happened," Carol remembered.

"This Is for Rodney King!"

On her way home from school that afternoon, Lora King decided to visit the neighborhood liquor store to buy her usual candy bar. She and her mother, Dennetta, adored the Korean American couple, Sue and George, who owned the store. "They were like our grandparents," Dennetta said. "They knew our whole family."

On her way to the store, Lora suddenly smelled smoke. The street was on fire. She raced home. "I was terrified. I didn't know what the hell was going on."

At home, her mother was already weeping, the TV news blaring in the background. Lora sat by the window, watching the violence spill across the street. "It was mass chaos, people running all over, fires and smoke everywhere," she said.

As her mother continued to cry, Lora heard people screaming, "This is for Rodney King!"

"HONK FOR PEACE." On May 1, 1992, photojournalist Yael Swerdlow captured Bobby Wade advocating for peace on the corner of Pico Boulevard and Fairfax Avenue. Two decades later they met by chance at Cedars-Sinai Hospital. Wade told Swerdlow that her photo was a "watershed moment in his life" and how proud his mother was of him.

"And that's when I put two and two together," she said. "That's when I realized it was bigger than what I can imagine."

"I've Got to See This Through"

"All units, all units, evacuate Florence and Normandie immediately."

Hyungwon Kang turned the volume up. The twenty-nine-year-old photographer was driving eastbound down Florence Avenue in one of the *Los Angeles Times* cars equipped with a police scanner for breaking news.

"I heard that, so I knew cops were pulling out there," Kang said. "It was getting ugly and dirty. And I wanted to document it, so I drove in."

Kirk McKoy, another *Los Angeles Times* photographer who worked with Kang, was already there, taking photos of the crowd. The first photo he shot was of a young man smashing a rock into the driver's window of a white Honda Civic hatchback.

But McKoy also witnessed acts of heroism. He documented the rescue of a man who had been assaulted and robbed at a nearby bus stop. "He lay there defenseless. And a man picked him up and said, 'Let me get you out of here before they kill you.'"

But it wasn't long before the crowd soon found their new target. As more photographers, reporters, and TV camera crews arrived at the intersection, they were immediately attacked. McKoy witnessed one protester ripping the camera off a photographer's shoulder. Earlier, Timothy Goldman, who was the first to start recording the violence at Florence and Normandie on his camcorder, escorted a *New York Times* photographer safely to his

The first picture taken by *Los Angeles Times* photographer Kirk McKoy after he arrived at the corner of Florence and Normandie in the late afternoon of April 29, 1992, showed a young protester smashing a rock into the window of a motorist trying to pass through the blocked intersection.

car. Another family rescued a *Boston Globe* freelancer, hiding him under a blanket as they drove him to the hospital.

Because McKoy, who was Black, towered at six-feet-four, no one bothered him at first, even though he was carrying a camera. "It definitely protected me when I first got down there," he said. "I'm six-four and 250 pounds, so I'm not a little guy. No one's gonna mess with me."

Despite his size, McKoy didn't stay safe for long.

"Take his camera!" someone shouted.

A group of protesters rushed McKoy. Adrenaline flooded his body as he pushed back against the crowd, managing to escape. He took refuge in a phone booth. Someone had ripped the phone off its mount, so he was unable to call his editor. He had no car.

McKoy was stranded. So he kept shooting photos.

"It hadn't entered my mind to be scared yet," he said.

"The Next Battle"

Meanwhile, Hyungwon Kang arrived at Florence and Normandie. On any other day, the police would have ticketed him for driving illegally through the median. But this was the only way he could avoid hitting the abandoned cars parked haphazardly throughout the intersection.

And there were no police around anyway.

Kang held up his camera with one hand out the window, snapping photos while clutching the steering wheel with his other hand. He managed to capture a photo of one of the last LAPD patrol cars evacuating the area.

As the chief photographer for the South Bay edition of the *Los Angeles Times*, it was Kang's job to scoop the competition when it came to breaking news. He was getting his scoop, but he was also witnessing the destruction of his "home sweet home."

Born in Gochang, 150 miles south of Seoul, Hyungwon Kang's family relocated to Los Angeles's Koreatown in 1977. His father wanted better educational opportunities for his four children. From 1981 until his retirement, Kang's father worked as the operator for a Unocal 76 gas station on La Brea Avenue in Inglewood near the Los Angeles Forum sports arena. Kang grew up working after school with his father at the gas station, learning how to fix cars at an early age.

Right now, his father stood guard there. The gas station remained safe the entire time. It was actually Hyungwon Kang who was in danger. Protesters threw rocks and bricks at his car. He realized they probably assumed the grey Pontiac Grand Am was an undercover cop car because of its police scanner and short antennae sticking out from the trunk.

Just then, he recognized his colleague, Kirk McKoy, standing stranded in a phone booth. He pulled up to McKoy, who immediately handed over a film envelope filled with several rolls he had just shot. He needed Kang to rush back to the *Los Angeles Times* photo desk so someone could develop the film for tomorrow's edition.

Kang knew his colleague was not leaving—and that he was running out of film. "We all carried around fresh rolls of film in bricks of boxes, about fifty rolls per brick," he said.

So Kang grabbed a half brick from his car and gave it to McKoy. "I replenished Kirk with fresh rolls of film, like fresh ammunition for the next battle," he said.

"We Don't Look Like We're Part of the Community"

Around 6:00 p.m. on April 29, 1992, *Associated Press* photographer Craig Fujii, thirty-two, was driving to the Forum to cover the L.A. Lakers–Portland Trailblazers playoffs game when he heard on the radio that violence had just broken out at the corner of Florence and Normandie.

Fujii was driving down Figueroa Street—just a few minutes away from that intersection. He figured he could take a few photos at Florence and Normandie and still make it in time for the basketball game.

He parked near Tom's Liquor and started snapping pictures with his Nikon thirty-five-millimeter camera. But instead of Fujii capturing something historical on his camera, he woke up later that night in the emergency room at Cedars-Sinai hospital with a welt the size of a ping-pong ball on his forehead. Where were his cameras? His glasses? The last thing he remembered was Tom's Liquor going up in flames.

An image later surfaced from Timothy Goldman's video revealing what had actually happened. Several young men, some of them gang members, had attacked Fujii while he was taking photos.

Even though demonstrators were attacking journalists, was Fujii also attacked because he was Asian? He believed so. "I'm an Asian face in South Central, and the only other Asians you saw owned liquor stores. I'm sure I was a target." Fujii's attackers couldn't know he was a fourth-generation Japanese American whose family had been forcibly incarcerated with other Japanese Americans during World War II.

Fujii's concussion and injuries were so severe that he still has trouble remembering what actually happened. "If you were just going to replay something over and over, a bunch of people coming at you and swinging at you and hurting you—if you had to replay that over and over in your brain, if you kept seeing it over and over, that'd be horrifying," he said. "The beauty of the way our brains work is sometimes we don't remember things that are horribly bad."

While Fujii recovered at the hospital, the Lakers-Trailblazers game was canceled.

The Truck Driver

Ten minutes after Fujii's attack, an eighteen-wheeler truck pulled up to the Florence and Normandie intersection. Traffic was bad, and the driver, Reginald Oliver Denny, had decided to take a shortcut.

The thirty-nine-year-old truck driver was hauling twenty-seven tons of gravel from a quarry to a plant in Inglewood. He blasted KZLA, the country music radio station, as he drove along the 110 Harbor Freeway. He wasn't listening to the news as he veered off Exit 17 for Florence Avenue, heading toward the plant. He had no idea what was happening.

Denny immediately saw something was wrong as he entered the Florence and Normandie intersection. People milled about in the middle of the street. Several abandoned cars were parked at odd angles. Glass bottle fragments and chunks of cinder blocks littered the intersection.

Suddenly, a young man opened the door on Denny's driver side. His name was Antoine Miller.

Just a month away from his twentieth birthday, Miller had already lived a lifetime of tragedy and trauma. His parents separated when he was a baby. He had been shuttled between numerous homes while his mother recovered from substance use. Around age twelve, Miller witnessed his grandmother shoot and kill his grandfather during an argument.

Before Denny could react, Miller and another young man

yanked him out of the truck's cab. Henry Keith "Kiki" Watson placed his foot on Denny's head, preventing him from moving. Police knew Watson as a "gang associate," although his parents insisted he wasn't a "gangbanger."

Watson, a twenty-seven-year-old ex-Marine, was in the middle of trying to turn his life around after arrests for firearms possession and holding up an armored car. He had recently been released from prison, was married, and had a young daughter. He juggled two jobs: driving an airport shuttle and working at a pet store. His family nickname Kiki was tattooed across his chest. "I'm not your typical gang member," he said.

But on April 29, 1992, Watson found old emotions and anger overwhelming him after the not-guilty verdicts were announced. "It was rage and anger, not just about Rodney King, but the injustices that were going on during that time," he later said. "Nobody specifically sought out Reginald Denny to cause him any harm. He got caught up in the moment, just like everyone else."

While Denny struggled to escape, Miller's best friend, Damian "Football" Williams, joined the attack. Miller had lived with Damian's family when they were younger. Nicknamed Football, Williams was a talented athlete who played football and baseball and boxed at the Marcus Garvey K–9 private school. He briefly had a shot at being recruited for college football. But the Crips, with their overwhelming presence and promise of a solid family structure, recruited him first.

By April 1992, the nineteen-year-old Damian Williams had become a father to a three-month-old baby. He wanted to leave gang life and focus on football. Maybe he could get a college scholarship and end up in the NFL. "That was one of my biggest dreams," he said. "So I could provide for my family and get my mother a way better life than she could ever imagine because of all the sacrifices she had made for me as a single parent."

But one older gang member told him, "It's too late."

On April 29, 1992, Williams entered the chaos. Just ten minutes before Reginald Denny stopped at the traffic light of Florence and Normandie, Damian Williams was one of the people who had attacked photographer Craig Fujii. He now clutched a cinder block in his hands. He slammed it directly against Denny's head.

After Williams struck the truck driver, he imitated the end-zone dance of an NFL player who had just scored a touchdown. He looked up at the TV news helicopters capturing all of this and flashed the Crips gang sign.

While Denny lay unconscious, a fourth man, Gary Williams (no relation to Damian Williams), rummaged through Denny's pockets. Gary, thirty-three, was a familiar figure at the nearby Unocal gas station, always hustling customers for change.

This hadn't always been Gary Williams's life. He was a conscientious student in high school who helped other children with their homework. As a teenager, he took care of his father, who died about a year after being diagnosed with cancer. And then, just a few months later, his mother died suddenly from a heart attack. His aunt raised him after that. Despite the double family tragedy, the teenager persevered, graduating from high school while still tutoring other students.

But after turning eighteen, Williams left his aunt to live on his own.

Gary's aunt saw her nephew live on TV as he stole Reginald Denny's wallet and ran away. "I kept saying: 'It couldn't be,' but it was," she said. "It was him."

But his aunt wasn't the only one who saw what had happened to Reginald Denny.

The Rescuers

Lei Yuille. Bobby Green. Titus Murphy. Terri Barnett.

These four young people couldn't believe what they were seeing live on their television sets. The violence was literally just blocks away from their homes. Where were the police?

Then they saw the attack on Reginald Denny. When Damian Williams hurled a cinder block against the truck driver's head, Bobby Green leapt off his couch and ran out. "That is enough," he said. "To me, he was another human being who needed my help."

Yuille, Murphy, and Barnett also reacted immediately, driving off to Florence and Normandie. Yuille, a nutritionist, arrived first. At this point, Denny's attackers had fled the scene. She was struggling to lift him up when Green showed up next to help her. Murphy and Barnett arrived next and waved frantically at the few LAPD patrol cars passing by. But none of them stopped. They realized the police would not rescue Denny.

It was up to them.

The closest hospital was three miles away. Bobby Green was a professional truck driver like Denny. But the truck's windshield was smashed so badly that he couldn't see through it at all.

Titus Murphy and Terri Barnett were friends, having worked together at Northrop before the aerospace and defense company closed shop in South L.A., laying off hundreds of employees, including Murphy.

Murphy clung to the hood of the truck while Barnett drove their Honda in front, leading the way. Because Green couldn't see through the windshield, Murphy and Barnett shouted directions to him.

Lei Yuille cradled Denny's head gently in her lap. She comforted him, talking constantly to keep him awake. "You're going to make it," she said.

A heroes' welcome: On May 5, 1992, the Los Angeles City Council honored the actions of several "Good Samaritans" who risked their lives to save others from danger during the 1992 Los Angeles civil unrest, including trucker Reginald Denny's rescuers, (front to back) Lee Yuille, Terri Barnett, Titus Murphy, and Gregory Alan Williams, who saved the life of motorist Takao Hirata.

When they arrived at the hospital fifteen minutes later, Denny went into convulsions. "Blood was shooting ten inches out of Denny's mouth," Murphy remembered. He jumped off the truck's hood and ran for help. Medical personnel told the rescuers "if we had been thirty seconds later, he would have died en route because he already had been choking on his own blood," Murphy said.

Doctors immediately performed surgery on Denny, whose skull had been fractured in ninety-one places, causing severe brain damage.

Green knew exactly where Denny's truck belonged, so he safely drove it back to company headquarters at Florence and Manchester.

Lei Yuille, Bobby Green, Titus Murphy, and Terri Barnett were Black. Reginald Denny was white.

They parted ways without knowing each other's names.

The Glass House

They called it the "Glass House."

Parker Center, the Police Administration Building built in 1955, got its nickname from its sleek modernist style and the palm trees and other skyscrapers reflected in its glass windows.

Around 6:30 p.m., several hundred protesters gathered outside the Glass House. It was a diverse crowd: Black, Latino, Asian, white. They carried signs: We Want Justice. Stop Beating My People. Gates Must Go. Justice for Latasha.

But Chief Daryl F. Gates had just left for a fundraiser dinner in the affluent, mostly white suburb of Brentwood.

The crowd chanted. "No justice, no peace!"

A line of police in riot gear assembled to protect the Glass House.

But as the sun set, it was too late. Protesters rushed toward

What had at first been a peaceful protest rally at the LAPD Parker Center in downtown Los Angeles turned violent after sunset as demonstrators knocked over a parking attendant booth. According to one TV news reporter recording the event live, the police were outnumbered. "They are doing nothing," the reporter said.

an empty guard booth in the north parking lot. They broke the windows and tore wooden boards off, lighting them on fire. The crowd surged, toppling the guard booth. They roared as several young people scrambled on top.

"As you can see right now, they're just jumping on it," said Linda Breakstone, a reporter with KABC-TV Channel 7 News. She had been covering the protest live with her camera crew for the past several hours. "They're tearing it up, they're smashing it with their feet."

"No justice! No peace!" the crowd chanted.

"What are the police doing now, Linda?" asked KABC-TV News coanchor Paul Moyer at the station.

"They're doing nothing," Breakstone replied. "They are doing nothing."

"We Are the Same"

Although the police had evacuated the flashpoint of Florence and Normandie, many civilians stepped in. Later, city officials would dub them the "Good Samaritans" and officially recognize and reward them for their acts of heroism.

These Samaritans did not consider themselves heroes. Although they were just as outraged over the verdicts as everyone else, they would also do anything to protect their community. Their actions defied the media's coverage of a city divided by race.

James Henry, a supervisor at a nearby aircraft and defense manufacturing company, his wife, and his ten-year-old son were having dinner when they saw five young men pull over a van across the street. They began attacking the driver, Raul Aguilar, a wedding photographer and student who had immigrated from Belize.

Henry, who was Black, rushed out and chased the men off. He covered Aguilar with a blanket. He flagged down a nearby

SWAT van, which took Aguilar to the hospital. "I didn't think at the time that I did something heroic," he said later. "I would just hope someone would do the same for me that I did for him."

· · ·

Gregory Alan "GregAlan" Williams wasn't a cop, but he played one on TV.

The thirty-six-year-old former Marine was a popular character actor who had appeared on many hit shows, including *Murder, She Wrote*; *L.A. Law*; and *The Fresh Prince of Bel Air*. His latest role was as Sergeant Garner Ellerbee on the hit NBC series *Baywatch*, about lifeguards patrolling the sunny beaches of Southern California. Sergeant Ellerbee was a good-natured cop who often was featured in lighthearted storylines, such as trying to corral a runaway golden retriever along the beach.

On April 29, Williams was working out at a gym near Florence and Normandie when he heard about the violence on the radio. He rushed out to the intersection, where he rescued Takao Hirata, a Japanese American motorist who had been beaten unconscious. The actor took Hirata to the hospital and contacted his family. Afterward, as Williams headed home, people saw Hirata's blood on his shirt and assumed the actor, who was Black, had been attacked. "It dawned on me that they could not tell his blood from mine," Williams said. "And so ultimately, when it comes down to it, we are the same."

· · ·

Los Angeles Times reporter John L. Mitchell was taking notes at Florence and Normandie for a story when someone threw a brick into a woman's car. The driver, Tam Tran, was a thirty-four-year-old Vietnamese American who had survived a refugee camp before moving to Los Angeles in 1989. Mitchell, who was Black, rescued Tran and drove her to the hospital. "I remember thinking how strange this planet was," he later wrote for the *Los Angeles Times*. "That someone could escape from Vietnam, travel halfway around the world and wind up at the intersection of Florence and Normandie in the middle of a riot: out of the frying pan and into the fire."

. . .

Reverend Bennie Newton never left home without his Bible. At 7:42 p.m. on April 29, the ex-convict, now a minister, found himself holding up his Bible against an angry crowd, shouting, "Kill him, and you have to kill me too!"

Photos by ROBERT DURELL / *Los Angeles Times*

The Rev. Bennie Newton, left, meets Fidel Lopez and his daughter Melissa just after the riots.

Reverend Bennie Newton and Guatemalan immigrant Fidel Lopez are reunited eight days after Newton saved Lopez's life. The two men became close friends and were planning a trip to Guatemala when Newton died on April 24, 1993, of leukemia at age sixty. Lopez, forty-seven, paid his respects at his friend's funeral the following week. "Last year, this good man save me," Lopez said. "This is a good country. We are supposed to live together and be in peace."

Newton, who was Black, was known for his advocacy work with prisoners. He was at the intersection of Florence and Normandie trying to preach peace when several demonstrators stopped a car and yanked out Fidel Lopez, a construction worker from Guatemala. They painted his body with black spray paint. One man smashed a car stereo on his head. Others doused him with gasoline.

They were about to light him on fire when Newton threw himself across Lopez's body.

"Please don't leave me here," Fidel Lopez begged Newton. All he could think about was his beautiful wife and three daughters. "Take me home."

Newton took his new friend home.

"This Ain't Right"

Tee, Nookie, and Trell were glued to the TV all day long. Grandma Ruth had forbidden the Harlins children from leaving the house. It was too dangerous.

And then the children smelled smoke drifting down the street.

Someone had set Empire Liquor Market Deli on fire. It would be the first of four attempts that night. The store had been shut down ever since Latasha Harlins was killed. Graffiti covered its boarded-up walls and windows. *"Burn this mother down!"* Over the past year, it wasn't unusual for someone to drive by and toss a bottle filled with lit rags against the store, starting small fires that quickly burned out. Unhoused people squatted inside the store, eating whatever food had not rotted away.

"I remember her going to the motel to get buckets of water to put it out," Shinese remembered. "She said, 'This ain't right.'" She and other residents lugged buckets and garbage cans filled with water up and down the sidewalk as flames climbed the walls.

Photographer Bart Bartholomew captured the frustration and fear of residents as the police abandoned the intersection of Florence and Normandie. But that fear soon turned into anger as protestors turned on the media, including Bartholomew. As the men shouted, "Get his film!" another man shielded Bartholomew and said, "We need to get you to your car and you need to get out of here." His rescuer? Timothy Goldman. The two men have stayed in touch to this day. Before being taken to the hospital, Bartholomew gave his remaining film to LAPD lieutenant Mike Moulin, who sent it to the *New York Times*. This photo of the LAPD leaving Florence and Normandie was published the next day.

"Stay Off the Streets"

At 11:00 p.m., Mayor Tom Bradley addressed the city in a live TV address.

"Stay off the streets," he said.

There was now a citywide sunset-to-sunrise curfew. Sales of ammunition were temporarily banned. The 110 Harbor and 10 Santa Monica Freeways had been closed. The National Guard was on its way.

"We believe that the situation is now simmering down, pretty much under control," he said.

Mayor Bradley was wrong. The situation was far from being under control.

The fires did not stop desperate residents from raiding stores for basic supplies, including food staples and even diapers, during the six days of civil unrest and nightly curfews.

Chapter 9
화 HWA

화 HWA—*SEVERAL DEFINITIONS IN ENGLISH, FROM "FURY" TO "FIRE"; SYMBOLICALLY, "ANGER."*

"You Have to Save Your Life First"

As afternoon turned to evening on Wednesday, April 29, Jin Ho Lee, a twenty-nine-year-old reporter who had started working at Radio Korea 1540 AM the year before, watched the station's switchboard light up.

Two miles north of Florence and Normandie, Koreatown was becoming a second flashpoint. Cosmos Appliance on Vermont Avenue was the first Korean-owned store set on fire. Owner Michael Kim and his family and friends hid in the back, frantically calling the police. "Nobody showed up," Kim said. "There was a fire burning across the street for three hours and nobody came."

Although no one was hurt, the Kims lost everything. "We took 15 years to build this up, and in two days it is gone," his wife, J. Kim later told reporters.

In the first few hours after the not-guilty verdicts, hundreds of calls from concerned Koreatown store owners flooded Radio Korea. Because of language barriers, they begged the radio station to call the police for them.

Jin Ho Lee and the other staffers called 911, only to find a busy signal.

Radio Korea's cofounder and vice president, Young Ho "Richard" Choi, took over. He had just wrapped up his shift as an on-air announcer at 2:00 p.m. He knew the LAPD trial verdicts would be announced soon. Before leaving, he had told his staff, "If any urgent news pops up, please, give me a call!"

As Choi drove home, he heard breaking news reports on the radio about Reginald Denny being attacked. He immediately turned the car around and went back to work.

Choi made the decision to stop all programming and instead take live phone calls all night. Radio Korea was now 911 for Koreatown. But as the calls mounted through the evening, he decided it was too dangerous for anyone to stay there.

He picked up the mic. "Ladies and gentlemen, although we came to America to eat well and live well, these riches are not as important as our lives," he announced in Korean. "Quickly lock up your stores and go home! You have to save your life first. No matter how important the store is, you better go home safely rather than losing your life."

But in twenty-four hours, Choi and Radio Korea would change their minds.

"How Can You Sit There and Not Do Anything?"

On the morning of Wednesday, April 29, Edward Jae Song Lee had surprised his family by cleaning their cars. His mom, Jung Hui, insisted on giving her son two ten-dollar bills, one for each car, as a thank you.

Out of habit, Eddie put one of the ten-dollar bills into an old kimchi jar on his desk. Every Sunday, he collected whatever cash was inside and used it as a donation during church service.

Eddie pocketed the other ten-dollar bill. He was planning to hang out with his friends later that weekend.

His nineteenth birthday was just three weeks away. He was still living at home with his family in Koreatown, taking classes at Santa Monica College, and working odd jobs like delivering pizzas to save up enough money for a summer trip to Korea. He wasn't sure what his plans were for the fall yet. Maybe he would enroll in dentistry school. Or maybe he would sign up for the police academy or military since he enjoyed participating in his high school's Reserve Officers' Training Corps (ROTC) program.

But that afternoon, immediate social plans were canceled after the not-guilty verdicts were announced. Eddie sat glued to the radio and TV for the rest of that day.

"He sat there, listening to Korean radio and watching Korean television and getting madder and madder," his sister Jenny remembered.

Eddie couldn't believe Radio Korea was advising store owners to go home.

"Everything we have worked for is now in flames," Eddie told his family as he watched images on TV of stores in Koreatown being set ablaze. "How can we just sit here and watch it happen? We Koreans should go out and protect our own."

His mother wasn't surprised by her son's outrage. "Since childhood, Eddie had a sense of justice and was full of energy," Jung Hui said.

But it was too dangerous for her son to leave the house. "I pleaded with him to stay and protect the family," she said. "I told him to stay beside us."

Eddie realized she was right. To his mother's relief, he did not leave.

It would be his last night at home.

"Let's Protect Koreatown!"

Shortly after the not-guilty verdicts were announced, about four hundred Korean Americans, most of them barely out of their teens, gathered outside the Koreatown Plaza located on the corner of Western Avenue and James M. Wood Boulevard. "Let's protect Koreatown!" they shouted. Many of them belonged to the Korean Young Adult Team, a volunteer security patrol group that protected Korean-owned businesses.

Jong Min Kang, the thirty-three-year-old president of the Korean American Business Association, had started this group in December 1991 because of increased attacks on Korean American businesses. Its volunteers guarded stores and escorted store owners to their cars.

One of these young volunteers was Roy Choi, a future TV celebrity chef and activist. As a child, he helped his mother by cleaning bean sprouts for dumplings at his family's restaurant. He joined the team to protect Koreatown. "The young kids, the twenty-year-olds, eighteen-year-olds, nineteen-year-olds, we kind of were tasked with like patrolling the streets," he said. "And so it took a couple days, but basically we started to kind of protect the borders."

The Korean Young Adult Team blocked Western and Vermont Avenues to stop a crowd of demonstrators from entering Koreatown. They organized groups to stand guard outside vulnerable storefronts and restaurants. They used walkie-talkies to communicate with each other. As they drove through Koreatown on the evening of April 29, they were shocked. *Where were the police?*

"All this was being looted," Roy Choi said. "Chairs and rocks, and everything being thrown through walls. If you go straight down Western on Venice, the whole plaza burned on fire. We were calling 911, and there was no response. I was here all three days. I didn't see any cops."

Jong Min Kang had no idea the civil unrest would erupt so

After the police were unable to contain the violence in Koreatown, Korean American store owners and volunteers armed themselves to protect their stores. Many wore white headbands, a Korean protest symbol.

quickly and get so out of control on the first night. "A lot of people were crying," he said. "So many people stole from stores, no police. Dark sky, dark sky, dark sky from the fires."

화 Hwa—Fire

At 3:47 a.m. on Thursday, April 30, scientists at the National Oceanic and Atmospheric Administration received unusual infrared images from a satellite orbiting above Earth.

These images showed an abnormally high concentration of heat spreading quickly across Southern California. The heat matched the temperature from the 1991 Mount Pinatubo volcanic eruption in the Philippines.

Scientists quickly discovered the source of this heat—Los Angeles.

There were so many fires happening at once in L.A. that satellites could detect it from space—an average of three fires flared every minute. More than 3,600 fires would be set in the next five days.

The city of Los Angeles shut down.

Bus service was canceled. Employers locked their offices and told employees to work from home. The U.S. Postal Service was suspended. All major sporting events, music concerts, and other entertainment events were canceled. Schools closed. By noon, the first two thousand National Guard troops were deployed, followed by the Marines. A citywide curfew took effect at sunset on Thursday. No one was allowed out on the streets at night.

"To Protect and to Serve"

On April 29, Sergeant Douglas Shur was working as a commander's aide at the Parker Center. He was assigned to a twelve-hour street patrol shift.

"My orders were not to let anyone go north of the Santa

Monica Freeway because of all the looting and burning on the other side," he said.

Shur was a third-generation Korean whose family had been in California since the early 1900s. The son of a decorated Army Ranger–turned–laborer, Shur spent his childhood in Compton, riding his bike and playing Kick the Can street games with his friends, most of whom were Black. Before becoming a cop, Shur had majored in zoology and biology at Cal State Long Beach. He was a researcher at a chemistry lab at the University of Southern California when his older brother Timothy joined the LAPD. Inspired by his brother's service, Shur joined the LAPD reserves in 1976, graduating from the police academy two years later.

Shur credited his science background for helping him compartmentalize his emotions. "Being in research, you go by the facts, so I had a more analytical approach. You want to be kind and fair, but you can't become attached because every incident would be emotionally draining. So it's just like how a surgeon views a patient."

But as the violence and fires surged for the next several days, the scientist in Sergeant Shur concluded, "In my observation, we didn't prepare enough."

• • •

Like Douglas Shur, Ben Lee's family had been in America for generations. His great-grandfather moved to Northern California from China to work as a laborer in the 1860s. Ben Lee's parents owned a market in Los Angeles. In high school, Lee ran track, played varsity tennis, and was a linebacker on the football team. But his passion was kung fu. He even worked as a stuntman on the ABC TV series *Kung Fu* starring David Carradine. "You may have seen me from the back," he said, laughing.

Ben Lee graduated with a degree in business administration from Cal State Los Angeles. He wasn't planning on becoming a cop until he and his friends were prevented from giving a martial arts demonstration during a Chinatown New Year's Parade because the LAPD mistakenly assumed they were gang members. Furious, he filed a complaint and at the station met a Japanese American sergeant named Shiro Tomita, who also happened to be the father of movie and TV star Tamlyn Tomita. Sergeant Tomita was impressed with Lee's integrity and encouraged him to join the LAPD. Ben enrolled at the police academy and worked as a beat cop before being promoted to detective in 1989.

On April 29, Detective Ben Lee, now thirty-nine, was enjoying a hot dog before working security at Dodger Stadium for an L.A. Dodgers–Philadelphia Phillies baseball game. Because cell phones did not exist back then, most of the thirty-six thousand people

Detective Ben Lee next to graffiti protesting the LAPD. Despite facing much hostility during his twelve-hour shifts, Lee worked hard to keep the peace and even put out some fires himself because the fire department was stretched too thin. "We wanted to let the community feel safer," he said.

in the stands had no idea that protests and violence had erupted earlier on the corner of Florence and Normandie.

But Detective Lee had a pager. It buzzed. He was ordered to meet at a command post in South L.A.

It was not long before baseball fans also heard the news from the stadium speakers. By the seventh inning of the game, the stadium was almost empty. The Dodgers would lose seven to three to the Phillies.

Ben Lee worked twelve-hour shifts, seven days a week, for the next month. On that first night, he and other police officers helped put out fires because there were so many and not enough firefighters. "People were like zombies wandering around," he remembered. "I will never forget the smell, the smell of just intense smoke everywhere. And we felt helpless."

• • •

April 29 was a slow day for Blake Chow.

The thirty-year-old Chinese American rookie cop had just wrapped up his day shift at the Central Division filing burglary and stolen-vehicle reports. Before leaving, he heard breaking news on the radio that protests had flared up at Florence and Normandie. "Do you want me to stick around?" he asked his watch commander.

"No, you can go home," his commander said. "We'll call you if we need you."

By the time Chow got home, his phone rang. It was his commander. "Hey, you need to be back at six o'clock in the morning," he said.

Chow left his house at dawn the next day. The sky was orange from the fires. Smoke hung in the air. The freeways were empty. "Wow," he thought. "This is what doomsday would feel like."

Chow and another rookie cop were assigned to patrol the streets together. "Around noon, people were coming in from other cities to loot some of the stores here in Los Angeles. We were stretched so thin and there were so many people out there, there was this feeling of helplessness."

When Chow started working at the LAPD, "Los Angeles was very, very violent." Because of the crack cocaine epidemic and gang problems, being a cop at the time was a very dangerous, high-risk job. "We had our guns out all the time," he said. "L.A. always had gangs, but the introduction of crack cocaine was a huge, huge milestone in what it did to the community." Assigned to the Rampart Division at the time, Chow estimated there were about 150 homicides that year. "There were a lot of attacks on police officers at the time," he said. "There were pipe bombs being put underneath police cars. When I came on in 1990, we were pretty close to losing an officer a year to some sort of violence."

Police academy training "mirrored" the rising level of violence in the community. "We were trained very, very aggressively because the mantra was you needed to go home safe, which is still the mantra," he said. "But the worst part is it drove a wedge between the community and the police department because we were going into neighborhoods like an occupying force."

By the time Chow joined the LAPD, the tension that had built over two decades was a powder keg waiting to explode. "Rodney King was just a fuse. That's what set off this twenty-two years of the impact of crack cocaine and change in tactics and our connections with the neighborhood. It just blew up during the riots."

Despite the danger, Blake Chow had always wanted to become a cop. Like Douglas Shur and Ben Lee, Chow hailed from an Asian American family who had roots in America since the turn of the century. His grandparents came to America in 1913. They worked as sharecroppers and farmers in the Sacramento Delta area of central California. Chow also came from a military family: his uncles served in every branch of the U.S. Armed Services. His father joined the navy and fought in the Korean War.

Chow's parents were "socially liberal," and their compassion influenced Chow, who decided he wanted to join the police force.

But his mother didn't like that idea. "There's no way you're going to be a cop," she told her son. "You're going to get killed or something will happen to you." So Chow ended up majoring in business at California Polytechnic State University, San Luis Obispo, and working as an auditor. "I hated it," he said. "I didn't feel like I was making a contribution to anybody." While working various accounting jobs, Chow attended the San Jose Police Reserve Academy and worked part-time with the San Jose Police Department.

But not everyone at the department welcomed Chow's presence. He experienced outright racism from several officers who often joked about his "yellow" skin color.

Although offended, Chow remained silent because his life depended on these other officers. "You had to laugh because that's what was expected," he said. "And if you were working by yourself, these guys had to back you up on radio calls, so you don't want to get so antagonistic that if you really needed backup, nobody would show up. So you kind of put up with it."

But in 1989, Chow realized he did not have to "put up with it." He was doing a patrol at a Christmas light display in the park when he found an Asian American child all by himself. "He was six years old and crying because he was lost and couldn't find his parents," he said. "We ended up reuniting him with his parents, and I'll never forget the look on his face." That was when Chow realized how important representation was as an Asian

Officer Blake Chow stands in front of an LAPD rescue vehicle used to patrol the streets during the 1992 L.A. uprising. "I think the worst thing I witnessed, and I still take this lesson to this day, is what can happen, what people can do when you have this mob mentality that they would not normally do," Chow later reflected. "And you had people that got caught up in the moment."

American—especially in law enforcement. Inspired, he decided to switch careers and applied for a full-time job at the LAPD the following year.

During his twelve-hour shifts in the days following April 29, Chow didn't eat or drink. He just went from looting call to looting call. People drove by him with sofas and television sets tied to the roof of their car. Others threw rocks and bottles at his patrol car. At one point, a man with an iron bar swung it in his direction because his window was open. Chow ducked just in time.

He remembered standing on the corner of Washington Boulevard and Central Avenue, watching people ripping the bars off store windows and passing stolen TV sets and stereos to each other.

"There wasn't anything we could do," he said. They were

outnumbered. "It was just really the most helpless feeling that you could possibly imagine, especially as a police officer, and we were powerless to do anything because it was just that out of control."

· · ·

On November 4, 1984, Philip Ahn, who had acted in almost three hundred movies and TV shows, was the first Korean American to receive his own star on Hollywood Boulevard's famous Walk of Fame.

Eight years later, twenty-seven-year-old LAPD officer Howard Choy stood in a skirmish line along that same street, forming a human barrier to keep demonstrators from torching more stores.

Choy was the only Korean American cop on the street. A Korean store owner rushed up to him. "All the Koreans would come up to me first because they couldn't speak English," he said.

"My store's burning," the store owner said in Korean to Choy. "Can you help us out?"

But Choy couldn't. If he stepped out of line to help the store owner, the police would lose control of the area. "There's nothing I can do," he said, heartbroken.

As Choy headed down the street with his unit, he turned around one last time. He saw the Korean store owner standing helplessly outside his store now engulfed in flames, just a few blocks away from where Philip Ahn's Hollywood star lay.

"He just stood there and watched his store burn," Choy said.

"A Volcano That Had Been Building"

Emile Mack felt like he was trying to put out every single fire.

The thirty-five-year-old Los Angeles Fire Department firefighter wasn't even supposed to be working that week. He was getting married in a few days. On Wednesday, April 29, Mack and his fiancée had spent the day taking care of last-minute arrangements for their upcoming Saturday wedding in Redondo Beach. On their way home around sunset, they noticed smoke billowing through the air. Dozens of fires blazed in the distance.

The experienced firefighter immediately knew that something was wrong. "We're going to get called in," he predicted.

Mack's prediction came true a few hours later. All LAFD firefighters were required to report for duty. He arrived at his fire station just after midnight. Mack had no idea that he was about to spend the next seventy-two hours fighting fires nonstop all over Los Angeles.

But Mack wasn't surprised by the civil unrest. "Here you had a very angry, frustrated community where an obvious injustice had taken place, and this is sort of like a volcano that had been building and building," he said. "There were other kinds of issues out there—lousy education, unemployment twice the rate of the general population. For us, it didn't start off with Rodney King."

On Thursday morning, Mack and four other firefighters were driving south on Vermont Avenue when they received a dispatch. A store at the corner of Vermont and 8th Street had been set on fire. They were in the first fire truck to arrive in Koreatown.

"By the time we got there, the store was engulfed in flames," Mack remembered. As they hooked up their hoses to a fire hydrant across the street, two cars slowed down in front of them. Before Mack and his crew could react, eight gun-toting gang members emerged. They began shooting at the Korean-owned store located behind the fire hydrant.

Several employees from inside the store burst out with guns, too. They shot back.

The firefighters were caught in the crossfire. "We hit the ground," Mack said.

Mack radioed their command center. "Shots fired!" he shouted. He and his crew dashed over to their truck and jumped inside. They drove around the block to escape the gun fight. When they returned a few minutes later, the two cars had sped off and the store owners had disappeared. Mack and his firefighters resumed their work. They hooked up their hoses and sprayed the store on the corner of 8th and Vermont.

But in the short amount of time they had been gone, the fire had spread down the street.

Not only was theirs the only fire truck in the area and outnumbered by the fires, but Mack had to keep an eye out for any other potential violence. "We were all by ourselves."

To his relief, a truck filled with armed National Guard members arrived.

Mack couldn't help but crack a joke. "You guys look good," he said, explaining they had just been caught in a gunfight.

One National Guard soldier leaned over and whispered, "We don't have any bullets." It turned out they didn't have time to stop by their call center before heading to Koreatown.

"That's okay," Mack replied. All that mattered to him was that they were carrying guns: that image alone would discourage any more shooting. "You still look good."

Three National Guard members protected the firefighters as they fought the fires.

Mack received another dispatch to stop the spread of fires down Vermont Avenue. As his crew drove out, buildings kept bursting into flames one by one. "It was like clockwork," he recalled. "I even looked at my watch. Every five minutes, the next block would go up in flames. Five minutes later, the next block. And then the next. Within an hour, from the intersection of Vermont and 8th all the way down to the Santa Monica Freeway, the whole street and this area was on fire. Dozens of fires. A blanket of smoke blocked out the daylight." Some fires were so powerful that steel beams melted and entire buildings collapsed.

What frustrated Mack and the others was that they could not stop to save every single burning building. "If the area becomes too dangerous, we have to pull out," he explained. "That's tough because you kind of become attached to the building you're trying to save and then you have to pull back."

As they drove through Koreatown, demonstrators barricaded certain streets with furniture to stop law enforcement.

"If we see a barricade, we are not stopping," Mack told their driver. "Just barrel through."

And they did. They smashed through a makeshift pile of shopping carts and trash on Vermont Avenue. A shopping cart flew straight into the air.

Mack's heart felt heavy. He was a Korean orphan adopted by a Black family from South Central L.A. "My two cultures were in conflict—were in odds," he said.

• • •

Emile Mack was born Yoon Young Do in Seoul, Korea. In 1959, his future parents Clarence Mack, forty-one, and Undine Mack, thirty-seven, were looking through photos of potential children to adopt from a Korean orphanage when Clarence put his finger on Yoon Young Do's photo and said, "He's the one."

Yoon Young Do (Emile Mack) was three years old when he arrived in L.A. to meet his new family.

"It just felt like I was already part of the family," Mack said. "It's not that I was 'accepted' but that I was just part of this family. From any of my family or friends around us, I never got a second look. It wasn't like, 'Here's this little Korean kid walking in, who the hell is that?' No one blinked an eye."

Growing up, Mack knew he was Korean. "If someone asked me, 'What are you?' I'd say 'I'm Korean.' But I would also say I've been raised African American because that is who I am. I'm Korean, but I grew up Black."

Mack was comfortable with his cultural and racial identity. But not everyone else was. Some Asian Americans would tell him, "You look like us, but you don't act like us." And some Black people would remark, "You don't look like us, but you act like us."

"So that was my world," Mack said. "I have a mixed bag of experiences—I've seen the prejudice and all the slurs, but I was also protected by the same groups."

Emile Mack (born Yoon Young Do in Seoul, Korea) with his father, Clarence Mack, who adopted Emile when he was three years old.

After graduating from high school in 1975, Mack attended UCLA. He became a firefighter by accident. He was planning to become a doctor when Craig Smith, his best friend since the ninth grade, asked Mack to help him study for the firefighter exam. Mack ended up taking the exam as well to support his friend. To his surprise, he not only passed the exam but developed a passion for firefighting. After graduating with honors in 1978, Mack immediately joined the LAFD with Craig. "Okay, I guess I'm not going to be a doctor," he joked.

At the end of April 1992, Mack and Craig found themselves fighting fires for three days straight. They never went home. There was no time to shower or sleep. The only food they had was one leftover slice of pepperoni pizza that they had to split.

By Friday, Craig asked Mack about his wedding. It was supposed to be the next day. Craig was his best man.

"Are you still getting married?" Craig asked.

"Yeah, are you still getting married?" chimed in a few of the other firefighters who were also part of the wedding.

Mack paused, not sure how to answer his friends. He looked up at the smoky sky and the burning palm trees.

"I don't know," he finally said. "I don't know if we're going to be out of here by then."

Radio Korea

RADIO KOREA HOST [in Korean]: "What's the address of your store? Could you repeat that?"

CALLER [in Korean]: "84th and Vermont . . ."

HOST: "Johnny's clothing store?"

CALLER: "That's a men's clothing store. Is that store being burned?"

HOST: "Yes, it is burning."

CALLER: "Oh my God. That's our store." (sobbing)

—*Live calls to Radio Korea, April 29 to May 4, 1992*

In February 1989, when KAZN Radio Korea debuted on AM 1300, its broadcast was so weak that some listeners had to go all the way up to a rooftop to get a signal.

But it was worth it. Radio Korea was a vital source of information for the Korean American community in Los Angeles. Many first-generation Korean immigrants were not fluent in English, so Radio Korea reporters would translate the *Los Angeles Times* and other English news sources into Korean on the air. In 1990, they were the first radio station to broadcast L.A. Dodgers baseball games in Korean.

The station had covered the increasing crime and killings of Korean American small-business owners in recent years. It not only reported on these crimes but attended funerals and did in-depth feature stories on the lives of families struck by tragedy.

"Every other month or every other week, we saw store owners get shot," said reporter Jin Ho Lee. "They kill for small change, they kill people for beer. It was a story of a broken American dream."

That broken dream became a nightmare on April 29, 1992, as angry crowds tore into Korean-owned stores, setting them on fire.

"The police weren't reachable," Jin Ho Lee said. "The fire department was not reachable. We sense something is very serious, so we open up and spread the information because if we don't spread the information and put people to safety, then who's going to do that?"

There were so many stores in danger that the staff put together a giant board filled with store names and addresses. "Our station quickly transformed into a disaster call center," Jin Ho Lee said. "We tallied the stores—liquor stores, swap meets, counting how many burned, found their owners' names."

But it was more than just numbers. "I cried several times interviewing people," Jin Ho Lee said. He never forgot one Korean woman who reported seeing smoke and fire in her neighborhood. He informed her that it was a store that had been set on fire. When he mentioned the store's name, she burst into tears.

"Oh, my God, that's my store," she said. "That's everything I had here in America."

Over seventy-two hours, Radio Korea became an alternate 911 call center and is credited with helping save many stores in Koreatown from burning down completely. Korean Young Adult Team members guarded the radio station as nearby buildings were set on fire. Korean restaurant owners delivered bowls of 설렁탕 seolleongtang bone broth to feed Radio Korea reporters working nonstop. Even acupuncture specialists stopped by with traditional Korean medicine.

Jin Ho Lee spent seventy-two hours straight fielding phone calls from desperate store owners. He slept under his desk. More than five hundred volunteers helped Radio Korea by delivering food to hungry reporters. The Pacific Bell company installed thirty telephone lines for free to help Radio Korea field as many calls as possible.

Radio Korea also set up a service center in the parking lot of a nearby church where Korean food companies and store owners sent hundreds of boxes of rice, ramen, and other food supplies for those whose businesses were destroyed.

Thanks to the radio station's efforts, many listeners donated money for the store owners. Children even called in to help. "My brother and I would like to donate $141 we saved in our piggy bank," said one young girl on the air.

Jin Ho Lee is proud of the role Radio Korea played. "A community radio station acted as a command center during the civil unrest," he said. "We feel proud that we did something for our community."

"Stand Your Ground"

Kee Whan Ha, president of the Korean American Chamber of Commerce and owner of the Hannam Korean grocery chain, was furious when he heard Richard Choi of Radio Korea tell store owners to go home on the evening of April 29. Because of Radio Korea's advice, Koreatown was left empty and defenseless.

"I don't see any police patrol car whatsoever," Ha said. "It is like Wild West in old days, like there's nothing there. We are the only one left."

By the following day, more than a thousand fires swept through Koreatown. Live TV news footage showed Olympic Boulevard engulfed in flames. Desperate shop owners barricaded their storefronts with their own cars, shopping carts, trash cans, milk crates, and even twenty-pound bags of rice. To add to the chaos, some tourists and suburban residents created traffic jams as they took joyrides down Olympic Boulevard, recording the fires on their video camcorders like it was entertainment.

Ha and his employees armed themselves and stood guard on the roof of Hannam market. Many demonstrators in the crowd also had guns. They fired at the store. Ha and his employees shot back.

In the cross fire, Patrick Bettan, a thirty-year-old man who worked as a security guard for the Hannam market, was shot and killed.

"I was standing a few feet away, so I see that his body has fallen down on the ground," Ha remembered. "I was so scared. We tried to call the fire department. 'Please help us.' But nobody listen."

It took six hours for a fire truck and medics to take Patrick Bettan's body away. His death would be ruled accidental. No charges were filed. "It's very painful, a human loss," Ha said.

Meanwhile, Ha drove over to Radio Korea and barged into their office, furious that the station had advised everyone to go home the day before. "We established Koreatown!" he shouted. "We've been here for the past 20 years . . . our time, our blood, our energy, our sweat. We can't have Koreatown just disappear and be destroyed in one day and be gone."

On Thursday, April 30, Radio Korea changed its tune. They told their listeners to go back to their stores, to fight back.

"The police have abandoned us," Choi announced live on the air. "We are the only ones to protect Koreatown. If we don't stay, Koreatown will burn to the ground. Arm yourselves. Stand your ground."

(*Top*) A security guard for California Market in Koreatown, along with armed employees and volunteers, guard their store from an angry crowd on the second day in a row of civil unrest. Many Korean immigrant men had gun training and experience because South Korea had established a mandatory conscription draft in 1957, requiring all male citizens ages eighteen to thirty-five to serve in its army, navy, or air force. (*Bottom*) Korean American volunteers shelter behind a forklift during a confrontation with demonstrators, many of them also armed.

Eddie—오빠 Oppa

It was Eddie Lee's second day staying at home.

He was relieved to hear Radio Korea was now advising its listeners to fight back. It was about time, he thought. The radio reporter compared the siege on Korean-owned stores to 행주대첩 Haengju Daecheop—the famous "Battle of Haengju."

Eddie was curious: what was this battle?

Jung Hui told her son about how in 1593, Japanese invaders had failed to take over the Haengju Fortress because the women inside used their 행주치마 haengju cheema skirts as aprons to carry rocks with which the Korean soldiers could fight back.

"How can you sit still and tell such a story?" Eddie asked. "Mother, you, too, must go out and fight."

But Jung Hui still forbade her son from leaving. "You cannot go," she said.

"Mom, this is not about Rodney King anymore," he protested. "This is about us Koreans."

"No, you must not," Jung Hui said. "Never. Ever."

Eddie knew he couldn't disobey his mother. He called his friends, inviting them over to plan how to help protect Koreatown.

His friends weren't surprised to receive a call from Eddie. "He wanted to help defend them," said James Lee, who had known Eddie since the third grade. "This is how he was. He cared about the community. And he was the kind of friend that, when he called, you went."

James Kang, twenty-two, was another friend who didn't hesitate when Edward invited him over. He raced out of the house with a golf club as a weapon. "They were breaking into stores like it was nothing, and the police were doing nothing about it," he said. "It was too much."

Eddie and his friends heard Jong Min Kang of the Korean Young Adult Team call Radio Korea, begging for reinforcements. Eddie told his friends they should join the team.

"Do not go," said Jung Hui. "If you don't protect our family, who will protect us?"

"Mom, don't you see that they are burning down our stores built up tirelessly for ten, twenty years in just a few days?" Eddie said.

"You are 100 percent right," Jung Hui said. "But I cannot let my only son run into that chaos."

Frustrated, Eddie burst into his sister's bedroom. "This isn't fair," he told her. "These people came to America and built up these businesses, and it's being burned down."

"Well, what are you gonna do?" Jenny asked.

"I have to do something," he said.

As a determined Eddie rushed out of her room, Jenny had no idea this would be the last time she would ever see her Oppa.

"American Pioneers"

On Thursday, April 30, Richard Park was working at his Wilshire Jewelry store in the Rodeo Galleria on 8th Street and Western Avenue when he heard Radio Korea urge store owners to stand their ground and defend their property.

Park owned two stores: Wilshire Jewelry and Western Gun Shop, located just a few blocks apart. Although a police squad car with four officers had parked outside, Park wasn't taking any chances. He told his employees, including his sister and sister-in-law, to pack away the jewelry and load the van. He wanted to shut down the shop and go home.

But it was too late. More than two hundred demonstrators

swarmed the shopping mall. Some were alleged gang members. Some were desperate, trying to hoard supplies for their families. Others were opportunists. Many had guns.

Before they could escape, gunshots rang in the air. To Park's horror, a bullet struck his sister's leg. His sister-in-law was also hit in the kidney and stomach.

"Please, call ambulance!" Park screamed in English. "Please, somebody hurt! Somebody crying! Please call ambulance!"

Park then called David Joo, the manager of his Western Gun Shop.

"Pack up some guns quickly," he told Joo. "We gotta leave here or we will die."

Park had hired Joo to manage his gun store because of his expertise. Joo was an avid gun collector who owned many antique guns. "I consider them works of art," Joo said. He trained for years at shooting galleries, had a license, and was conscientious about gun safety.

Joo became fascinated with guns after watching classic American Western movies as a child, from *High Noon* to *A Fistful of Dollars* to anything starring John Wayne. In fact, Joo originally thought John Wayne was Korean because the movies were dubbed in Korean.

After studying psychology in college in Korea, Joo moved to Colorado in 1985, where he worked at a martial arts studio. He relocated to Los Angeles three years later and passed his American citizenship test in 1991. Becoming an American citizen was a dream come true. He loved living in California, which "reminded me of a big ole Western with its big fields and the desert."

After Park called, Joo immediately brought over a half-dozen weapons to the jewelry store, including semiautomatic pistols and rifles.

"When I arrived, it was like a war zone," Joo said. "I was terrified. Bang! Bang! Bullets were coming from everywhere." Although Joo was wearing a bulletproof vest, he couldn't help but raise his hands over his head. "I could literally see bullets flying by me," he said. "I thought I might get shot. I never thought we would have this big incident together, to have to fight a thousand shooters."

Meanwhile, the police, who were outnumbered, drove off. Joo and Park were now on their own.

As Joo and Park shot back, a KABC TV Eyewitness News van pulled into the parking lot. The cameras rolled as KABC reporter Linda Moore described the scene. "Just a few minutes ago, some of the Korean shop owners here . . . started pulling out weapons. These are all loaded guns. Koreans are starting to shoot at some of the people here."

But many Korean Americans questioned how the events were reported. "The mainstream media depicted Koreans as aggressive people shooting at everyone," said Peter Pak, editor of the Korean-language *Korea Times* newspaper. "When the police officers left us, we had no choice but to defend ourselves. . . . The mainstream media misunderstood the intention of Korean Americans, which was self-defense."

"They were standing up for their own survival," agreed *Los Angeles Times* photojournalist Hyungwon Kang, whose photos of the events in Koreatown would later win a Pulitzer Prize.

"They said they were fed up," Moore continued to report live on the air. "Next thing I knew . . . three of them were holding guns and they just started firing at everybody and anybody. [We] were right in the middle of it. It all happened so quickly. To tell you the truth, I thought they were blanks at first. I couldn't believe that these guys had actually pulled out loaded guns. There's just a simmering point and they just boiled over. I mean, I saw it happen, I was talking to the gentleman, I saw it in his eyes."

For the next several days, TV news stations constantly reaired close-ups of Joo and Park aiming their guns and shooting. But the cameras didn't show what the two Korean American men saw on the other side—an angry crowd of two hundred demonstrators, many of them armed.

So Joo participated in as many interviews as he could, wanting to tell his side of the story.

"I want to make it clear that we didn't open fire first," he told the *New York Times*. "At that time, four police cars were there. Somebody started to shoot at us. The LAPD ran away in half a second. I never saw such a fast escape. I was pretty disappointed."

During the gunfire, friends were able to drive Richard Park's sister and sister-in-law to the hospital. Both women survived. Despite the two hundred rounds fired, no one had been killed. Police later investigated the store and found over eighty bullet holes in the front wall of Park's jewelry store. They determined that Joo and Park had shot in self-defense, and no charges were filed.

Park felt America had betrayed him. He and his family had worked fifteen-hour days for the past twenty years only to lose everything. "I love this country," he said. "America is a dream. But that day that happened, nobody helped me. Everybody ran away. Now everything is gone."

Meanwhile, David Joo had trouble sleeping. Severe tinnitus and a burst eardrum from the loud gunfire caused a constant ringing in his head, requiring medical attention. But even worse, he had also come down with a case of what Koreans call 화병 hwabyung, or "fire disease," which the American Psychiatric Association later classified as "suppressed anger syndrome."

"Hatred," he said. "I had hatred for everyone. I was angry

about what happened. We had no reason to be the victim of the riots. There was no reason to be looting the Korean people and Koreatown."

But Joo eventually found his happiness again. His 화 hwa faded, and his faith in America returned. Three years later, in March 1995, Joo testified before Congress during a House subcommittee hearing on gun laws. "When law and order breaks down, citizens have a right to protect themselves," he said. "It's our most basic right, and I think it's the most important freedom we have as Americans."

Asked what makes him still love America, Joo said without hesitation, "Freedom."

"You can have anything you want. America reminds me of a Western. Wild fields, big desert. Opportunities." He smiled. "We have to appreciate the American pioneers."

미국 Miguk: "Beautiful Country"

It was Soo Myung Koh's turn to stay awake. The forty-eight-year-old owned a stall at the Compton Swap Meet near Wan Joon Kim's Cycadelic Records. Instead of rap records, Koh sold business suits at his four-hundred-square-foot stall with his small but dedicated staff of Mexican American and Black employees.

On the night of April 29, Soo Myung Koh was one of the few stall owners who remained, guarding the Compton Fashion Center in shifts, armed with handguns and rifles.

Like most Korean men, Koh knew how to use a gun. After the Korean War ended in 1953, the Korean government had made it mandatory for all men ages eighteen to twenty-eight to join the military for a three-year conscription. So when the protests turned violent, many male Korean store owners used their military training to arm themselves.

"I was ready for this," he said. "We had to protect ourselves."

Koh was born in 1944 in Seoul, the only son of four children. "Yes, I have memories," he said in English. "Seven years old. First they're coming from north to Seoul. When tanks come in, I watching that. My dad grabbed me and take me home. After that, all Korea is occupied by North Korea. So we start running and hiding."

"I was a very nice boy," Koh continued. "My mother and father, some kind of worried about me. I was very much like an adventure and rock climbing and camping and hiking and climbing the mountain. So the only son I pretty precious in Korea so I did wrong things."

In other words, because Koh was the only son, he was "precious." His parents worried when he went hiking or did anything physically risky. His love of hiking led to his studying forestry at Dongguk University. But after graduating, he had trouble finding work because "Korea was a developing country."

Koh decided to try his luck in America. He always had a fascination with America, having watched Hollywood cowboy movies starring John Wayne and listening to country music growing up. His favorite song back then was John Denver's "Country Roads," whose lyrics painted a romantic picture of America: "Almost heaven, West Virginia / Blue Ridge Mountains, Shenandoah River / Life is old there, older than the trees / Younger than the mountains."

Koh moved to San Diego in September 1978 and opened his own stall at the Compton Swap Meet in 1985.

He made only twenty dollars on his first day there. But he did not give up, expanding into selling business suits. He woke up around 5:00 a.m. every morning to drive his wares over. His stall was open every day from 10:00 a.m. until 7:00 p.m.

Koh was proud of owning his own business to support his family. "One thing," he said in English. "First generation, me and the older people, very much they were struggle and settle down to United States. Very, very hard to work and we were thinking only for family. I want to bring my family over here. So first generation is great! We did it!" He smiled.

When Koh first moved to America in 1972, he had taken a cross-country Greyhound Bus tour, from Yellowstone National Park in Wyoming all the way to Key West, Florida. There, he had gasped at the unexpected sight of dolphins and turtles swimming in the ocean as his bus drove over the 113-mile Overseas Highway of the Florida Keys.

Growing up, Koh knew Koreans had named America 미국 Miguk, which meant "beautiful country." As he gazed in wonder through the window at the magnificent vista of blue ocean that seemed to stretch out forever, he finally understood why Koreans called this country beautiful. "This is paradise," he marveled. "After I finished my trip, I decided I gonna stay here. I'm not gonna go back to Korea."

And now here he was, twenty years later, clutching a shotgun outside the Compton Swap Meet, as fires burned in the distance.

"I am disappointed in America," Soo Myung Koh thought, his heart breaking. "America has let me down."

"It Was Unreal"

The fires were everywhere.

On April 30, fourteen-year-old Kirk Kim was flying home to Los Angeles from visiting his aunt in Maryland. As his plane approached the Los Angeles airport, he glanced out the window. "There were patches of fire all over L.A.," he remembered. "I had no idea what the hell was going on."

The fires were so dangerous that dozens of flights, including Kirk's, were diverted to other airports.

After Kirk finally arrived home, his father, Wan Joon "Pops" Kim, explained everything that had happened in the past twenty-four hours.

The next day, Kirk and his family drove back to the Compton Fashion Center to find out if Stall No. Z-7 was still standing.

"It was unreal," he remembered as they drove through Compton, which looked like a combined ghost town and war zone as the National Guard patrolled the empty streets.

Wan Joon was worried because his stall was located right by a large window. It would be so easy to break the glass and steal all their records.

But when they arrived, they saw a group of their loyal customers guarding the front entrance and the window next to Stall No. Z-7.

Cycadelic Records had survived the night.

"Yeah, Mr. Kim, ain't no one gonna do shit to your store," a customer said. "We were right here the whole time."

"They protected our store for sure," Kirk said. "My dad hugged everyone and kept saying thank you."

After Mayor Bradley lifted the citywide curfew and declared the civil unrest over on May 4, 1992, Wan Joon returned to the Compton Swap Meet and opened up Cycadelic Records. "It was business as usual," Kirk said.

The next day, May 5, was Kirk's fifteenth birthday. He recalled, "I had my mom's famous 미역국 miyeok guk," the traditional Korean seaweed birthday soup. It was a small birthday celebration with no big presents because of the civil unrest. But Kirk didn't care: his birthday present was his family.

"Honestly, I was just happy that I was home," he said.

Eddie—형 Hyung

As night fell on Thursday, April 30, Eddie Lee and his friends were in James Kang's maroon 1988 Chevrolet Lumina, tagging along with another car driven by Korean Young Adult Team volunteers. Eddie sat in the passenger seat with John Kim, and their friend Sam Lee sat in the back.

Koreatown residents had already dubbed the Korean Young Adult Team "the superheroes during the riots." But Eddie's friend John Kim felt far from a hero.

"Do you want the truth?" asked John Kim, who now works at a transportation truck company. "The real truth? I was a bad kid."

At the time, John's seventeenth birthday was three weeks away. Born in Korea, he had moved to America at age seven with his mother and two sisters after his parents' divorce. Although he learned how to speak English fluently, John still preferred speaking in Korean. John usually called Eddie by his Korean name, Jae Song. And because Eddie was almost exactly one year older—they both had birthdays in the same week of May—it was customary for John to refer to him as 형 Hyung, the Korean word used by the male gender for "Older Brother."

John met his Hyung in middle school. They were friends for about a year before parting ways to go to separate high schools. John's mother had various jobs, from being a janitor to working at a shrimp factory. John remembered her coming home with chemicals all over her reddened fingers. "We were poor working class, but my mom took care of me always," he said. "I never felt I was poor."

Although John was a shy kid, he began rebelling in high school. Growing up in a high-crime area, John said it was easy for him to be influenced by peer pressure. "I was into gangs and drugs," he said.

Because he kept getting into trouble, John's mother shuttled him back and forth between California and Korea. He had recently moved back to Los Angeles and reconnected with Eddie. The two friends often went camping on weekends in the Santa Monica Mountains in Los Feliz, bonding under the stars.

But this time, John and Eddie were overlooking Koreatown, which was on fire. Because Eddie had belonged to his high school's ROTC team, he owned a .22 handgun. John had suggested he bring it just in case. They could just wave the gun in the air to scare off any trouble. No one would know it was empty. So Eddie held onto the unloaded gun while John carried the bullets separately.

John hoped his Hyung would not have to use the gun that night.

"A Shooting Star"

Around 10:00 p.m., Eddie decided they should go home. He felt bad for having argued with his mom. He didn't want her to be scared. As they headed home, they heard a store owner on Radio Korea report that a crowd had gathered outside Kang Seo Myun Oak, a popular Korean noodle restaurant located on the corner of Hobart Avenue and Third Street.

The restaurant was near Eddie's house, so he impulsively decided they should swing by on their way home. James Kang, who was driving, followed the other Korean Young Adult Team members to the dimly lit intersection of Third and Hobart.

Angry demonstrators filled the street. Some people in the crowd had guns. So did the Korean American store owners and volunteers perched on a nearby rooftop.

No one knows who shot first. Police later described the scene as a "combat zone." "There was a lot of fire out there, a lot of gunshots," said David Escoto, a homicide detective at Wilshire Station.

Eddie stuck his head out of the window to get a clearer view. A bullet struck him in the throat. He fell back in his seat.

Another volley of shots rang out. More than a dozen bullets struck the car. The other Korean Young Adult Team's car sped off.

"James, start the car!" John Kim screamed.

"I'm trying, but I can't move it!" James panicked. "I'm stuck!"

Before James could hit the gas pedal, one bullet struck him in the gut, then another shattered his hip. Sam Lee was shot in the face and arm. John ducked to avoid being hit.

As the police arrived, they shouted for a cease-fire. But no one listened. The police joined the battle, shooting off twelve rounds. Detective Escoto estimated that the men on the roof shot between thirty and fifty rounds of ammunition during the gun battle.

And then silence. The shooters on both sides had run out of bullets.

"Eddie was alive," James Kang remembered. "He was breathing."

John Kim was the only one who witnessed Eddie getting shot. He still remembers exactly where the bullet entered, pointing to the middle of his own throat to demonstrate. "As soon as he got shot, I heard a sound," he said. "It sounded like this. Grrrrrr. Grrrr." Eddie was trying to breathe.

John crawled out of the car. He opened the other door and yanked Eddie out. "He wanted to say something but couldn't," John said.

Because John was smaller than Eddie, he struggled to carry his friend across the street. At one point, he dropped Eddie on the ground. "I'm sorry," John said, gasping for breath.

Sam and James also stumbled out of the car. The four young men collapsed outside the glass entrance of a Korean-owned pizzeria called Pizza Go just across the street.

At that point, most of the crowd had run away. The armed men on the rooftop disappeared. Police confiscated about fifteen handguns and rifles.

The car that carried Eddie Lee and his friends sits at the intersection of West 3rd Street and Hobart Boulevard, its front windshield shattered by bullets from the cross fire between demonstrators and store owners. Police interview Eddie's friends outside the Pizza Go restaurant. Eddie has already died from his wounds.

Three police officers questioned John, James, and Sam as they waited for the ambulance to arrive.

Eddie lay a few feet away on his back, blood soaking his shirt. It took about half an hour for the ambulance to arrive. Which was the same amount of time he had left.

"He was alive for another 30 minutes," said James, who lay bleeding next to him. "He was a fighter. He didn't want to die. I know Eddie. You could tell he was fighting for his life."

As John Kim watched Eddie struggle to breathe, he flashed back to the last time he and Eddie had gone camping together just outside of the city in the Angeles National Forest. He remembered how they had sat by their campfire, looking up at the night sky.

"We saw a shooting star," he said, tearing up. "As soon as we saw that comet, Jae Song started talking about his grandmother who had passed away. He missed her. I said I was sorry. He was a nice guy."

John rolled over. He sat up and pressed his hands against Eddie's throat. "I tried to stop the blood," he said. "But it was coming out from all over here." He pointed to his throat and chest, the image forever seared in his memory. "And in the back."

As John desperately tried to stanch the flow of blood, he kept comforting his friend. "You're going to be okay, Jae Song," he whispered in Korean. "You're going to be okay."

"Mistaken Identity"

Three blocks away, *Los Angeles Times* photographer Hyungwon Kang was snapping pictures of armed Korean men protecting their grocery store.

Just then, a car peppered with bullet holes pulled up. It was the other Korean Young Adult Team who had driven with Eddie and his friends all night. Their driver told the photographer that there was "huge trouble" at a nearby mini-mall.

Kang jumped in his car and drove over. He spotted Eddie, John, James, and Sam lying outside Pizza Go.

He immediately started taking pictures.

"Eddie Lee was already on the pavement," he recalled. "They had pulled him out of the car. He was on the pavement in the parking lot, just bleeding to death." Eddie's blood streamed like a river down the driveway. "It was horrific."

At 10:30 p.m. on Thursday, April 30, 1992, Edward Jae Song Lee died.

He lay on his back in the parking lot of the Pizza Go restaurant, just half a mile from his house.

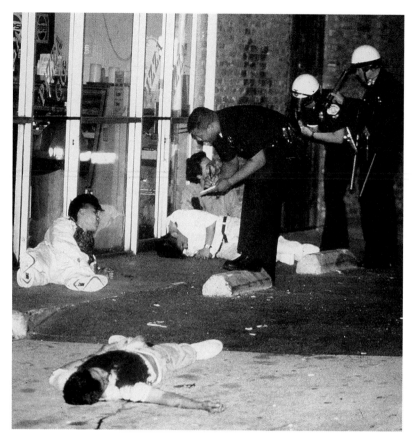

Police interview (left to right) John Kim, James Kang, and Sam Lee as their friend, Edward Jae Song "Eddie" Lee, lies in the foreground, dead. James and Sam were also shot but survived. John Kim, the only one unharmed, didn't want to go home. His clothes still covered in Eddie's blood from carrying him across the street, the shell-shocked John ended up guarding another store just six blocks east of where his best friend died. "I didn't feel nothing at that time," he said. "I stayed up all night. I never went home."

• • •

A police investigation later concluded Edward had been accidentally killed in the cross fire.

"He was not shot by a police officer," stated Captain Julius Davis of the Wilshire Division police station.

The district attorney's office concluded this was a case of

"mistaken identity." The armed Korean American business owners and volunteers had confused Eddie and his friends with looters.

"Mom, Something Has Happened to My Brother"

"According to our source, a Korean American was killed last night."

Jenny Lee couldn't stop crying as she listened to Radio Korea. "Mom, something has happened to my brother," she said. "I think the victim yesterday might have been Eddie."

Jenny and her parents hadn't slept at all. It was dawn on Friday, May 1. The entire family had stayed up all night waiting for Eddie. But he never came home.

"My heart was beating so fast," Eddie's mother, Jung Hui, said. "I felt uneasy. I had this ominous feeling all over my body."

Jung Hui called Radio Korea. "Announce that Jae Song should call us and let us know where he was," she begged in Korean to the on-air reporter.

• • •

Later, Jung Hui picked up a copy of the most recent *Korea Times*. The front-page headline said, "First Korean Victim." But to Jung Hui's confusion—and relief—the blurry black-and-white photo showed a man wearing a black T-shirt.

"This couldn't be my son," she thought. "When my son went out, he wore a white shirt and blue jeans. I was clutching at straws. The face was my son's, but his clothes were not. He could not have possibly changed them."

Jung Hui and her husband decided to stop by the *Korea Times* building in hopes they might have more information on Eddie. They asked a newspaper reporter where their son could be.

"I was told he was in the morgue," Jung Hui said.

"Can We All Get Along?"

"You've got to say something."

On Friday, Rodney Glen King's civil attorney Steven Lerman called him. Where was he?

For the past forty-eight hours, Rodney Glen King had been in seclusion. He was shocked and devastated by the civil unrest that had broken out across the city.

Especially in Koreatown. "I felt very sorry for all those business owners," he later said. "They were just innocent people working hard to make money and take care of themselves and their families. They definitely got the worst of it."

Overnight, President George H. W. Bush had officially deployed 3,000 soldiers of the Seventh Infantry; 1,500 Marines; 6,500 National Guard troops; and 1,000 FBI, SWAT, Border Patrol, and U.S. Marshal's Service law enforcement officers to California.

"I will use whatever force is necessary to restore order," President Bush declared. "What is going on in L.A. must and will stop. As your President, I guarantee you, this violence will end."

Instead, the L.A. civil unrest sparked similar demonstrations and acts of violence and fires in cities across the country, including San Francisco, New York City, Atlanta, Toledo, Denver, and Las Vegas.

Public pressure mounted for an official statement or any kind of reaction from Rodney King. A nervous Glen finally agreed to speak. The press conference in Beverly Hills was the first time he had appeared in public in the past fourteen months. Reporters, TV crews, and news helicopters swarmed the area.

"I could barely breathe," he remembered. "The whole thing was weighing so heavily on me."

At 2:45 p.m., Lerman introduced Rodney Glen King to the press. He handed a four-page statement to Glen to read out loud.

But Glen took one look at the pages and decided not to read it.

"I was going to speak my own words," he said. "These words were coming from my heart."

Rodney Glen King finally broke his silence.

"People, I just want to say, can we all get along? Can we get along? Can we stop making it horrible for the older people and the kids? . . . We'll get our justice. They've won the battle, but they haven't won the war. We'll have our day in court, and that's all we want."

And like Marquette Frye from 1965, Glen's eyes filled with tears and his voice shook as he expressed his horror over the violence he had seen on TV.

"We've got to quit," he said. "We've got to quit. After all, I mean, I can understand the first upset, for the first two hours after the verdict. But to go on—to keep going on like this and to see this security guard shot on the ground, it's just not right."

Rodney King chose to speak from his heart instead of reading an official statement prepared by his attorneys. "Can we all get along?" he asked.

That "security guard" Glen mentioned would turn out to be Edward Jae Song Lee. Earlier that morning, Glen was devastated by Hyungwon Kang's photo in the *Los Angeles Times*, describing Eddie as a "slain sentry."

"It's just not right because those people will never go home to their families again," he said in reference to Hyungwon Kang's photo of Eddie.

Glen ended his speech with a plea to everyone.

"I mean, please, we can get along here. We can all get along. We've just got to. I mean, we're all stuck here for a while. Let's try to work it out. Let's try to beat it. Let's try to work it out."

"The Last Hope"

At the morgue, Eddie's mother, Jung Hui, was still in denial, even when the police officer handed over Eddie's belongings. A wallet, two dimes, a pen, and a pair of eyeglasses.

"I was holding the last hope that it might not be my son," she said.

But when Jung Hui and her husband, Young Hi, had to identify the body, she finally realized—this was her son.

Eddie had died from multiple gunshot wounds to his chest, abdomen, neck, and shoulder.

"I cried out aloud and called for his name, but he did not answer," she said.

• • •

Later that day, Jung Hui bought a copy of the May 2, 1992, edition of the *Los Angeles Times*. She turned to page A-3.

A huge color photo taken by Hyungwon Kang filled the top half of the page. The headline above it read "Arms, and the Agony."

The photo caption stated, "Slain sentry: Police officers interview three men Thursday night who were guarding a pizzeria when gunmen wounded them and killed a companion at 3rd and Hobart Streets." The names of the "three men" and "companion" were not listed in the story.

In the photo, three police officers stand over John Kim, James Kang, and Sam Lee. The three young men lie sprawled outside the glass entrance door of the Pizza Go restaurant, bloodied and dazed.

In the foreground, Eddie Lee lies on his back. His left hand rests gently on his waist, his right arm outstretched to the side. His feet, clad in white tennis shoes, point outward. His head tilts slightly to the right side. If not for his blood-soaked shirt, he looks as if he is simply sleeping.

As Jung Hui looked at Hyungwon Kang's color photo, she realized why she had been confused earlier.

"About that black T-shirt," she said. "In the _L.A. Times,_ the picture was in color. What looked black in the Korean newspaper was my son's blood."

Chapter 10
한 **HAN**

한 HAN—FEELINGS OF SORROW, GRIEF, AND REGRET, BUT THE
SADNESS IS ROOTED IN ANGER AND OPPRESSION.

한 Han

On Thursday, April 30, *Los Angeles Times* photographer Kirk McKoy stood at the corner of La Brea Avenue and Washington Boulevard. The entire block was ablaze, blistered by heat. Smoke choked the air.

Only one building remained standing. McKoy aimed his camera at it.

In his photo, published the next day, red and orange flames fill the entire left side, still flickering, as if the fire is alive. The building on that side has been burned down to its skeletal frame, a twisted metal-grate fence collapsed out front. Trash covers the sidewalk. Despite the smoke, a small patch of blue sky peeks through at the upper right-hand corner.

A haunting message is spray-painted against the remaining wall of a building that has almost burned to the ground, telling passersby, "Look what you created."

The building on the right side has not caught on fire. Yet. Its white metal door swings open, revealing a dark interior.

Someone has spray-painted four words in all capital letters across the surviving building's grey brick façade. The black, jagged letters shout at the world in both sorrow and rage.

"LOOK WHAT YOU CREATED."

This was 한 han.

"We Never Thought of Dying Before"

The Korean Young Adult Team did not sleep for three days as they fought to protect Koreatown.

They weren't scared.

Until Eddie Lee was killed.

"In truth, we weren't scared because we didn't know anything," said Han Sung Chang, one of the original twenty-four members of the team. "We would have been scared if we knew anything. We never thought of dying before."

After Eddie's death, the Korean Young Adult Team wore white 망건 manggeon headbands to avoid future mistaken-identity problems.

During the Joseon Dynasty (1392–1897), Korean men wore a white 망건 manggeon headband to keep their topknot in place under their 갓 gat, a traditional, wide-brimmed hat. In modern times, Koreans wore white headbands symbolic of that era during protests to symbolize determination and unity during a crisis.

"Since then, we promised to put white bands on our heads . . . to prevent friendly fire," Han Sung Chang said. "To Jae Song and his friends who were shot, to their parents and to the others who lost their stores or businesses: I would like to say that I am very sorry that I was unable to protect them. I am so sorry. . . . It breaks my heart."

"Right Now, It Doesn't Seem Real to Me"

Overnight, Edward Jae Song Lee became famous, which was the last thing his family wanted.

"As soon as people found out about Edward, it was chaos," his sister, Jenny Lee, remembered. "Next thing you know, reporters were all over our lawn. We had no privacy. My parents didn't have time to process what happened. Instead, they had to talk to reporters. The phone rang constantly, over and over."

Jenny's eighteenth birthday was in November. Her 오빠 Oppa would not be there to celebrate with her. "I feel so lonely going to school without him," she sobbed to her mother.

It pained Jung Hui to see her daughter crying all the time. She realized how much her son had taken over her role as a parent. "He always took care of Jenny, who is physically weak. He cooked for her when she wasn't feeling well. Every morning, Jae Song dropped Jenny off at school. It seems like Jenny grieves over the loss of her brother who was like her guardian more than her mother."

"Right now, it doesn't seem real to me," Jenny told reporters. "Like, it doesn't seem like he's really dead. Seems like he's out somewhere. He's gonna come back home soon."

"We Knew We Had to Fight to Have Our Stories Be Told"

On the morning of Wednesday, April 29, John H. Lee was surfing. He rode his shortboard at the Windansea Beach in La Jolla. It wasn't for the faint of heart: due to the rocky shore and strong currents, only experienced surfers rode these waves.

"One of the pivotal moments early on in my life was surfing,

John H. Lee in his official staff ID photo as a newly hired reporter for the *Los Angeles Times*. In 1992, he spent his birthday huddled behind a barricade in a store in Koreatown, interviewing the store owner and his family about their anguish during the civil unrest.

standing up on a board and a wave at age eight," he said. "Catching a wave and riding it created a feeling that you chase all your life."

The youngest of three sons, John H. Lee grew up in San Diego, where they were the only Korean American family in their mostly white neighborhood. Now twenty-nine, he was a metro reporter for the *Los Angeles Times* San Diego bureau. Before joining the *Times*, the UC Berkeley English major had worked for K. W. Lee's *Korea Times English Edition*. "K. W. Lee is like 'Columbo,'" John said. "Nothing gets past him."

As one of the few reporters of color working at the *L.A. Times* in 1992, John H. Lee saw a lack of accuracy and fair representation of their communities in the paper. "We reporters of color were united in our disdain for the management structure of the *L.A. Times*. We knew we had to fight to have our stories told."

When the young reporter heard about the civil unrest at Florence and Normandie after the not-guilty verdicts, he realized he had access to sources no one else at the newspaper had— including his own mother who lived in L.A. and was listening nonstop to Radio Korea.

"I used what my mom was relaying from Radio Korea and sent updates to the city desk about what was happening in South L.A.," he said. "It was news to them."

The next day, the *Los Angeles Times* assigned John H. Lee to cover Koreatown. As he arrived in L.A. after the 125-mile drive from San Diego, he saw plumes of black smoke and palm trees burning. "It felt like scenes from the bombing of war-torn countries. When we arrived in Koreatown, we saw rice bags blocking the entrances, stacked like sandbags. I just saw guys with guns."

One store owner was grateful to learn John H. Lee was with the *Times*. "We haven't seen any other reporters, just helicopters in the sky," he said. "Do you want to meet the Lee family?"

This was the first time anyone at the *Los Angeles Times* had heard about Edward Jae Song Lee. Korean media covered a press conference at the Lee family's house. John and another *Times* reporter, Tammerlin Drummond, were the only American journalists present.

"I told [Eddie] don't go, don't go," Jung Hui Lee told reporters.

"The feeling I got was she blamed herself for not stopping Eddie from leaving the house," John H. Lee said, still haunted by her pain.

• • •

Although John's thirtieth birthday was later that week, he didn't have time to plan for any celebration. Instead, he found himself kneeling behind a row of refrigerators barricading the Cosmos Appliance store on Vermont Avenue. John's heart filled with 한 han as he observed store owner Michael Kim and his friends, several who were Korean army veterans, arming themselves with .45 Colt guns and clips. He learned how gang members had shot into the store for two nights in a row and how a pickup truck had rammed into the front entrance so looters could steal everything except for the refrigerators.

"You have to explain how we feel," the store owner's fifteen-year-old niece told John.

In that moment, John realized his responsibility as both a journalist and a Korean American. Representation had to matter in what he wrote next. "It was a call to arms that I was writing to myself," he said.

"This Is about People Feeling Desperate"

Edward "Eddie" Travens was close to getting his driver's license. His sixteenth birthday was in June. To his excitement, his uncle let him practice driving in his Cadillac.

At 9:25 p.m. on Wednesday, April 29, the outgoing teenager was driving with his older brother, Allen, twenty-one, and their friend Dan Ortiz to a neighborhood video store to rent a movie for the weekend.

As they waited for the traffic light to turn green at the intersection of San Fernando Road and Mission Boulevard in the San Fernando Valley, an unknown man ran up to their car. "Where are you from?" he asked.

Before they could answer, the man pulled out a gun and shot at the car before running away. He was not caught. Travens was hit five times. His friend took over the car while Allen held his brother in his arms.

Eddie Travens died around midnight at the hospital, less than twenty-four hours before Eddie Lee would die outside Pizza Go. Travens, whose father was white and mother was Latina, was counted among the nineteen Latinos killed during the civil unrest.

Like the Korean American community who criticized the media for stereotyping their community, the Latino community was also upset by the media bias portraying them mainly as "looters."

Héctor Tobar was angry when his white editors had asked him to "go out and find some Latino looters." Tobar was a rising star reporter at the *Los Angeles Times* who had written numerous front-page stories.

"Héctor, you go out and see if you can find some Latino looters for us, because we saw a lot of Latinos looting in the riots on television," Tobar remembered. "Go see if you can find some. And I was so personally insulted."

During the L.A. uprising, Latinos made up 51 percent of all arrests. Almost a third of the sixty-three people killed were

As 3,600 fires swept throughout Los Angeles, desperate residents grabbed whatever supplies they could from mom-and-pop stores and major department-store chains like Sears.

Latinos. Early reports estimated that up to 40 percent of businesses destroyed were Latino-owned, including more than five hundred newsstands carrying the popular Spanish-language newspaper *La Opinión*.

In 1990, Latinos made up 40 percent of Los Angeles's population according to the Census Bureau (who identified them back then as "Hispanic"). There was a well-established middle-class community of Mexican American families who had planted roots there generations ago. In the previous decade, Central American immigrants also began moving into the Pico-Union district and South L.A. By 1990, South L.A.'s population was 45 percent Latino and 48 percent Black.

This population surge led to more stereotypes in the media. When TV news crews filmed Latinos raiding stores, they were frequently described as "looters," "illegal aliens," "thugs," and "gangbangers."

But the reality was that many of these "looters" were families living below the poverty line and in food deserts. The burning stores were their only connection to basic necessities like baby formula and cleaning supplies.

"I saw a lot of people getting essentials, not just televisions," remembered criminal defense attorney Angela Oh. "People were getting dishtowels, dish soap, and diapers, stuff that when you saw it was really sad."

Many in the Latino community would later call the 1992 L.A. civil unrest the "levantamiento"—uprising.

"Latinos were a very important but underwritten part of the story" when it came to the 1992 Los Angeles civil unrest, said University of Southern California professor Manuel Pastor. "So much of the Latino unrest was about the situation of working poverty. But everyone pays a lot more attention to the spark rather than the tinder."

"Everything Snapped"

Najee Ali, the former Crips gang member who had attended the trial of Soon Ja Du, found himself caught up in the fury on the first night of protests. He and several other demonstrators had driven over to Wilshire Boulevard and Western Avenue in the heart of Koreatown, where they broke windows and threw Molotov cocktails.

"The number-one enemy for us was Koreans, who we felt were oppressing us," he said. "Everything snapped." He believed the original protest at Florence and Normandie was "a rebellion, a revolt of Black men saying, 'We're tired of being murdered and abused by everyone in society, so we're gonna fight back.'"

But Ali noticed the large numbers of families looking for basic necessities in these ransacked stores. He realized for them, this had nothing to do with the protests against the LAPD.

"They didn't care nothing about Latasha, Rodney King, or no one else," he explained. "They saw it as an opportunity to overcome economic hardship and poverty. This went from a revolt to the largest civil unrest in American history."

As Ali watched the fires in Koreatown, he thought about his baby daughter. He had to stay alive for her. He was at a crossroads in his life, trying to leave gang life forever and forge his new passion for activism.

This was his 한 han.

So he went home.

"But I didn't say anything to try to bring peace or reconciliation or unity," Ali admitted. "I didn't discourage anyone. And I feel guilty now thirty years later. I could've done more. If nothing else just to say, 'Hey, let's not do that. That's not the way.' But instead, my voice was mute, just like as I felt the Koreans' voice was mute when Latasha was murdered. I felt like 'Hey, you guys left us on our own, you're on your own now.'"

"Did I Really Cause This?"

For the twelve men and women who served on the jury for *The People of the State of California v. Laurence Powell, Timothy E. Wind, Theodore Briseno, and Stacey Koon*, the past five days had been a nightmare.

The jury felt like they were the ones on trial. Jury foreman Dorothy Bailey wondered if this "national hate" was all their fault. "Did I really cause this?" she wondered, unable to sleep for the first three nights after the verdicts were announced. She wasn't the only one. Other jurors also experienced insomnia, weight loss, and even stomach ulcers.

Jurors were distraught over accusations of racism. "This is the worst experience of my life," said one juror. "I don't know what's in the heart of others. But I know in my heart I'm not a racist."

The press hounded the jurors. They received death threats. Some went into isolation. Others left Los Angeles, not sure they would return.

"I've gotten some calls saying that I'll have to live with this for the rest of my life," said a shaken juror, describing the civil unrest as "a little hell."

This was the jury's 한 han.

"We Want Peace"

When Radio Korea broadcast an announcement that a peace rally would be held in Koreatown on Saturday, May 2, they had no idea that more than thirty thousand Korean Americans would show up. They came from all over California. They ranged in age from children to people in their eighties. It was the largest Korean American protest in American history.

Protesters carried signs written in English and Korean: Why Are Korean Americans the Fall Guys for All Social Injustice? The Blame Lies with the U.S. Government. Stop Making Us Scapegoats. No Racism, No Violence. Mutual Respect. Justice for King.

Korean American community leaders, military veterans, and a speaker from the South Korean National Assembly delivered speeches asking for peace and understanding.

A visibly distraught Jong Min Kang spoke next, flanked by members of his Korean Young Adult Team, all wearing their 망건 manggeon headbands. "We don't know how long this situation will last," he said, "but until the day it ends, we will do our best. Even if we make some mistakes . . . we are risking our lives to protect the lives and property of our Korean Americans."

More than thirty thousand Korean Americans showed up for a peace rally in Koreatown on May 2, 1992, with signs supporting Rodney King and condemning racism. This was the largest gathering of Korean Americans ever in the country, inspiring a future generation of Korean American activists and politicians.

Afterward, Edward Jae Song Lee's family led a three-hour march from Olympic Boulevard to Western and Vermont Avenues, holding Eddie's 영정 사진 youngjeong sajin, a traditional Korean funerary portrait framed with black ribbon. Marchers carried brooms and garbage bags to sweep up the broken glass and debris. Restaurant owners handed out plates of food, while teenagers poured cups of water.

Black and Latino marchers wore white headbands in solidarity and included Mexican American movie star Edward James Olmos, who had also led volunteers in clean-up efforts for the past three days and met with California governor Pete Wilson to discuss how to rebuild the city. A group of elderly Korean men in the parade noticed young Black and Latino spectators holding up the Korean flag and went over to hug them.

"We want justice! We want peace!" the crowd shouted. They sang Korean folk songs and "We Shall Overcome."

Activist and freelance photographer Tong Cho "T.C." Kim, whose parents' bookstore had been set on fire but not destroyed during the civil unrest, was taking photos of the parade for the Los Angeles-based *KoreAm Journal*, the most widely circulated Korean American magazine in the country founded in 1990. As he perched on the roof of a National Guard truck, he spotted a group of diverse people from the crowd join traditional Korean folk dancers in the parade, imitating their steps. He started to cry. "I'm like, 'Oh, this is so beautiful,'" he said. "This is the picture, this is what I wanted to see."

This picture of solidarity also meant the world to David Lin, who brought his broom to the parade to sweep the trash off the streets. The twenty-six-year-old Chinese American engineer by way of Taiwan and Minnesota had just moved with his wife to Los Angeles after graduating from the Massachusetts Institute of Technology. Lin, a devout Christian who belonged to a local Chinese American church, had recently partnered with Victory Outreach, a downtown L.A. church to help the unhoused and recently paroled prison inmates. "God wants people to be in harmony," Lin said. "He wants people to love each other, neighbors to care for each other."

The parade reached its destination—the intersection of Hobart Avenue and 3rd Street where Edward Jae Song Lee had been killed.

Eddie's family and friends held up his portrait and prayed outside Pizza Go. His parents and sister held each other.

"They're All Together"

At the same time the Koreatown Peace Parade was being held, the 120 guests for the wedding of LAFD firefighter Emile Mack and Jenny Kawada fought their way to Redondo Beach. Several exits off the 110 Harbor and the 10 Santa Monica Freeways had been shut down since Thursday. They would not fully reopen until the next day.

But Mack's wedding was today.

"We've got to get through to Redondo Beach," one guest insisted to a California Highway Patrol officer monitoring a roadblock. "We're going to a wedding."

On May 2, 1992, Emile Mack and his bride Jenny Kawada-Mack wed in Redondo Beach in front of 120 family and friends who all managed to get there despite several freeway closures. After the ceremony, Mack and his groomsmen, including best man Craig Smith (pictured to Mack's right), tried to return their rented tuxedos, only to find out the store had burned down. "The store's gone," the store owner told Mack. "There's nothing."

The CHP officer was shocked. "Are you kidding?"

But everyone made it. Mack and his best man and fellow firefighter Craig Smith and their wedding parties stood at the altar as the bride walked down the aisle.

"All my groomsmen were there," Mack said. "They're all firefighters. They were all there."

During the wedding reception, Mack found the deejay weeping. "What's wrong?" he asked.

"Just look at this," the deejay said. "This is so beautiful. Black people, white people, Mexican, Asian . . . they're all here. They're all together."

Mack realized the deejay, who was white, had noticed his family and friends dancing and laughing on the dance floor—including his bride, Jenny Kawada-Mack; his best man, Craig; and his parents, Clarence and Undine Mack.

Mack smiled. Of course they were together.

"I'm Just a High School Kid"

All week, Carol Kim had been watching non-Korean reporters describe Korean American store owners as "vigilantes."

"I'm watching all these businesses burning down to the ground, and then these white TV news reporters on the street are sticking their microphones into the faces of Korean business owners who are just beyond devastated," she said. "They're wailing, they're crying, they're like in complete disbelief watching their businesses being looted or burned, and then you have these white news reporters saying in English, 'Why are you crying?' Like, really?"

The seventeen-year-old high school senior, who grew up in Koreatown, was an aspiring journalist and had just been accepted into the University of California, Irvine, where she planned to study media and communications.

Her family lived just a few miles from the KABC Channel 7 News station on Prospect Avenue. "The Koreans were being portrayed, instead of the victims . . . as the aggressors," she said of their coverage. "I was like, 'Okay, we're going to protest against the KABC-TV News station.'"

On Sunday, May 3, 1992, Carol and her cousin sat in the backyard of her house, armed with magic markers, making picket signs. Stop Unfair Media Coverage! We're Americans, Too!

They called Radio Korea. "Listen, meet us at KABC studio on Prospect Avenue," they told the reporter live on the air. "We're going to protest about the media's coverage."

When they arrived at the KABC station, three of their church youth-group friends were waiting for them. "This is like a ragtag group of know-nothing kids, and we give them our handmade posters, and we're just standing there," she said.

Luckily for the teenagers, a couple of members of the Teamsters were taking a work break on the other side of the studio gate. "What are you doing?" asked one of them.

"We're here to protest the media's unfair news coverage of the Korean community and the L.A. riots," they announced.

"Okay, here's what you have to do," the teamster said. "You can't just stand here, or you'll get arrested for loitering. You have to keep walking." He pointed to the sidewalk. "Go in a circle."

"He basically gave us a tutorial on how to strike," Carol Kim remembered, laughing.

For the next ten minutes, the five teenagers marched around, holding up their handmade posters, chanting "Unfair media!"

Carol Kim felt a little silly. "I didn't know if the call to Radio Korea was even going to be answered. Was anyone even going to show up? Like, for all I knew, it was just going to be us doing this for maybe a half-hour and we're not going to get any attention."

And then they heard honking.

"It was like a Hollywood movie scene," she marveled. "Like those famous war battle scenes where all of a sudden the brigade comes charging down."

A line of cars filled the street. A crowd rushed over, waving their own protest signs. People handed out water bottles and cellophane-wrapped paper plates filled with Korean 김밥 kimbap rice rolls to feed everyone.

Within the hour, more than three hundred Korean Americans were marching along with the five teenagers, shouting, "Unfair! Unfair media!"

"We drew quite a crowd," she said. "It was actually causing a bit of traffic, so KABC ended up sending out one of their TV reporters to talk to us."

The story aired that evening during the broadcast of KABC Channel 7 Nightly News. It was also shown nationally on *Nightline* with Ted Koppel.

"And so that's my unsophisticated ragtag organizing as a high school student who didn't know a thing," Carol Kim said proudly. "This was like pre-cell phone. There was no internet, no Tweet storm. This was literally old school. I'm just a high school kid, but the community responded. People showed up."

"We Are Being Scapegoated"

Three days later, on Wednesday, May 6, a prominent national news program finally presented the Korean American point of view.

Angela Oh, the criminal defense attorney who had spoken out during the Soon Ja Du–Latasha Harlins shooting case, appeared in an interview with anchor Ted Koppel on ABC's *Nightline*.

"In the aftermath of the Los Angeles riots, another color of rage," Koppel said. "Tonight, we'll hear from a group that was a target of the violence. Korean Americans."

Koppel asked Oh about the alleged conflict between the Korean American and Black communities. "You must have heard it again and again from Black citizens in that community. 'They just don't get it. . . . We've been here for hundreds of years, these Koreans are the ones who are here for a few years or a generation or two, if there's a culture gap, let them learn our culture.' To which you say what?"

"To which I say, that is exactly what the goals are of most immigrants that come to this country," Oh replied, explaining that Korean immigrant families *did* have the intention of

On May 6, 1992, thirty-six-year-old criminal defense attorney Angela Oh gained national prominence as the voice of the Korean American community after her *Nightline* interview with ABC news anchor Ted Koppel. Her appearance led to hate mail from anti-Asian racists and even criticism from some older and more politically conservative Korean Americans who viewed Oh as a "left-wing radical." But Oh remained positive—and pragmatic. "I'm a die-hard optimist," she said. "I feel very strongly that people are capable of coming together. . . . We are able to do it if we choose to do it."

assimilating into America. But the expectation that Korean immigrants must assimilate overnight was "extremely unfair and extremely unrealistic."

"She expressed the Korean experience very well," praised Black-Korean Alliance member Marcia Choo. "We continue to be defined by rude Korean merchants, who are a very small portion of the community. There is no balance. We have very little exposure in the mainstream media. . . . We are largely invisible and voiceless."

During the *Nightline* program, Oh criticized the media's coverage of the Korean American community. "I want to make a statement about this whole Black–Korean thing that the media has been portraying," she said. "It's a very damning thing that the media is doing. Because the fact of the matter is I know that my Korean American brethren, and my Black brothers and sisters, my Native American brothers and sisters, my Latino brothers and sisters, we feel no hatred innately for one another. This is a myth that's being created by the press. . . . We aren't victims. Make no mistake. Korean Americans do not view themselves as victims. We are being scapegoated. We know it."

Given how rare it was to see nonstereotyped images of Korean American—and Asian American—women on-screen, Angela Oh's strong and confident *Nightline* appearance was groundbreaking.

U.S. Representative Maxine Waters, a Democrat from California, praised Angela Oh's appearance "as a lesson in how to make sense out of the worst of times and how to keep us turning from each other."

"At the time, I was carrying a lot of anger, so my energy was coming from a place of intensity and passion," Oh said. "I was upset over the unnecessary destruction of a lot of immigrant lives and livelihoods. I was ready to meet that moment."

"We Lost Our Son"

Earlier that day, both Eddie Lee and Eddie Travens were laid to rest.

A Catholic mass was held for Eddie Travens in San Fernando. On the way to his final resting place at the San Fernando Mission Cemetery, someone had spray-painted "Rest in Peace, Eddie B." on the Interstate 5 overpass near Laurel Canyon Boulevard. The "B" stood for his mother's maiden name, Ballasteros.

Five thousand people attended Edward Jae Song Lee's funeral, held at the Ardmore Recreation Center (now known as Seoul International Park) in Koreatown.

Most of them did not know Eddie. But they came out to support his family and the community.

An NBC News helicopter hovered above the park, which was just six blocks from the Lees' house. Hundreds of international newspaper reporters and TV news crews crowded the area. High-ranking government officials and politicians from Korea also attended the funeral, from Unification National Party politician Kim Dong Gil to Democratic Party member and future president of South Korea Kim Dae Jung. Eddie's friend James Kang, still in serious condition, attended the funeral in a wheelchair, wearing his hospital gown, an IV drip attached to his arm. "It didn't need to happen this way," he said, bitter. "I still can't forgive for this. I have hatred for a lot of people now. That's all I have is hatred and anger."

Giant wreaths of flowers surrounded the podium, gifts from the Korean government and the U.S.-Korean ambassador's office. The

Lees sat in the front row onstage with Eddie's official funeral portrait, the 태극기 Taegeukgi South Korean flag draped over his casket.

Mourners held up protest signs in English and Korean: We Want Peace. Chief Gates Needs to Explain the Intentional Delay of the Arrival of the LAPD. We Need Justice. In Loving Memory: Edward Song Lee. We Grieve Together as One Family for the Loss of Our Brave Son.

Eddie's friends, including John Kim, served as his pallbearers for the burial service at the Forest Lawn Memorial Park cemetery in the Hollywood Hills. A man in full military uniform from the Republic of Korea Marine Corps stood with the Korean flag in a white car, leading the funeral procession down Olympic Boulevard through

Edward Jae Song Lee's coffin follows a young pallbearer carrying his portrait as family and friends head to his final resting place at the Forest Lawn Memorial Park cemetery in the Hollywood Hills.

the heart of Koreatown. It was the same route Eddie used to walk when participating in the annual Korean Festival parade as a child.

His mother was the first to toss a ceremonial handful of dirt over his casket. "How can I sprinkle dirt on your body?" she wept in Korean. "Don't you feel cold down there?"

One of the Korean pastors comforted Jung Hui, telling her, "He is gone. But his spirit lives within us forever."

In that moment, Jung Hui remembered how her son had picked up the bowl of noodles during his traditional Korean 돌잡이 doljabi first-birthday fortune-telling ceremony. The noodles symbolized long life.

She realized his fortune had come true.

Edward Jae Song Lee's name would live on forever.

"Don't Say Goodbye"

After the funeral, Jung Hui stood outside Eddie's room. She had not been in there since he had died.

"I keep looking at the front door as if he will soon open that door yelling, 'Mom! I'm hungry!'" she said. "Sadly, he doesn't show up to me anymore, even though I still can feel his breath on every corner of this house, and still can hear his voice and his stomping sounds. I feel empty. The house looks so vacant. I am waiting for that door to open, but he is not there."

She finally opened the door.

As usual, his room was messy, camping gear and piles of books cluttering the floor. She smiled at the music box with a miniature spinning Elvis Presley figure. Her son loved Elvis Presley, Ritchie Valens, and other classic rock musicians from the 1950s and 1960s. He always listened to an oldies rock 'n' roll radio station while getting ready for school in the mornings.

An old kimchi jar sat on his desk. There was a $10 bill

inside—the same bill she had given him for washing their cars on the day before he died. He had saved it in the jar for a future church service donation.

An open Bible lay on Eddie's bed. "Jae Song was reading the Bible before he ran out of the house during the riot," she said. She closed the Bible before checking to see what verse he had read. "Those were the last Bible verses he read before he went to Jesus," she said. "I regret that I did not mark that page."

She then found one of his notebooks in which he had been practicing his 한글 Hangul, the Korean alphabet. She smiled at his "clumsy handwriting" until she realized he had been writing the lyrics to one of his favorite songs by veteran Korean pop singer Lee Seungchul—"Don't Say Goodbye."

"I felt like something hit me hard," she said. "Did he leave a message for a mom he left behind? Why did he write these lyrics and leave them on his desk?"

As she read her Eddie's handwriting . . .

안녕이라고 말하지마 Annyeong eerago malhajima.
나는 너를 보고 있잖아 Naneun nuhleul bogo itjanah.

안녕이라고 말하지마 나는 너를 보고 있잖아
Don't say goodbye. My eyes are on you.
그러나 자꾸 눈물이 나서 널 볼 수가 없어
The tears are welling up. I cannot see you.
안녕이라고 말하지마 우린 아직 이별이 뭔지 몰라
Don't say goodbye. We don't even know what that means.

"Who can mend my broken heart?" she asked.

Chapter 11

OUT OF THE ASHES

"All Signs of Normalcy Have Returned"

On Monday, May 4, 1992, Mayor Tom Bradley ended the four-day, dusk-to-dawn curfew. He believed the civil unrest was "under control" now that more than twelve thousand Marine, Army, and National Guard members had been deployed.

"All signs of normalcy have returned," the mayor declared.

During this "normalcy," army troops slept on the stage at the Hollywood Bowl. At Venice Beach, closed due to toxic debris caused by the fires, National Guard soldiers in riot gear escorted surfers trying to sneak a few waves off the sand. More than half of the buildings burned had contained asbestos and other dangerous chemicals, forcing some residents to evacuate their homes temporarily for shelters set up at nearby high schools.

Entire blocks were without electricity and gas. Cars lined up at gas stations only to discover the tanks were empty. Armored

A man comforts a distraught store owner after her store is destroyed, one of the many displays of compassion and comfort among residents during the civil unrest. (*Opposite page*) On Monday, May 4, 1992, despite the still-lingering smoke and smoldering buildings, businesses and schools reopen after several days of a citywide curfew and shutdown.

trucks could not deposit money into banks, so people could not access their accounts. Mail delivery was halted. Supermarkets were unable to restock, so people hoarded milk, bread, eggs, and toilet paper.

Koreatown had suffered a disproportionate 45 percent of all damage—amounting to almost half a billion dollars. More than two-thirds of the 2,300 Korean-owned businesses that were destroyed had no insurance. Many people lost their life savings. Almost 40,000 people were forced to file for unemployment.

Many Korean American store owners who did have insurance struggled to fill out endless and complex forms because of the language barrier. Their children helped translate these forms. Korean American doctors, pharmacists, bankers, and other experts answered questions in Korean live on Radio Korea about everything from visas and insurance to counseling services.

More than $2.5 million was raised by Radio Korea, the Korean American Coalition, and other community organizations to provide clothing, food, and legal services for displaced Korean American business owners and their families.

But the money wasn't enough to erase their 화 hwa—their anger. And this suppressed anger soon flared into 화병 hwabyung, the "fire disease."

Many store owners, employees, and families reported insomnia, depression, paranoia, suicidal ideation, and physical illness due to the stress and despair over their losses. But language barriers and a lack of adequate cultural sensitivity training for mental health professionals in America made access to mental health care services difficult for Korean immigrants.

Back then, South Korea also had one of the highest suicide rates among "developed" countries for various complex reasons, including

a reluctance to seek professional psychological counseling and therapy unless it was an emergency. That ingrained cultural reluctance continued for many Korean immigrants, even in America.

"You internalize family issues, domestic violence issues, your own depression," explained activist T.C. Kim. "You keep it to yourself; you don't go and share it with other people."

But the 1992 L.A. uprising was a turning point as thousands of Korean Americans flooded local counseling centers, seeking therapy for the first time in their lives.

"The whole perception about mental health changed," said T.C. Kim, who was inspired by the uprising to become a community leader and nonprofits consultant. "After the riots, the whole PTSD, family, and anger issues came about, and people were like, 'Okay, counseling is for anybody who feels depressed or suffering pain, anger, it could help all those people.' The attitude toward getting mental health changed."

Black-Owned

Just as they had during the Watts rebellion in 1965, many Black store owners posted Black Owned signs in their windows during the 1992 civil unrest.

But not all of these signs worked.

Firestone Tire on 52nd Street and Crenshaw Boulevard burned to the ground.

Dobson's Food Market, a staple for locals in Leimert Park for fifty years, was now ashes.

The Kinney shoe store, Wherehouse Records, and the Security Pacific Bank on La Brea Avenue, all were gone. Jazz Etc., a popular nightclub, destroyed. Black doctors' medical offices, banks, Black-owned liquor stores, all vandalized and torched.

The Thrifty Drug chain, which had lost four outlets during the 1965 Watts rebellion, lost three more stores in 1992.

Because the L.A. fire department was overwhelmed with thousands of fires erupting all at once across the city, many Black store owners were forced to put out the fires themselves. Payless Market owner Cornelius Pettus was on his own as he fought an out-of-control fire that had erupted next door at the Ace Glass store on the corner of 57th Street and Western Avenue.

"The roofs are wood," Pettus said. "So if one catches fire and that fire spreads another ten feet, not only would my facility burn, the whole block would burn because there's no stopping it."

The flames climbed thirty feet in the air, torching some of the telephone wires. The Ace Glass sign melted. As Pettus threw a pail of water into the fire, he feared being electrocuted. He heard

For seventy-two straight hours, Payless Market store owner Cornelius Pettus battled alone to stop a fire from a neighboring store from reaching his own business. "It was overwhelming for the fire department because when a fire department gets a call, they go to where they're dispatched to," Pettus explained. "They got so many calls, they were passing by burning structures to get to the place where they were sent to go."

gunshots as cars passed by. "A lot of things could've gone wrong," he said.

During the next seventy-two hours, a nearby shopping center, a hamburger stand, and a video store all burned down. As Pettus battled the blaze on his own, all he could think about was his wife and their two young children.

"Your life flashes before you," he said. "I mean, what do you do?"

On April 30, the day after the verdicts were announced, James Fugate was working at Eso Won Books, which he had cofounded with Tom Hamilton in 1988 in South L.A. to promote Black authors. They had just relocated their store to Inglewood earlier that year. That morning, a protester entered the store.

Fugate grew tense. This was his second time experiencing civil unrest, the first being the 1967 Detroit rebellion when he was a child. To his relief, the protester noticed the books and realized this was a Black-owned store.

"He looked around and said, 'Okay, I see what this store is all about,'" Fugate recalled. "He said, 'We're not going to loot this store.'"

But another Black-owned bookstore wasn't so lucky. The Aquarian Book Shop on Martin Luther King Jr. Boulevard was America's first and oldest Black-owned bookstore, founded in 1941. Just one month earlier, civil rights icon Rosa Parks had appeared at the Aquarian for a book signing.

On April 30, someone set fire to the Aquarian Book Shop. Owners Dr. Alfred Ligon, a physician, and his wife, Bernice, were helpless to stop it. "There's nothing we can do," Ligon said.

The Aquarian and its five thousand books burned to the ground. The Ligons could not afford the insurance to rebuild the $175,000 worth of damage.

A magazine was the only item to survive the fire.

"We Have to Come to the Same Table"

On November 17, 1992, the Black-Korean Alliance broke up.

Despite the BKA's progress over the past six years, members agreed talk was not enough. They were a volunteer group with no money to hire a staff. Everyone was frustrated, burned out, and disillusioned.

"The BKA from the beginning was set up to fail because we had no funding," said UC Riverside professor and BKA member Edward Taehan Chang. "We had no sustainable way to continue this . . . and membership was voluntary. Anybody can come and go. No membership dues, nothing. There is no accountability or responsibility. Its main focus was on dialogue and cultural understanding. That is important, but you can only go so far. The Black–Korean L.A. riot issue is far more structural than just improving dialogue."

"We need people working together on concrete problems," agreed BKA cofounder Larry Aubry. "Organizing around education, housing, economic development, and community-based policing."

"My dad was trying to get beneath these superficialities and really have people talk honestly about things," reflected Larry Aubry's daughter, Erin Aubry Kaplan. "My father always said it was very difficult work for both sides. But he felt it was really important, that this is something that affects everybody, not just Black people. It's all of us. We have to come to the same table."

Activist and BKA member Marcia Choo said the city's civil unrest exposed a much bigger problem beyond their communities. "There are tensions, but it's not just a Black–Korean conflict. Problems of racism, hopelessness and despair are bigger than what the (alliance) was about."

But Jerry Yu, executive director of the Korean American

Coalition, remained proud of what the BKA did accomplish in its short life. "I met a lot of people through BKA. That was the strength of BKA—it brought people together to talk about these things."

"Sorry, Mr. Lee"

But amid all this despair, hope still bloomed. Many Korean American store owners began to rebuild. They found out they were not alone.

At first, Chung "Brother" Lee felt abandoned when his second store, Watts Market, was set on fire. The owner of Farm Fresh Dairy in Watts had recently purchased the nearby store.

But now all that remained of Watts Market were four walls. Everything else, gone.

"I worked hard for that store," he said, weeping. "I don't know my future. Where can I go?"

Later, Chung Lee visited what remained of his store to assess the damage and find out how much it would cost to hire a demolition crew.

What he saw shocked him—and moved him to tears.

Although only the skeleton of four walls still stood, the rubble, shattered glass, and twisted metal frames had been completely cleared out. It was ready to be rebuilt.

A sign on the property read "Sorry, Mr. Lee."

It turned out Brother Lee's customers and neighbors who lived in the nearby Jordan Downs housing project had organized a clean-up with former NFL football star Jim Brown's Amer-I-Can gang rehabilitation advocacy organization. For two weeks, they wore hard hats and rented a dumpster to clean up all the debris. They hadn't forgotten Chung Lee's kindness and generosity—how he had donated sodas and snacks to their children's Little League

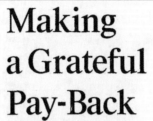

Making a Grateful Pay-Back

Watts Market Customers Pitch In to Help Out Korean-American Merchant

By PENELOPE McMILLAN
TIMES STAFF WRITER

The small Watts Market was one of hundreds of businesses destroyed in the riots, but it was special to the community that surrounded it.

"Sorry, Mr. Lee," reads a sign scrawled across the front of what had been a thriving market on 103rd Street.

Chung Lee, a Korean-American merchant, had operated the store for seven years and was known for his efforts to help his customers, many of whom live in the Jordan Downs housing project across the street.

So when his store was burned during the riots, his customers rallied to

MEL MELCON / For The Times

After the 1992 Los Angeles uprising, there was a significant effort by the media to highlight positive stories about solidarity between the Korean American and Black communities, including this one on how loyal customers helped rebuild a beloved store owner's business.

games. How he held Korean barbecues over the holidays for customers. How he had hired Black youth and trained them to run sales at the store.

"We were trying to show him there is a relationship between the Black community and the Korean community," said one of his customers.

Brother Lee was so grateful that he donated $2,300 to the Ameri-I-Can group. He promised his community that he would rebuild the store.

"I want to come back," he said.

Mama

No one messes with Mama. Her customers made sure of that.

When the unrest began on April 29, loyal customers rushed

into "Mama's Market" on 54th and Van Ness and told the store's beloved owner, Chung-Bok "Mama" Hong, to leave. They warned her about possible riots and looting.

Hong and her husband followed their advice and locked up the store. The next day, Mama's Market was still standing. In fact, it was one of the few buildings in the area that remained intact.

Mourner places flower on table during Thursday's memorial service for grocer Chung-Bok Hong, who was killed by robbers last year.

A Community Remembers 'Mama'

By K. CONNIE KANG
TIMES STAFF WRITER

A year after a popular Korean American grocer was killed by robbers, a multiethnic gathering Thursday remembered Chung-Bok Hong as a noteworthy contributor to improving relations between African Americans and Koreans by her quiet deeds that exemplified love.

Hong, 52, called "Mama" by her customers, was struck down on Feb. 3, 1999, in front of her husband and son when two gunmen robbed them in the parking lot of her convenience store at 54th Street and Van Ness Avenue.

Her customers adored her because they said she treated them with respect and kindness, no matter what their social or economic status.

"I had an opportunity to love her for 11 years in our community," said Kerry Lewis, who spoke at a neighborhood representative at an English-Korean memorial service at St. Brigid Catholic Church in South-Central. "And, I want to tell you what she meant to me. She

'She meant love, she meant understanding, she meant friendship.'

Kerry Lewis, at English-Korean memorial service in South-Central

meant love, she meant understanding, she meant friendship."

Though Hong has passed on, Lewis said, her generosity and love will live on in the people who were touched by her.

"Love is something that not even death can take away," the Rev. Leonard Jackson, of the First African Methodist Episcopal Church, said during the 90-minute service, attended

Photos by KIRK McKOY / Los Angeles Times

Jong-Pyo Hong wipes away tears during the service for his late wife.

by more than 100 Koreans, African Americans and Latinos. "Love can overcome hate. Our challenge today is . . . to love thy neighbor as thyself."

Jackie Brown, who frequented Hong's store for more than four years, said that for a long time after the merchant's death, she was so grief-stricken she could not bring herself to go near the place. Brown said she felt as though she had lost a

member of her family.

"Mama was a very special lady who was sweet but also feisty when she needed to be," she said.

Brown, a jazz singer with a rich mezzo-soprano voice, sang a "special song" she had written to honor her at the memorial.

This is not goodbye. I can see you when I look at the sky. When I look at the trees, feel a warm breeze or see a butterfly, you are there, you are everywhere. Mama, they told your story around the world. It touched so many people. You are loved, you are missed, you always will be remembered.

Hong's husband, Jong-Pyo, said the outpouring of love for his wife and the family expressed by friends like Lewis and Brown has been a tremendous source of strength and comfort to him and his children.

"We are a family," he said of his African American customers, "so much so that sometimes we would even argue with each other."

Ellis Cha, president of the Korean

Please see MAMA, B11

On February 3, 1999, Chung Bok "Mama" Hong was shot by two armed robbers outside her store and died in her husband's arms. More than three hundred people attended her funeral, which made national headlines. "Mama contradicts [that] stereotype of African American and Korean American relations," said Los Angeles city councilman Mark Ridley-Thomas at her service. "This can set an example of what ought to be." Family, friends, and customers celebrated Mama at a special memorial service on February 3, 2000, to commemorate the one-year anniversary of her death.

Why? Her mostly Black and Latino customers had stood outside all night, protecting her store.

Chung-Bok Hong hugged her customers and thanked them. To her surprise, they thanked *her* for being their "loving angel," saying, "We will always love you, Mama."

The New Police Chief

On June 28, Daryl F. Gates resigned as chief of police for the Los Angeles Police Department.

Former FBI and CIA director William H. Webster, who led a panel investigation on the Los Angeles civil unrest, blamed Gates for having "failed to provide a real plan and meaningful training to control the disorder."

One month earlier, Amnesty International had released a study concluding that the LAPD and Los Angeles County Sheriff's Department used excessive force, especially against Black and Latino suspects. "Amnesty International's findings suggest that there have been a disturbing number of cases in recent years in which law enforcement officials in Los Angeles have resorted to excessive force, sometimes amounting to torture or other cruel, inhuman or degrading treatment," the report stated.

"The record on police brutality is appalling," said Ian Martin, secretary general of the human rights organization.

Gates dismissed Amnesty International, calling them "liberal do-nothings" and "a bunch of knucklehead liberals." He also criticized the media, especially the *Los Angeles Times*, for what he called "irresponsible" reporting. Although he acknowledged that the LAPD beating of Rodney King was wrong, he blamed the media for sensationalizing the case. "It was a terrible thing. Everyone agrees with that. But you made it into something spectacular. You made it something bigger than the Gulf War."

REFUSING TO STEP DOWN
Gates' supporters gather at the Police Academy to cheer him on weeks after the beating of
King. The incident drew calls for his ouster from Mayor Tom Bradley and others.

(*Top*) LAPD chief Daryl F. Gates at a March 1991 rally held in his support at the Police
Academy after the beating of Rodney King. Although Mayor Tom Bradley and others
called for Gates's resignation, he refused to step down. It was only after the civil
unrest the following year that he finally resigned. (*Bottom*) LAPD police chief Willie
L. Williams. The former head of the Philadelphia Police Department, Williams took
over as the first Black chief of police for the Los Angeles Police Department.

As Gates walked out of the Parker Center for the last time, a crowd of loyal police officers cheered him on, chanting, "We love you, Chief!"

Willie L. Williams was sworn in as Gates's replacement. The forty-eight-year-old former Philadelphia police commissioner became the first Black chief of the LAPD.

"We will be addressing concerns about police abuse and concerns about the misuse of force, and about sexism and racism, and we're going to look at our training," he announced. "We're going to take a whole fresh look at the department from A to Z."

As the city and the LAPD struggled to clean up and rebuild, questions of justice remained.

"Justice Was Half-Served"

"I was just trying to stay alive, sir."

At 1:30 p.m. on Tuesday, March 9, 1993, Rodney Glen King took the stand to testify against the four LAPD police officers who had beaten him two years earlier.

People lined the block outside the Edward R. Roybal Federal Building on Temple Street at 6:00 a.m. for a chance at only a dozen courtroom seats available for the public.

One year after the first trial of LAPD officers Stacey Koon, Laurence Powell, Timothy Wind, and Theodore Briseno, a second trial was taking place. This time, a federal grand jury had indicted all four officers for violating Rodney King's civil rights. Briseno, Powell, and Wind were charged with "willfully and intentionally using unreasonable force under color of law" and Sergeant Koon for "willfully permitting and failing to take action to stop the assault," thus depriving King of his constitutional rights.

This case was being tried at the U.S. District Court in downtown L.A. The jury consisted of eight men and four women.

Of the twelve jurors, nine were white, two were Black, and one was Latino.

King testified that he may have heard racial epithets during the beating. He remembered police officers chanting, "What's up, killer?" and using anti-Black slurs. When cross-examined, King admitted his memory was spotty. "I'm not actually sure which word it was."

King also testified that he had seen George Holliday's video of his beating about ten times. "It makes me sick to my stomach to see it."

Ira Salzman, the defense lawyer for Sergeant Koon, tried to prove King had been coached by his attorneys. "Who told you it was a baton, your lawyer?" Salzman asked.

"Sir, no one had to tell me that," King replied. "I felt it."

King's appearance at the trial was important not only for the jury but also for the world to learn what happened that night from King's point of view.

"He looked good," admitted defense attorney Michael P. Stone. "He was very mild-mannered and polite and very thoughtful. All of these things spelled credibility."

While on the stand, a nervous King noticed how the courtroom was as "quiet as a church." In that silence, once again, he felt his ancestors watching over him.

"I was finally able to tell my story," he said. "This, I realized, was the reason I had ordered myself to stay alive that night, so that one day, I would be heard. I finally got to speak for myself. It felt good to finally represent myself and use my voice."

• • •

On April 2, 1993, Rodney Glen King celebrated his twenty-eighth birthday.

Fifteen days later, the jury delivered their verdicts on whether the four LAPD police officers had violated King's civil rights.

Los Angeles held its breath.

Gun sales had doubled in Koreatown during the federal trial proceedings. David Joo, the manager of the Western Gun Shop, saw his weapon sales increase, from three to four guns a day to almost twenty per day. Joo encouraged his customers, who were mostly Korean American first-time users, to learn proper gun safety practices at local shooting ranges. As a result, the number of new Korean American clientele at the L.A. Gun Club pistol range jumped from 2 to 30 percent.

The new LAPD police chief Willie Williams planned to deploy 7,800 police officers in case civil unrest broke out. President Bill Clinton also pledged $1.7 million to pay for overtime for L.A.'s law enforcement.

But this time, there was no uprising.

On April 17, the jury delivered their verdicts.

Stacey C. Koon and Laurence M. Powell: guilty.

Timothy E. Wind and Theodore J. Briseno: not guilty.

Koon and Powell were both sentenced to thirty months in prison. Koon, released in 1995, published his memoir and still lives in California. Powell also resides in California, but no longer talks publicly about the King case and trial.

Although they had been acquitted, the LAPD fired Wind and Briseno shortly after the federal civil rights trial. Wind worked for the Culver City Police Department from 1994 to 2000 before moving out of state with his family. Briseno also maintained a low profile, working various jobs, including as a security guard, and eventually left California for the Midwest.

As for Rodney King, he believed "justice was half-served."

"But I was at peace after the verdict," he said.

"Let's Get on with Life"

On Monday, August 23, 1993, over a year after he had been robbed and severely beaten at Florence and Normandie, Craig Fujii faced his attacker, twenty-year-old Damian Monroe "Football" Williams, in court.

Since they had been filmed beating truck driver Reginald Denny on April 29, 1992, Damian Williams, Henry Watson, Antoine Miller, and Gary Williams had been nicknamed the "L.A. Four." The charges against them included assault, robbery, and attempted murder. As one of the five people attacked by Williams right before trucker Reginald Denny arrived, Fujii was called to testify in court and identify his attacker.

The jury for this trial was much more diverse than for the trials for the LAPD–Rodney King and Soon Ja Du–Latasha Harlins cases. Out of the nine women and three men, five were white, three were Black, three were Latino, and one was Asian American.

"Do you recognize this person?" the attorneys asked Fujii. "Where were you at this time?"

Fujii testified that because of his concussion, he could not recall much of what had happened on April 29, 1992. He did not even remember how he ended up at the hospital.

"I get incredibly nervous speaking in front of groups of people," Fujii said later. "I don't love public speaking. I bet I was a pretty bad witness."

· · ·

Three days after Fujii's testimony, Reginald Denny took the stand. As he watched the video of his own attack, Denny could not identify anyone. "I couldn't tell you," he said. "I don't remember."

The only thing Denny remembered was how confused he was

by the chaotic traffic on the street. "I couldn't quite figure out what was going on. It was total madness."

After the attack, Denny had awakened with ninety-seven broken bones in his face, including his jaw and left eye socket. His skull was so fractured that he suffered brain injuries and had trouble talking and walking. Denny has never fully recovered from his injuries.

Before leaving the courtroom after his testimony, Denny reached over to embrace the mothers of Damian Williams and Henry Watson.

"I told him I loved him," said Georgiana Williams. "I respect this man. I admire him. This man has no malice in his heart."

Joyce Watson, Henry Watson's mother, agreed. "When he hugged me, it was so warm. I said: 'God bless you.' I feel so much better. I have prayed for that man."

Three months later, Henry Watson and Reginald Denny would reunite on the popular TV talk show *The Phil Donahue Show*. Watson apologized to Denny, calling him "an innocent victim. . . . I'm sorry for the injuries Mr. Denny suffered."

Denny shook Watson's hand and told the studio audience that he sympathized with him. "This is a civil war," he said. "This is not me against Mr. Watson—it's not a personal vendetta. The problems were happening before Mr. Watson and I were born."

• • •

After five weeks, the jury reached a verdict.

They ruled Damian Williams and Henry Watson not guilty of attempted murder. But Williams was found guilty of one felony count for mayhem and sentenced to ten years in state prison. Watson was ruled guilty of a misdemeanor assault against Denny but did not go to jail because he had already spent seventeen months previously at the L.A. County Jail for another crime.

The remaining L.A. Four members had separate trials. Gary Williams was sentenced to three years in jail for the attempted robbery of Reginald Denny and the assault on another man. Antoine Miller was found guilty of grand theft and sentenced to seventeen months in jail and twenty-seven months on probation.

Reginald Denny told the press that he agreed with the verdicts. "Let's get on with life," he said.

• • •

Damian Williams was released after four years. But in May 2003, he was arrested again and convicted for the fatal shooting of a man in Southwest L.A. in 2000. He was sentenced to forty-six years in prison.

Over the years, Williams has had time to reflect upon his life. "I had a choice," he said. "I could have stayed on the front porch and continue to grow the way my mother intended for me to grow, but I made a bad decision, I came off the porch and I went in the streets and I got caught up. So most people would say, 'Oh we're a product of our environment.' No, I'm a product of bad decisions."

Describing himself as "far from perfect," Williams no longer wants to be the angry "young teenager in the streets" but to do "good work" and help those who are suffering with his example. "I believe in myself," he said. "I'm free."

• • •

In 1997, Craig Fujii left journalism to attend nursing school, inspired by the emergency room workers who saved his life. He works as a nurse practitioner in Honolulu.

Since 1992, Craig Fujii has forgiven his attackers. "We are the product of the people that have come before us and everything they experienced, and that includes good things and bad things," he said. "So if you've survived to this point, what a miracle. We have to look forward and not be bitter."

Fujii sometimes wonders what might have happened had he and Williams met under different circumstances. They were both young men at the time who shared similar interests, including sports.

"It may turn out that we would just be sitting and talking, and I'm sure he was a fun, interesting guy," Fujii reflected, his voice tinged with both sadness and hope. "I'm guessing he wasn't angry and unhappy all the time or particularly violent. It was just the circumstances where people were getting up in arms and angry about the verdict and so it all came to a head at one time. But I'm guessing, if we had the chance to sit down and talk or have lunch, he'd be a perfectly decent person."

"No One Wins Here"

There would be a third and final trial on behalf of Rodney Glen King—a civil suit against the LAPD seeking compensation for medical bills, psychological suffering, and loss of income resulting from the beating. On April 19, 1994, the jury decided the case in King's favor. The final amount was $3,816,535.45.

"I would like it to end," Rodney Glen King announced to the public. "No one wins here in this type of situation."

Chapter 12
사이구 SA I GU

사이구 Sa I Gu—4.29

The L.A. riots.
The L.A. rebellion.
The Los Angeles civil unrest.
The Los Angeles uprising.

What are we supposed to call what happened in Los Angeles in 1992?

For a long time, it was most often referred to as the "L.A. riots."

"A riot is the language of the unheard," said Dr. Martin Luther King. But over the years, the term *riots* has sometimes been used to trivialize justified protests as meaningless violence, from newspapers describing the Watts rebellion as a "Negro riot" in 1965 to former President Donald Trump denigrating the Black Lives Matter movement as "looters, criminals and rioters" in 2020.

Today, the 1992 Los Angeles civil unrest is usually referred to as an "uprising." But UC Riverside professor and original Black-Korean Alliance member Edward Taehan Chang said that "rebellion" and "uprising" can imply that all Korean Americans played a role in systemic racism back in 1992, when many were victims of it. So Korean Americans have given their own name to the 1992 Los Angeles civil unrest: 사이구 Sa I Gu.

In English, Sa I Gu means four-two-nine, referring to the first day of civil unrest—April 29. Koreans have always nicknamed important events after numbers. For example, 한국 전쟁 Hanguk Jeonjaeng, the Korean War, is often referred to as 육이오 Yuk Ee Oh—the numbers six-two-five, referring to the first day of the war on June 25, 1950.

Sa I Gu is now considered a political movement and the day Korean American identity was born. It also inspired the first generation of elected Korean American politicians. In 1992, Republican Jay Kim became the first Korean American elected to the U.S. House of Representatives, representing California's 41st District.

But he would not be the only one. In 2021, for the first time in history, four Korean Americans were sworn into Congress: Young Kim (Republican from California, 40th District), Michelle Park Steel (Republican from California, 45th District), Andy Kim (Democrat from New Jersey, 3rd District), and Marilyn Strickland (Democrat from Washington, 10th District).

Radio Korea's Richard Choi believed that Sa I Gu "played a big influence in how they decided to run for office and enter the political realm. . . . The Korean community needed political power. In order to live here in the U.S., you must have political power, you must have a presence."

And the four Korean American representatives from the 117th Congress made their presence known. Representatives Steel and

Young Kim made front-page headlines for condemning anti-Asian hate crimes during the early years of the COVID-19 pandemic.

A photograph of Representative Andy Kim kneeling down on the floor of the United States Capitol to clean up the garbage left behind on the night of the January 6, 2021, insurrection went viral. He credited his Korean immigrant parents for that moment. "After January 6th, what I did that day was not heroic, it was not special, it was very ordinary," he said. "But I think it's that sense of humility, that kind of attention to service and quiet patriotism that my parents taught me."

Representative Strickland was the first biracial Black-Korean woman elected to Congress, and she wore a traditional Korean 한복 hanbok dress during her Congressional swearing-in ceremony to honor her mother. "Admittedly there is prejudice and racism against Blacks in the Korean community, and there is the same thing in the Black community against Koreans because for some people, we just don't know each other yet," she said. "And so if someone like me can be a bridge between the two communities, I'm willing to do that."

"Korean immigrants realized if we want to stay and live and work in America, we have to become part of the United States and take ownership," Edward Taehan Chang explained. "We are no longer guests. We are no longer just immigrants. A majority of Korean immigrants didn't really embrace the term 'Korean American' until after the L.A. civil unrest in 1992. Sa I Gu was the birth of Korean American identity."

Veteran journalist K. W. Lee agreed, saying Korean Americans today are the "children of Sa I Gu." He never forgot the sight of more than thirty thousand Korean Americans marching for peace in Koreatown on May 6, 1992, after the L.A. civil unrest had ended.

"That's when I was reborn again," Lee said. He began to cry. "I became Korean American."

After the 1992 Los Angeles uprising, called Sa I Gu by the Korean American community, veteran journalist K. W. Lee lectured at college campuses across the country. "You are the first and last line of defense for your parents," Lee said at the Korean American Students Conference held at the University of Washington in 2005. "Remember that! You have to define your destiny in your own terms. . . . When you have thirty thousand demonstrators in America, it's the largest . . . demonstration in America. They are carried out by your parents who don't speak . . . English. And you guys were present at it. That's when I was reborn again. I became a Korean American."

A Child of Sa I Gu

After Sa I Gu, Carol K. Park had trouble sleeping. She continued to work at her parents' gas station in Compton until she was twenty-six years old. Even after her mother sold the gas station, Carol woke up nightly to terrifying dreams of being shot and killed. She stopped eating and lost forty pounds in less than one month.

Carol had been suffering from post-traumatic shock syndrome and 화병 hwabyung for over a decade. "My therapist said my brain was finally able to assess and take in all those years of constant trauma," she said.

Carol remains good friends with the gas station's new owner, Hany Elyamany, an Egyptian immigrant her mother hired when Carol went to college. Carol's mother, Son Lye Park, died in 2018 at age sixty-seven.

"We know Mrs. Park for a long time," Elyamany said. "She was a very well-respected lady and hard worker." Elyamany, who speaks Arabic, English, and Spanish, smiled, adding that Mrs. Park taught him some Korean. "Of course I speak Korean. 감사합니다! Gamsahamnida! Thank you!"

Painful memories still exist for Carol at the gas station. A quarter-sized hole in the bulletproof glass booth remains. "A bullet hit this. Crack! It's been here since I was a kid. This has never gone away." She placed her finger against the nicked glass. "Look at where it's at. Right where the cashier's head is. I always looked at this and got nervous."

Inside the cashier's booth, plastic containers of Elyamany's hummus sit alongside the same boxes of "love roses" Carol sold as a child during the height of the crack cocaine epidemic. Taco trucks and a booth selling fried churros sit outside the station, reflecting Compton's Latino population surge.

Carol still owns the same *Anne of Green Gables* books from childhood, their tattered covers taped together. "Reading really saved me because it was my escape from that world. Anne was just looking forward to the future, and I remember thinking, 'That'll be me one day when I will not have to work at this gas station, where Mom will be okay and we will all be okay, and the family will be able to move forward.'"

Carol became a writer herself. She majored in English at UC Riverside and currently works as a PhD candidate and researcher with Professor Edward Taehan Chang at the Young Oak Kim Center for Korean American Studies.

Carol Kwang Park stands outside her parents' former gas station in Compton in January 2022. Bullet holes remain in the walls and bulletproof glass windows. She holds two of her favorite *Anne of Green Gables* books, which comforted her whenever she worked as a child cashier at the station.

In 2017, Carol's book, *Memoir of a Cashier: Korean Americans, Racism, and Riots*, was published to critical acclaim. Veteran journalist K. W. Lee praised Carol as a "child of Sa I Gu" who was "destined to become the first and last line of defense for her heroic mother's generation of silence and sacrifice."

Compton Kirk

On January 15, 2015, the Compton Fashion Center on North Long Beach Boulevard closed. The Compton Swap Meet became a Walmart store.

The meat and poultry department replaced Wan Joon "Pops" Kim's Stall Z-7. Frozen pizzas line the walls now instead of 1990s gangsta rap vinyl records and framed photos of Pops with famous rappers.

But Cycadelic Records still exists. Kirk Kim helped his father transition from a physical space to selling rap music online. To serve the increased Latino population in South L.A., Cycadelic Records also includes Latin music and Chicano gangsta rap.

Fans and music industry insiders call Kirk Kim "Compton Kirk." He divides his time between California and Korea, managing international hip-hop artists. In 2017, he created and hosted several "Club Compton" nightclub events in both Los Angeles and Seoul to introduce hip-hop to new Korean fans. For fun, he fixes up low-rider cars at Hub City Customs in South L.A.

"Compton Kirk" wasn't surprised by hip-hop and rap's popularity in Korea. "The genre often cries about the injustice of a government or people," he said. "Korea has been through war, suffered injustice. Hip hop for us is about expressing these things artistically. I will always be here for that."

Kirk Kim stands underneath a mural of President Barack Obama in Compton in September 2022. Many people in his neighborhood recognize him and call him by his nickname, "Compton Kirk." He still works in the music business, promoting concerts and managing music artists across the world.

• • •

Wan Joon "Pops" Kim died on March 13, 2013, from lung cancer at the age of seventy-nine. Boo Ja "Moms" Kim died a few years later in 2016. She was seventy-six. "It was very hard for her," Kirk Kim said. "I always tell people she died of a broken heart."

A few days after his father had died, Kirk was working at their stall when a man stopped by, wanting to find "Pops."

"He told me he had stolen a rap CD as a kid and the police caught him, and my dad told them to let him go," Kirk said. It turned out this man was the same twelve-year-old boy who had shoplifted a CD more than thirty years ago. Pops had forgiven him and let him keep the album.

"This guy had a horrible life and was in jail for fifteen, twenty years," Kirk said. "All he could think about that whole time was what my father did for him when he was a kid. As soon as he got out of prison, he came to our stall and wanted to thank him."

Kirk told the man that his father had just died. The two men embraced and cried.

Afterward, Kirk went outside for a break. He stood in the parking lot near the same spot where his father used to rest in his car, gazing at his favorite pine tree standing tall in the distance until he fell asleep.

The tree is still there.

K-Town

What has changed in Koreatown since 1992?

A lot.

Koreatown, nicknamed K-Town, is a mix of old-school Korean stores and restaurants along with giant billboards of K-pop stars hovering over hipster dance nightclubs, 노래방 noraebang (karaoke) bars, trendy coffeehouses, massive H-Marts, and remodeled shopping plazas. Drive down busy Olympic Boulevard, and it looks as if the fires and violence and looting of 1992 never happened.

One of the many Koreatown stores that burned during the 1992 civil unrest in Los Angeles. The shopping mall was later rebuilt and still exists today.

In recent years, Koreatown has become the backdrop for music videos by such stars as Justin Bieber and Ariana Grande. Korean American rapper Jay Park filmed his song "K-Town" at the same Hannam market where owner Kee Whan Ha and his employees faced demonstrators.

Today's K-Town reflects the new worldwide prominence of Korean pop culture. Korean-language TV drama series, known as K-dramas, have become popular, including *Squid Game* released in 2021, which was Netflix's most-watched show that year. The 2019 Korean movie *Parasite* was the first Korean and non-English-language movie to win the Academy Award for Best Picture, and in 2021, *Minari* was the first Korean American movie nominated for multiple Oscars.

K-pop, the music genre created in Korea in the early 1990s with influences from R&B and hip-hop, has become a global music phenomenon. Psy's "Gangnam Style" became the first music video on the internet to reach one billion views, and superstar group BTS regularly sells out shows and became the first K-pop act nominated for multiple Grammys. Their fans, dubbed Army, included a large percentage of Black fans called Black Army. When BTS played two sold-out shows for 120,000 people at Pasadena's Rose Bowl in 2018, their diverse fans, including Black Army, sang along in Korean.

K-Town's demographics have also changed. In 2023, more than 50 percent of its residents are Latino. K-Town's street markets sell queso duro viejo and edible loroco flower buds used in pupusas and other traditional Central American cuisine alongside Korean food booths serving 갈비 galbi short ribs and spicy 김치찌개 kimchi jjigae stew. In 2013, Vermont Avenue between 11th and Adams Streets in Koreatown was officially renamed El Salvador Community Corridor. The Koreatown Run Club and the Koreatown Youth and Community Center are among the new organizations that provide resources and family events to connect Korean American and Latino families.

Hannam grocery chain owner Kee Whan Ha, who had convinced Radio Korea to urge store owners to defend their businesses in 1992, believes bridges have been built between the Korean American and Black and Latino communities since the L.A. uprising.

"It's much better," Ha said. "We have a lot of relationship with the African American community, as well as the Latino community." He said Korean American small-business owners have also made stronger connections with the police department. "We know that we cannot survive ourself. We have to have a relationship with other communities."

"Strength in Numbers"

Sa I Gu inspired more Korean Americans to join the police force. In 1983, 75 percent of LAPD officers were white. But in 2023, out of the 9,146 officers sworn into the LAPD, 26 percent were white, 53 percent, Latino, and 9 percent, Black; Asian American–Pacific Islander officers jumped from 1 percent to 8 percent over the past forty years.

In January 1996, Paul M. Kim—whose Korean name, Myung-Chun, means "bright sky"—was the first Korean American to be promoted to the rank of captain in the history of the LAPD, and was later promoted to commander in 2002.

Four years later, in 2000, Douglas Shur was the second Korean American to become a captain, leading the Rampart Detective Division in Koreatown. He retired in 2009 and now works as a consultant. "I hope that I was fair," he said, reflecting on his twenty-eight years of service. "I kept my integrity intact. To protect and to serve the public is the motto that rings true in our profession."

Blake Chow became the first Chinese American commander in the LAPD. Upon promotion to deputy chief, he served as the Commanding Officer, Transit Services Bureau and Operations West Bureau. He was promoted four years later to Assistant Chief and is now the Director of the Office of Special Operations. As of 2023, he was the LAPD's highest-ranking Chinese American officer.

"One of the best things that ever came out of the riots was that we as a department started taking an introspective look and asking, 'Is our relationship with the community good, and if it's not, what do we need to do to make sure that we don't have this wall between us again?' And so that was really the start of what we called community policing. We hired a lot of people who were more reflective of the community. Now we have these relationships with the community that are just unlike anything we had back then."

Ben Lee was promoted to supervisory detective before retiring in 2009. He continues to serve as a level 1 reserve officer at the LAPD Academy. After retiring in 2021 as a sergeant field supervisor, Howard Choy volunteers with his church by delivering food to those in need.

In September 2022, the 49th Annual L.A. Korean Festival was held in Koreatown, featuring its traditional parade. Because 2022 marked the thirtieth anniversary of Sa I Gu, the crowd cheered especially loudly for KALEO—the Korean American Law Enforcement Organization.

KALEO promotes advocacy and cultural understanding between Korean American officers and the community. The group started in 2018 with 30 members. By 2023, more than 350 Korean American officers were members.

KALEO president and LAPD reserve officer Ben Pak believes

In September 2022, when the 350 members of the Korean American Law Enforcement Organization led the annual Koreatown Parade down Olympic Boulevard, the crowd cheered and gave them a standing ovation.

the LAPD still needs more Korean American officers to prevent a future Sa I Gu. "We're underrepresented," he said. "There's got to be strength in numbers, and that's one of the reasons I created the Korean American Law Enforcement Organization. If we don't step up, then we have no strength."

The *Los Angeles Times*:
"Our Reckoning with Racism"

Twenty-eight years after the 1992 Los Angeles uprising, the *Los Angeles Times* apologized.

On September 27, 2020, the newspaper published a front-page story with the headline, "Our Reckoning with Racism: Committing to Change at the *Times*—The Failures of This Institution, Our Apology and a Path Forward."

The newspaper admitted that "an insidious problem marred the work of the *Los Angeles Times* for much of its history."

That problem? Racism.

In 2020, Black Lives Matter and Stop AAPI Hate protests swept the country due to the killing of truck driver and security guard

On September 27, 2020, after Black Lives Matter and Stop AAPI Hate
demonstration rallies across the country, the *Los Angeles Times* editorial board
published a front-page article, apologizing for its biased and uneven reporting of
past events, including the 1992 Los Angeles uprising. The paper vowed to improve
its coverage and hire more diverse staffers.

George Perry Floyd Jr. by a Minnesota police officer and the rise
in anti-Asian hate crimes during the COVID-19 pandemic lock-
downs. As a result, the *Los Angeles Times* did much soul-searching.
"Our nation now faces a long-delayed reckoning with systemic
racism," its editorial board wrote. Since it began in 1881, the
newspaper had been "deeply rooted in white supremacy." By not
hiring a more diverse and equitable newsroom, they had created

a "lonely place for journalists of color." The newspaper preferred telling stories "largely for and about white people."

Yet the *Los Angeles Times* would win a Pulitzer Prize for its coverage of the 1965 Watts rebellion, even though there were no Black full-time reporters in its newsroom back then. Robert Richardson, a twenty-four-year-old Black man who worked as an *L.A. Times* classified advertising messenger, volunteered to report. He called editors from phone booths on the streets of Watts with his dispatches. Richardson was the first one to report protesters shouting the now famous phrase, "Burn, baby, burn!" Afterward, the *Los Angeles Times* promoted Richardson to "reporter trainee."

Twenty-seven years later, the *Los Angeles Times* won a Pulitzer for covering another rebellion—the 1992 Los Angeles civil unrest. The Pulitzer Prize committee praised the newspaper for its "balanced, comprehensive, penetrating coverage under deadline pressure."

But in its 2020 editorial, the *Los Angeles Times* admitted that its "balanced" coverage of the 1992 L.A. civil unrest was off. As in 1965, the *Los Angeles Times* still had very few reporters of color, especially of Asian and Korean descent. The newspaper had to recruit veteran journalist K. Connie Kang from San Francisco to help with their coverage because their only other bilingual Korean Americans on staff were reporter John H. Lee and photographer Hyungwon Kang. In 1964, she was the first Korean American female reporter to be hired in the country (for the *Democrat and Chronicle* based in Rochester, New York), and she cofounded the Korean American Journalists Association in 1982. The *Los Angeles Times* hired her full-time later that same year.

The newspaper also apologized for inflaming tensions between the Black and Korean American communities, which, in part, resulted in the disproportionate damage in Koreatown during the 1992 civil unrest. "[The *Times*] sensationalized Black-Korean conflict."

The *Los Angeles Times* pledged to be more accountable and to increase its staff diversity.

"On behalf of this institution, we apologize for the *Times*' history of racism. We owe it to our readers to do better, and we vow to do so. We know that this acknowledgment must be accompanied by a real commitment to change, a humility of spirit and an openness of mind and heart."

· · ·

Former *Los Angeles Times* reporter John H. Lee, who covered the 1992 L.A. uprising, remains cautious about the newspaper's apology.

"I feel frustrated that it's taken them so long to acknowledge that," he said. "It makes me wonder what they are getting out of it. Does it buy them credibility now in future coverage of race relations? It's definitely frustrating that they were not able to acknowledge that at the time it was happening. It could've avoided so much suffering. I think the real measure of any meaning in that *mea culpa* is how is this going to affect the way they pursue coverage in the future?"

The Rooftop Koreans

In 1992, *Los Angeles Times* photographer Hyungwon Kang's powerful images of Korean American store owners perched on store rooftops, armed with guns to protect their property, won the Pulitzer Prize.

Twenty-eight years later, on May 25, 2020, Kang's photos reemerged after a live video aired on Facebook of a Black man named George Floyd being arrested by four police officers, one of whom knelt on his neck despite Floyd's repeated pleas of "I can't breathe." He died of cardiopulmonary arrest due to neck compression. As Black Lives Matter protests galvanized by Floyd's death erupted across the country that summer, Kang's same photos of armed Korean American store owners were reduced to a pop culture meme known as the "#RooftopKoreans."

Alt-right and pro-gun "Right to Bear Arms" advocates co-opted this joke meme to criticize the #BlackLivesMatter demonstrations and other similar movements.

"Bring back the #RooftopKorean and the looting will stop," one person posted on Twitter (rebranded as X three years later). Similar posts included "Roof top Koreans getting ready to hunt!" and "Don't mess with 'Roof Top Koreans.'"

This racist reduction of what Korean immigrant store owners suffered during the 1992 L.A. uprising disturbed UC Riverside professor Edward Taehan Chang.

"What we see here are white supremacists using 'Rooftop Koreans' images and video to justify their own position," Chang said. "This has potentially very damaging consequences to incite racial division and hatred between Korean Americans and other communities of color, particularly African American communities. It speaks to a common divide and control strategy perpetuated by white supremacists."

Hyungwon Kang believes people should not lose sight of the tragic aftermath for many of these store owners, several of whom he witnessed waving toy guns in fear and desperation. "They were merely trying to protect what was rightfully their own. When their stores went up in flames, they lost life savings; they lost everything."

April 29, 2022:
사이구 Sa I Gu Thirty Years Later

In March 2022, Korean American community advocate Hyepin Im called Shinese Harlins.

Im, founder and president of the advocacy group FACE (Faith and Community Empowerment), wanted to do something special for the thirtieth anniversary of Sa I Gu. For many years, she had worked to provide social and outreach events for the Korean American and Black communities, along with working for Reverend Mark Whitlock's economic development program at the First AME Church.

So she created the SAIGU (Serve. Advocate. Inspire. Give. Unite) campaign to commemorate the upcoming anniversary with special events and seminars to inspire local leaders to create more outreach programs for both communities.

But Im believed her SAIGU campaign could not move forward without Latasha Harlins's family. She reached out to Shinese, who answered her phone immediately. The two women began to talk.

On April 29, 2022, Hyepin Im, Shinese Harlins, Lora King, and Najee Ali met L.A. mayor Eric Garcetti on the corner of Florence and Normandie for an event to commemorate the thirtieth anniversary of Sa I Gu.

"The city has survived and changed in the years since," said Mayor Garcetti. "But in other places, we still see a city broken and broke."

Hyepin Im reminded the audience that solidarity would help "lift up the truth. . . . At the end of the day, we're all in the same boat."

Shinese Harlins presented Im with a Latasha Harlins Foundation T-shirt, saying, "The only way we're going to make progress is to stand together, stand tall, keep God first."

Lora King echoed her father's sentiment of keeping hope alive. "I think if we operate out of a place of love and hope, that will take us so much further."

Najee Ali called out for healing.

"Thirty years later, I'm here to say I'm sorry," he said. "I apologize for the role I played in not calling for unity and peace thirty years ago. We were angry about the murder of Latasha Harlins, and we had a right to be, but we didn't have the right to turn on our fellow L.A. citizens. There was so much property damage and hurt and pain. I'm all about healing today."

After the uprising in 1992, Ali, known then as Ronald Todd Eskew, served sixteen months in prison for armed robbery. He was caught stealing baby clothes out of a Thriftee store for his then three-year-old daughter. During his time in prison, he read *The Autobiography of Malcolm X.*

"I realized Malcolm X was someone who I identified with because he came from a broken home, poverty, despair, had run-ins with law enforcement, committed petty crimes like I did, got sent to prison and converted to Islam," he said. "So in reading his book, I finally wanted to get my life together, and I converted to Islam and changed my name to Najee Ali."

Ali concluded that the media had played a huge part in turning the 1992 L.A. rebellion into a riot. "One billion dollars of property damage, the majority of it in Koreatown that was targeted on purpose by young Black men angry at Latasha's murder and what we perceived was the Koreans' indifference," he said. He believed the media's erasure of the Korean American community led to this perception. "Korean Americans had a toy drive for Latasha.

(Left to right) Shinese Harlins, Hyepin Im, Najee Ali, Mayor Eric Garcetti, Lora King, and other community members hold hands at a press conference commemorating the thirtieth anniversary of the 1992 Los Angeles uprising. "My late father, Rodney King, became synonymous with police brutality to some people," said Lora King. "But our family remembers him as a human being—not a symbol. He never advocated for hatred or violence and pleaded for peace as the city burned by asking, 'Can we all get along?' That's my father's legacy . . . unity."

The majority of my people didn't know about that. There was no social media then, even posting things like, 'Hey, this is what's going on.' "

Although Ali believes there is still a lot of hard work ahead for both communities, he is hopeful. "The SAIGU campaign is so important and so critical. Now we can honestly say that Black leaders, faith leaders, community leaders, we do have relationships now with the Korean community. We're in dialogue. There's a true friendship."

At the end of the press conference, Im, Harlins, King, and Ali held hands together with Mayor Garcetti and raised their arms to the sky.

엄마 Umma: Mother

Jung Hui Lee touched her heart and began to cry softly. Her husband, Young Hi, bowed his head in grief.

It was April 20, 2022. The *Korea Times* (Korean-language newspaper) was hosting a Sa I Gu thirtieth anniversary conference. Speakers included U.S. representatives Young Kim and Michelle Park Steel, L.A. City Council members Herb J. Wesson and John Lee, and photojournalist Hyungwon Kang.

During Hyungwon Kang's speech, he showed the audience some of his most famous Sa I Gu photos. People in the room gasped audibly when his 1992 photo of Edward Jae Song Lee dying outside the Pizza Go restaurant appeared on-screen.

It had been thirty years since Eddie's parents had seen this photo.

Jung Hui Lee was scheduled to close the conference with a brief speech. She had not spoken publicly about Sa I Gu and her son's death in many years.

Eddie's 엄마 Umma took a deep breath and spoke from her heart.

"You just saw a picture of my son," she told the audience in Korean. "I couldn't look at his pictures at the time, and still I cannot look at them closely. . . . Feeling responsible, Jae Song went out to guard fellow Koreans who were not able to protect themselves. If he didn't have those thoughts, he would have been here today with me."

Jung Hui spoke about her 한 han, saying the past thirty years were "excruciating." But she believed her son's "sacrifice" was now a "stepping stone" for the Korean American community to rebuild.

"Jae Song would have been surprised if he saw how much our community has developed," she said. "It's time to leave the regrets and pains of the riot behind and to move forward so that Jae Song's precious sacrifice and his courageous spirit will not be in vain."

Chapter 13
정 JEONG

정 JEONG—LIKE 화 HWA AND 한 HAN, THERE IS NO DIRECT
ENGLISH TRANSLATION OF THE KOREAN WORD 정 JEONG. THE
CLOSEST TRANSLATIONS ARE "LOVE" AND "COMPASSION."

정 Jeong: Love, Korean-Style

All Korean Americans have their own definition of 정 jeong. Affection. Trust. Loyalty. Tenderness. Empathy. K. W. Lee once described 정 jeong as a bond of love and trust that arises from a "journey of tears."

But no matter how you define it, 정 jeong is shared between people.

On May 14, 1992, *Los Angeles Times* reporter John H. Lee wrote a personal essay about his experience covering the violence in Koreatown during Sa I Gu and how he realized 정 jeong drew people together. "It is out of a sense of 정 jeong that we share each other's pain," he wrote. "The emotional drain of seeing arsonists and looters wrack my Koreatown . . . never have I felt such soul-yanking 정 jeong as when I reported on the victims' plight, and those who answered their pleas for help."

After Sa I Gu, activist and Black-Korean Alliance member Marcia Choo was asked to speak at several conferences about her activism. At one conference, she found herself on a panel with Latasha Harlins's Aunt Denise. When an audience member asked about Choo's reaction to a Korean American having shot Latasha Harlins, Choo replied, "Stop trying to parse this into a Black-Korean issue. Why don't we all work together so that no child ever gets killed? Latasha is all of our children."

Choo remembered how surprised and touched Denise Harlins looked by her declaration.

Afterward, Choo ran into Denise Harlins in the bathroom. "I took her hand and said, 'I'm just so sorry,'" she said.

Denise Harlins nodded. The two women stood still, holding hands in silence.

"I want to believe in that moment between two women, Black and Korean, that there was a connection," Choo said. "That's 정 jeong."

흑인의 생명은 소중하다

After George Floyd's death in 2020, Black Lives Matter rallies were also held in Korea. From anti-Black racism arising from the segregated white and Black American troops during the Korean War to the use of blackface in the early years of K-pop in the 1990s, which was later denounced, there was a huge reckoning in Korea about why Black lives must—and should always—matter.

But in the Korean language, there is no literal translation of the English phrase Black Lives Matter.

So Koreans created this phrase instead: "흑인의 생명은 소중하다"

Heukinui Sangmyeongeun Sojoonghada, which means "Black lives are precious."

This is 정 jeong.

A New Empire

Empire Liquor Market Deli no longer exists. In recent years, the Numero Uno Market chain took over the building. Chile de árbol, plantains, papaya, and fresh corn and flour tortillas now stock the shelves, reflecting the changing demographics of South Los Angeles, from four-fifths Black to two-thirds Latino. Only about a quarter of the original Black population still resides there.

Soon Ja Du and her family have not spoken publicly since 1991. They have worked very hard to maintain their privacy—and to find peace.

I reached out directly to the Du family multiple times, requesting an interview. They said no. Soon Ja Du's children are fiercely protective of their mother and family.

This is 정 jeong.

"A Journey of Healing"

Although the Harlins family eventually left South Los Angeles, Latasha Harlins remained.

In February 2021, the Algin Sutton Recreation Center, where Tasha, Tee, Nookie, and Trell used to play, unveiled a memorial mural designed by visual artist Victoria Cassinova. It features Latasha Harlins's portrait with birds in flight in the background along with her handwritten poem "We Queens."

The center also unveiled its newly remodeled playground, now called the Latasha Harlins Memorial Playground.

For years, it was too painful for Tasha's grandmother Ruth to walk by this youth center. She always cried when she heard chil-

I am very reliable
and trustworthy
honest.
I have a lot of
talent, and I know
whatever I set my
mind on something
I can accomplish
I show people I care by
giving what I have
to people who
actually need it.

WE QUEENS

Latasha Lavon Harlins
January 1, 1976 - March 16, 1991

In February 2021, the city of Los Angeles commissioned visual artist Victoria Cassinova to design a mural in Latasha Harlins's memory for the Algin Sutton Recreation Center where Tasha, Tee, Nookie, and Trell used to play. "The people in [this] neighborhood don't know who Latasha was because these are new generations," said Shinese ("Tee") Harlins. "So now is our time to speak up so we won't forget her name."

dren laughing in the playground. Today, Ruth smiles whenever she walks by Tasha's mural and the playground that now bears her name and image.

"Now, every time I pass by, I say, 'Oh, this is my granddaughter cause I miss her and I love her,'" she said.

· · ·

Moroccan cashmere. Champagne toast. Lavender and spring apricot.

These are among the scents Shinese Harlins created for her handmade candle-making business, Sensuous Soul.

"Candles are my vibe," she said. After watching instructional videos on YouTube and taking classes, Shinese was accepted into

Convergence in 2022, a six-month business incubator program for aspiring entrepreneurs. Jane Oak, an attorney and deacon at the Korean American Tapestry LA Church in South Los Angeles, created the program to help diverse and underserved small-business owners.

Shinese was assigned to her business mentor, David Lin. Coincidentally, Lin was the same twenty-six-year-old Chinese American who had volunteered to sweep up the debris in devastated areas of Koreatown and South Los Angeles during the 1992 civil unrest. The two bonded quickly, with Lin nicknaming Shinese Sunshine.

"She's just very bubbly, very bright with a very warm and loving personality," Lin said. "She has this indomitable spirit that says, 'I'm gonna keep going, do my best, work hard, and make my dream come true.'"

More than thirty years after Latasha Harlins was killed, Shinese still lives with post-traumatic shock syndrome, experiencing occasional bouts of anger and depression.

Whenever she feels the onset of PTSD, she lights a candle and meditates. "It helps me let go of my childhood pain. It's part of my journey of healing."

Her healing was disrupted just a few years after her cousin was laid to rest. Paradise Memorial Park in Sante Fe Springs, just outside Los Angeles, was the first Black-owned cemetery on the West Coast, originally established in 1927 when segregation separated Black and white even in death. In 1995, one of the largest grave desecration scandals in the country happened at Paradise Memorial Park. Tasha's grave was among several hundred burial plots resold illegally by the family who owned the cemetery. They were later found guilty of fraud and received jail time and fines. State officials took over the cemetery, which has been closed ever since, except for visitations by family and friends.

Tasha's family does not know if her coffin still exists. But her grave marker is still there, faded and worn, her image nearly washed away by the weather. The marker simply reads, "Our Loved One. Latasha Harlins. 1976–1991."

The earth is so soft that several tombstones sit crooked, having sunken slightly into the ground. The grass grows tall, hiding many grave markers. It's a place most people have forgotten.

Except for the families of those still resting there.

Every January 1, on Latasha Harlins's birthday, Shinese visits her cousin's grave. For Tasha's forty-sixth birthday on January 1, 2022, Shinese planted a black star-shaped balloon with gold and silver stars and the words "Happy New Year!" by her marker. This is 정 jeong. The sun shone brightly. It was a beautiful day.

"You Saved My Life"

After the 1992 L.A. uprising, George Holliday retreated from the public. He remained a freelance plumber and avoided the media. He wanted his privacy—and his life—back. On September 19, 2021, thirty years after he videotaped the LAPD–Rodney King beating, he died from complications of COVID-19. He was sixty-one years old.

The only time George Holliday ever met Rodney Glen King was by coincidence.

In 1992, shortly after the civil unrest had ended, both men happened to be at the same gas station. Holliday was filling up his car when someone shouted out his name.

It was Rodney King.

"I didn't recognize him because the only pictures I had seen of him were of his face all swollen and beaten up, but now he'd recovered," Holliday recalled.

"You don't know who I am, do you?" King asked.

"No," Holliday said.

"Well," Rodney King said, "you saved my life."

"Let's Try to Work It Out"

Rodney Glen King continued to battle alcoholism, leading to several more arrests for drunk driving and allegations of domestic abuse (for which he was later acquitted) over the next decade. In May 2008, he checked into the Pasadena Recovery Center, agreeing to be filmed for the VH-1 reality TV series *Celebrity Rehab with Dr. Drew* and *Sober House.*

During rehab, Glen wrote a "forgiveness letter" to the officers who beat him. "I need to forgive the officers who beat me the way they did because being angry with them is not helping me. The police officers that did that to me must have personal problems, and all I can do is forgive them and put them in my prayers."

Glen stayed sober. He fell in love with Cynthia Kelley, a juror in his civil suit. After their engagement, they were featured on *The Oprah Winfrey Show.*

He became a grandfather to Lora King's daughter Jailyn. He taught her how to swim. When she was four years old, he loved beading friendship bracelets with her.

At dawn on June 17, 2012, Cynthia Kelley found her fiancé lying at the bottom of the swimming pool in their backyard. She called 911.

At 6:11 a.m., Rodney Glen King died. Like his father, Ronald King, who had died years before in the same way, Glen's death was ruled an accidental drowning.

June 17, 2012, was Father's Day.

Glen was forty-seven years old.

• • •

Today, everyone remembers Rodney Glen King's famous quote, "Can we all get along?"

But Glen meant much more than that. He had ended his original statement with these words: "We're all stuck here for a while. Let's try to work it out."

Today, everyone is still trying to work it out as this cycle of systemic racism continues. Glen's daughter, Lora King, founded the Rodney King Foundation, which provides scholarships for Black fathers and helps raise money for local charities and organizations.

On March 1, 2022, Lora King met George Perry Floyd Jr.'s sister Bridgett Floyd for the first time at the Smithsonian's National Museum of African American History and Culture in Washington, D.C. While there, Lora grew visibly upset watching George Holliday's video of the LAPD beating her father. Bridgett Floyd hugged her.

Asked what keeps her from giving up hope in the face of what seems to be a never-ending cycle of systemic racism, Lora echoed what her father thought about on that fateful night of March 2, 1991.

"I'd say God and our ancestors," she said. "I think our ancestors went through way more than we did. There was a time when we weren't even allowed to talk to each other. Once upon a time, I couldn't have someone from another race sit on my couch. So those are the types of things that give me hope to keep going. You have to think about your ancestors and what they went through for you to have this very opportunity that you have."

• • •

In 2022, ten years after Rodney Glen King died, his granddaughter Jailyn entered the ninth grade. She loved reading books, sketching art and Japanese manga in her dozens of journals, and seeing her favorite K-pop musicians in concert.

In Jailyn's history class, her teacher assigned everyone to do a research project on a person who had made a significant "impact" in America. Jailyn pulled her teacher aside. "Can I do my project on my grandpa?" she asked.

Her teacher said yes.

"So I made a five-page slide presentation and a five-paragraph essay on him," she said. "My main point was how he had kept peace throughout all of it. I think most people would say if they were unjustly beaten for no reason and didn't get justice for it, they'd be angry. But he wasn't. And I thought that was really impactful."

• • •

The Forest Lawn Memorial Park cemetery in the Hollywood Hills, located next to the Warner Brothers Studios movie lot, is home to many celebrities: Carrie Fisher, who played Princess Leia in the Star Wars movies; concert pianist and Las Vegas entertainer Liberace; Grammy award–winning R&B, pop, and jazz musician Al Jarreau; trailblazing comedian and actor Richard Pryor. Dosan Ahn Chang Ho's sons, Hollywood actors Philip Ahn and Ralph Ahn, rest at Forest Lawn, too.

Rodney Glen King is also here.

Like Tasha, Glen has a modest marker planted in the earth: "Rodney G. King. Beloved son, brother, grandfather, uncle, cousin, friend. 4/2/65–5/17/12. 'Can we all get along.'"

Whenever Lora King and her children visit Grandpa, they

bring cleaning cloths and scissors. Lora kneels in front of her father's marker, trimming the grass along the sides. She polishes the bronze metal plaque with a soft cloth.

On September 26, 2022, Lora and her mother, Dennetta Lyles King, visited Glen.

They knelt by his side, gently brushing the dirt away so everyone could see his name.

This is 정 jeong.

"Wait and Hope"

On the night of April 30, 1992, police detained and questioned three men in connection with the shooting of Edward Jae Song Lee and his friends. Two of the suspects admitted shooting in the direction of their car, which led to legal action by the Lees and the families of Eddie's friends. Although Jung Hui wanted justice for her son, she decided to withdraw from the case because it had become too painful for her. Afterward, one of the suspects, a Korean American college student who was only two years older than Eddie, knelt before her, weeping. "He had a lifetime ahead of him," Jung Hui reflected later. "I cared about his future."

This is 정 jeong.

• • •

Edward Jae Song Lee is buried about a quarter mile away from Rodney Glen King at Forest Lawn.

The bronze marker inlaid in the earth at his gravesite has his photo engraved at the top with the following words in both Korean and English: "On April 30, 1992, during the Los Angeles riots, Edward Lee went out into Koreatown to help those who could not protect themselves, unaware that his selfless act of courage would result in the loss of his own life. . . . As a seed must fall to the earth and die to itself in order to grow, may Edward's sacrifice continually remind us of the need to seek peace and pursue love."

Jung Hui Lee visits her son every month. Like Lora and Dennetta King, she has her own set of cleaning supplies. Brushes, scissors, wax, and rust-cure primer spray cans. She even uses chopsticks and wire hangers to secure any flowerpots she brings for her son. She carries her supplies in the same worn, black leather bag that Eddie saw when she worked the night janitor shift at the bank.

"We have used this bag for thirty years," she says in Korean, holding up a brush and soft cloth. "I brush his face with these, and I use this for polishing the brass plate. The moss grows easily and covers his face."

As Jung Hui tends to her son's grave, her husband, Young Hi, pours water from an old milk gallon container on the flowers left behind for Eddie and his neighbors. Jung Hui sweeps the soil, grass, and leaves away from the engraving of her son's image on the marker. "Honestly, I come here not only to see my son but also to wipe his face," she says. "During summer, it gets too hot, so I bring a small parasol and make a shade for his face."

She looks around the cemetery, surrounded by mountains in the distance. "Oftentimes I see five, six, or seven deer wandering around here. But they are not here today."

After Eddie died, Jung Hui struggled with severe depression. She could not leave the house, not even to go grocery shopping, except late at night to avoid seeing people. She had blood pressure issues and fainted so much that she had to be admitted to a hospital. "I thought I could not live like this anymore," she said.

But when her daughter Jenny's lupus flared up, Jung Hui had a conversation with her son's spirit. "I talked to Jae Song and told him, 'I have to take care of Jenny. I cannot follow you.'" She joined a grief counseling group. She began to take long walks to strengthen her heart. She stopped hiding.

"I feel like I have been freed," she said.

• • •

In high school, Eddie's favorite book was Alexander Dumas's *The Count of Monte Cristo.*

"He said he would go to the Korean bookstore and buy me a Korean translation of the book as a gift, but he was not able to keep his promise," Jung Hui said. "I told him I already had read it when I was younger, but he encouraged me to reread it. I regret that I did not ask him which part was his most favorite and why he liked it."

But Jung Hui still remembers the last line of her son's favorite book: "Wait and hope?" There is a question mark at the end of that sentence.

As she packs up her bag of cleaning supplies at Eddie's grave, Jung Hui has her own questions.

"After I die, I don't know who is going to clean and polish his memorial plate," she frets. "That's why both of us come here while we still can. Who will take care of Jae Song's grave after both of us die? Who is going to remember him? Who is going to remember us?"

Eddie. Tasha. Glen.

Who is going to remember them?

It is a simple question that has a simple answer.

We all will.

AUTHOR'S NOTE

For me, *Rising from the Ashes* is not just a book.

It is a journey that started with my dad, the first person in our family to go to America.

Young Sik Yoo was twenty-one years old when he flew from Seoul, Korea, to Anchorage, Alaska, on June 24, 1960. He, along with K. W. Lee, was among the first Korean immigrants to attend Tennessee Tech University (known back then as Tennessee Polytechnic Institute), where he majored in mechanical engineering.

My dad was one of only a handful of non-white people in Cookeville. Tennessee Tech was originally founded in 1915 as a racially segregated public institution. Although my dad is not white, he was considered an "international student" and allowed to matriculate. After the 1964 Civil Rights Act outlawed segregation, the university accepted its first Black student, Leona Lusk Officer, that same year.

Despite being one of very few non-white people in Cookeville in 1960, my dad had no problem making friends. He attended church, picnicked with classmates at the state park waterfalls, and went on a few dates. He was featured in a story in the Tennessee Tech *Oracle* college newspaper with the headline, "Oriental Students Impressed by Tech's Differences." My dad talked about his love for kimchi and rice and how the pagoda-style roof of the

Cookeville Railroad Depot, built in 1909, reminded him of his family's house in Korea and made him feel homesick.

"Your father was gracious to people," my uncle Kyung Sik "Kenneth" Yoo said.

When my uncle was also accepted as an engineering student at Tennessee Tech, my dad gave him a tour of Cookeville after he arrived. When they visited the town's movie theater, my dad warned him about the strange bathrooms. They had two different doors.

"Your daddy told me, if you go anywhere, they have two signs," my uncle remembered. "'White Only' and 'Colored Only.'"

He paused. "We didn't know which door to go through."

My dad and my mom, Young Kim Yoo (a nurse), made sure my younger brother David and I never had to make that choice. Although our parents raised us to be open-minded, it was difficult growing up in a mostly white small town in Connecticut in the 1970s and 1980s where kids made "slant eyes" and called us racist slurs. Although we were American, we were sometimes treated like outsiders.

When my family relocated temporarily to Seoul in 1977 for my dad's new engineering job, suddenly everyone looked just like us. But we were still treated like outsiders—because we were born in America and only spoke English.

We didn't fit into either world.

We moved back to the United States in 1982, where I have lived since.

I still do not speak Korean. Although I love 김치찌개 kimchi jjigae, I sometimes love lasagna more. My whole life, I have always wondered if I was "Korean enough."

In writing this book, I realized there is no such thing as being "Korean enough." Instead, I learned that I *am* enough. Although

I had to rely on the help of Korean translators for many of my interviews with Korean American sources for this book, I recognized, understood, and sympathized with their experience. Their resilience and hope transcended all language barriers.

I am grateful to everyone who joined me on this journey to help me learn about what happened in 1992 Los Angeles, from interviews with people who experienced the civil unrest at ground zero to the academics and experts whose knowledge expanded my understanding of the foundation of the systemic racism that led to the uprising. Their stories taught me that amid the violence, systemic racism, social prejudice, and heartbreak, courage and compassion far outweighed pain. The stories from those I interviewed for this book are not only universal but also empowering for all of us who have had to rise above the noise in order for our voices to be heard.

THIS BOOK IS DEDICATED TO

Latasha Lavon Harlins (January 1, 1976–March 16, 1991)
Edward Jae Song Lee (May 24, 1973–April 30, 1992)
Rodney Glen King (April 2, 1965–June 17, 2012)
For their families and loved ones.

Rest in peace.
Rest in justice.
Rest in power.

For K. W. Lee of the Korea Times English Edition *and Larry Aubry of the* Los Angeles Sentinel *for mentoring Korean American and Black journalists, raising awareness of our stories, and championing voices of color.*

For my family: my dad, Young Sik Yoo; my mom, Young Hee Kim Yoo; my husband, Kyle McCorkle (and our cats Oreo, Beethoven, and Charlotte); my brother, David Yoo; my sister-in-law, Jessica Jackson Yoo; my nephew, Griffin; and my niece, Lucy.

故 라타샤 라본 할린스 양 (1976년 1월 1일—1991년 3월 16일)
故 이재성 열사 (1973년 5월 24일—1992년 4월 30일)
故 로드니 글렌 킹 님 (1965년 4월 2일—2012년 6월 17일)
그리고 그 분들의 사랑하는 가족들과 친구들.

평화 안에서 편히 쉬기를.
정의 안에서 편히 쉬기를.
힘과 능력 안에서 편히 쉬기를.

재미 한인과 흑인 저널리스트들의 멘토로서
우리들의 이야기를 세상에 알려주시고,
힘써 유색인종들의 목소리가 되어주신,
코리아 타임즈 영문판의 저널리스트 이경원 선생님,
로스엔젤레스 센테니얼의 칼럼리스트 故 래리 오버리 선생님.

제 가족들: 아버지 故 유영식 님, 어머니 유김영희 님,
남편 카일 멕코클 님 (우리 고양이 오레오, 베토벤, 샬롯),
동생 데이빗 유 (유환욱), 올케 제시카 잭슨 유
그리고 조카들 그리핀과 루시.

이 모든 분들께 이 책을 바칩니다.

ACKNOWLEDGMENTS

"파이팅" is a common Korean word of encouragement, often used as a cheer at sporting events or during a difficult time. It is a "Konglish" term—a mix of Korean and English, pronounced "paiting," which rhymes with "fighting." It means "Let's go!"

파이팅! Let's go!

Thank you to my brilliant editor, Simon Boughton, and to Kristin Allard, Naomi Duttweiler, Pat Wieland, and everyone at Norton Young Readers for your guidance and wisdom during the writing and publication of *Rising from the Ashes*.

Thank you to my literary agent, Tricia Lawrence, and to Erin Murphy, Dennis Stephens, and everyone at the Erin Murphy Literary Agency for believing in my book and supporting its journey to publication. I am grateful for Tricia's expertise, advice, and, most important, our friendship.

I am grateful for the incredible support and hard work of my TV agents, Nancy Etz and Grant Kessman of CAA, my manager Steve Simons of the Shuman Company, and my lawyers James Mandelbaum and Erez Rosenberg of Jackoway Austen Tyerman Wertheimer Mandelbaum Morris Bernstein Trattner & Klein, PC, and their support staffs.

. . .

Grateful thanks and all my 정 jeong to Jung Hui, Young Hi, and Jenny Lee, Shinese Harlins, Dr. Christina Rogers, Vester Acoff Jr., Ruth Harlins, and Denise Harlins (1963–2018), Lora Dene King and her children, Dennetta Lyles King, Erin Aubry Kaplan, K. W. Lee, Diana Lee Regan, and Sonia Lee Cook.

• • •

Much 정 jeong and special recognition to two prominent Asian American journalists who were also role models and friends. They both died from COVID-19 within the same two-week period in early 2021 before the first vaccine became available for the general public: Corky Lee, the self-proclaimed "Undisputed Unofficial Asian American Photographer Laureate" and photographic justice photojournalist (September 5, 1947–January 27, 2021); and Jimmy Lee, managing editor of *KoreAm Journal* (April 22, 1972–February 7, 2021).

• • •

I am grateful for the following people who rose above and beyond the call of duty to help me with my research and interviews for this book.

Karen Myers professionally transcribed the hundreds of hours of in-person interviews. Thank you for your patience, diligence, and incredible accuracy. It was a pleasure to work with you—and to bond over our cats!

My friends and fellow writers Annelise Kollevoll Medina and Monroe Maxwell transcribed the video documentaries, films, and news footage of the 1992 L.A. uprising for me. Your professional and timely work freed up my time so I could focus on the writing.

Many thanks to my longtime friend and writer Greg Lanier who also designs and manages my website.

Professional translator and sensitivity reader Aerin Park interpreted, proofread, and edited all the Korean-language author interviews and media articles into English. Currently, there is no universally embraced Romanization system for the Korean language. Therefore, various Romanization systems (such as "Revised Romanization" and "McCune-Reischauer") have been used in this book. 감사합니다, Aerin! Thank you!

And it was an honor and privilege to work for the past four years with photographer and writer Hyungwon Kang. He not only accompanied me on many in-person interviews and research trips, but he also helped translate some quotes live on the spot for me. We had many reporting adventures in Los Angeles together! I am grateful for Hyungwon's generosity of time, expertise, and friendship, and especially for becoming my unofficial 오빠 Oppa—my big brother.

Rest in peace and 정 jeong to store owner Soo Myung Koh (May 13, 1944–February 18, 2022), who died from COVID-19 during the reporting and writing of this book.

• • •

Thank you to everyone who agreed to talk with me about their experiences and share their expertise of the 1992 Los Angeles uprising.

I also want to thank those who declined to be interviewed because their experiences are, to this day, severely traumatizing. I appreciate and respect your decisions: your silence still speaks volumes.

The following is an alphabetical list of those sources who agreed to speak on the record. I am grateful for your consideration, generosity, and willingness to make sure we never forget what happened in 1992 and how we can work together in solidarity to ensure peace for our future generations: Najee Ali, Cam T. Ashling, Karen Grigsby Bates, Dr. Edward Taehan Chang, Eric Choi, Marcia Choo, Blake Chow, Howard Choy, Connie Joe Chung, Dr. Sarah Park Dahlen, Eric Deggans, Jonathan Dixon, James Fugate and Tom Hamilton of Eso Won Books, Craig Fujii, Shinese Harlins, Peter Hong, Hyepin Im, David Joo, Joseph Juhn, Hyungwon Kang, Dr. Jerry Kang, Juri Kang, Erin Aubry Kaplan, Alex Kim, U.S. Representative Andy Kim (NJ-03), Carol Kim, David Kim, retired Los Angeles County Deputy Sheriff David Sangbong Kim, Do Kim and the K. W. Lee Center for Leadership, Heidi Kim, Jae S. Kim, John Kim, Kirk Kim, Paul Kim, Tong Cho ("T.C.") Kim, U.S. Representative Young Kim (CA-40), Dennetta Lyles King, Lora Dene King, Karen Koh and her father Soo Myung Koh, Dr. Scott Kurashige, Stewart Kwoh, Ben Lee, Edward Lee, H. J. Lee, Jenny Lee, Jin Ho Lee, John Lee, Councilmember John S. Lee (Los Angeles City Council, 12th District), Jung Hui Lee, K. W. Lee, Will Yun Lee, Young Hi Lee, Tia Legoski, David Lin, Emile Mack, Kathy Masaoka, Kirk McKoy, Kalaya'an Mendoza, Jane Oak, Angela Oh, Ben Pak, Peter Pak, Carol K. Park, Dr. Edward J. W. Park, Robert Peterson, Cornelius Pettus, Diane Lee Regan, Dr. Allissa V. Richardson, Dr. Christina Rogers, Douglas Shur, U.S. Representative Michelle Park Steel (CA-45), U.S. Representative Marilyn Strickland (WA-10), Reverend Mark Whitlock, Bill Wong, my uncle Kenneth Yoo, and my mom, Young Kim Yoo.

· · ·

Thank you to the journalists, academics, librarians, research archival specialists, and courthouse staff employees who provided expertise and access to important primary sources for this book. Your scholarship helped ensure everything in my book was presented in a fair, accurate, and authentic manner: all the members of the Black Korean Alliance (BKA); Dr. Edward Taehan Chang and Carol K. Park at the Young Oak Kim Center for Korean American Studies; Eric Choi; Anne Park and Khee Park of the Korean American Scholarship Foundation Western Regional Chapter; Connie Joe Chung of Asian Americans Advancing Justice—Los Angeles; Jennifer Dewar, Archives Assistant; and the entire staff of the Volpe Library's Archives and Special Collections at Tennessee Tech University; Ralph Drew of the *Los Angeles Times*; Friends of California Citrus Park and the staff of the California Citrus State Historic Park; Terri Garst and Sung Kim of the Los Angeles Public Library; Jessica Geiser, Special Collections and University Archives, University of California, Riverside; Tricia Gesner and the staff of AP Newsroom; the staff of Getty Images; Michael Holland, Records Management at the Los Angeles City Clerk's Office; Jungeon Hong and Yuriy Shcherbina at the Korean Heritage Library/USC Digital Library; Jess Huang; Alexander Kim of Three Kings Public Affairs; Do Kim, president of the K. W. Lee Center for Leadership, and its staff; Stewart Kwoh of Asian Americans Advancing Justice—Los Angeles; H. J. Lee and everyone at Legacy Project: SaIGu L.A. Riots and KoreanAmerican Story.org; Stephanie Levy and the entire staff of the Archives and Records Center of the Superior Court of California in the County of Los Angeles; Jeannie Lin of the National Association of Chinese Americans; Janice Rhoshalle Littlejohn; Katie Maloney and the staff of the University of Southern California Sol Price School of Public Policy; Roby Massarrotto; Dean Musgrove and Gene Blevins of the *Los Angeles Daily News*; Byung J. ("BJay") Pak of Alston & Bird, Partners; Pam Pritt and Jake Stump of *WVU Maga-*

zine at West Virginia University; Yael Swerdlow and Tabby Refael of the *Jewish Journal*; *KoreAm Journal* founders Jung Shig Ryu and James Ryu and their entire staff (now archived at CM: Character Media); Sindy Saito, Taylor Torregano, and everyone at Spectrum News 1; Dr. Ebony Elizabeth Thomas; Héctor Tobar; Ron Waite of the *Kingsport Times News* and Rob Walters of Six Rivers Media; LaDale Winling and Robert Nelson; Jeff Yang, Phil Yu, and Philip Wang, authors of *Rise: A Pop History of Asian America from the Nineties to Now*; Bonnie Youn of Georgia Asian Pacific American Bar Association; Pat Zeider, assistant archivist; the entire staff at the Pasadena Museum of History; and the staff of ZUMA Press.

· · ·

I would also like to thank the city of Los Angeles. I have spent more than half my life in this beautiful, historic, diverse, complicated, sometimes infuriating but always inspiring city. I love L.A.!

For my research, I traveled all over L.A. County, downtown Los Angeles, Altadena, Pasadena, Compton, Watts, Riverside, Sacramento, and other places. I watched the sun rise at the Korean Bell of Friendship in San Pedro, donated in 1976 from the Republic of Korea to the city of Los Angeles to honor the Bicentennial and the veterans of the Korean War. I hiked down the Devil's Gate Dam to a small watering hole where Rodney King used to swim as a child. I stood at the exact spot where Latasha Harlins and Soon Ja Du met on March 16, 1991, at the former site of Empire Liquor. I visited the intersection in Lakeview Terrace where LAPD officers Theodore J. Briseno, Stacey C. Koon, Laurence M. Powell, and Timothy E. Wind beat Rodney Glen King. I paid my respects to Tasha, Eddie, and Glen at their graves. I spent days revisiting the famous "hot spots" of the 1992 L.A. uprising. Koreatown. Florence and Normandie. Parker Center. The First AME Church.

Radio Korea. The parking lot of Pizza Go where Eddie Lee died. Rodeo Galleria where David Joo and Richard Park defended their stores. Tom's Liquor, now Tom's Market.

Although many of these places no longer show signs of civil unrest, some areas remain abandoned, empty lots. Others are the birthplace of shiny, new shopping malls where it looks as if 1992 had never happened. But if you look closely, you can still see the signs of their past—through the communities and residents who still live and thrive there today to make sure this history does not repeat itself.

Los Angeles Times

CIRCULATION:
1,164,388 DAILY / 1,531,527 SUNDAY

FRIDAY, MAY 1, 1992
COPYRIGHT 1992 / THE TIMES MIRROR COMPANY / CCXI 158 PAGES

DAILY 35¢
DESIGNATED AREAS HIGHER

Looting and Fires Ravage L.A.
25 Dead, 572 Injured; 1,000 Blazes Reported

COLUMN ONE

South L.A. Burns and Grieves

■ Life has been hard in the neglected area for years. But now, as self-inflicted wounds mount, residents fear for the future.

By JONATHAN PETERSON
and HECTOR TOBAR
TIMES STAFF WRITERS

In a smoky parking lot in South Los Angeles, Ruby Gaines, 58, stared in disbelief at the wreckage of her local grocery store. "I'm a diabetic. This is where I get all my juices and foods," she said, peering at mounds of glass and soaked debris. "What am I going to do now?"

A few miles away, Paul C. Hudson arrived at his family-run savings and loan, a community fixture since 1947 in a neighborhood that has a grave shortage of banks. On Wednesday night it burned down. "Just the exterior wall was left standing," he said.

Anthony Wright and his wife, Joye, meanwhile, sat in lawn chairs, as radio news blared from their pickup truck. Just a few blocks away, hundreds of people were on a looting rampage on Vermont Avenue.

Hard times fuel the fury, said Joye Wright, a teacher's aide. "I'm not a recreation for minority communities. It's a depression."

Long before this week's spasm of destruction, daily life in parts of South Los Angeles was grueling in ways much different from elsewhere in the city. In ordinary, mundane ways—from a shortage of grocery stores and credit at normal interest rates to a scarcity of jobs and the more publicized ills of crime and drugs—it was often hard to get through a typical day.

Now, the rising toll in human life, torched businesses and destroyed property are adding insult to an already dangerous, frustrating existence.

On Thursday, some residents spoke in determined voices about getting on with the job of rebuilding their community. There were brave pronouncements of commitment to the future, promises that shell-shocked South Los Angeles would gird itself up and, with the aid of new investment, move forward after the rioting subsides.

"We have an obligation to reopen," said Paul Hudson, president of Broadway Federal Savings & Loan, whose green, two-story headquarters on 45th Street survived the Watts riots but not the current mayhem.

However, there were other voices that—

Please see FEAR, A34

Los Angeles County sheriff's deputies keep watch on a group of people arrested after a store on Martin Luther King Boulevard was looted.

STEVE DYKES / Los Angeles Times

Opportunists, Criminals Get Blame for Riots

By VICTOR MERINA
and JOHN MITCHELL
TIMES STAFF WRITERS

As Los Angeles firefighters and police spent a weary day and night battling arson blazes and looters, stunned residents and business owners grappled with the question of who is torching and pillaging their communities. The answer seemed to be both criminals and opportunists.

The rampage, which began Wednesday within hours of the verdicts in the Rodney G. King beating case, continued Thursday with scenes reminiscent of a war zone—smoke billowing from dozens of fires, looters bustling out of stores with merchandise, and gunfire echoing through the streets periodically.

But amid the pall, there also was a carnival atmosphere among some participants and onlookers who reveled in lawless neighborhoods to watch, join the looting or record events with video cameras. And there was the bizarre picture of gleeful teen-agers and families, as if on a weekend outing, ignoring outnumbered police and loading up on looted goods.

Although young black men constituted many of the rioters and there was the suspicion of many black and Latino rioters, substantial numbers but not with the numbers needed to hustle the situation.

Gates speculated, however, that had LAPD officers not retreated when rioting first flared, they might have incited even greater violence.

But as the chief sought to defend

Please see RIOTERS, A12

LAPD Slow in Coping With Wave of Unrest

■ Response: But the rapidly unfolding violence might have overwhelmed any police department.

By DAVID FREED
and TED ROHRLICH
TIMES STAFF WRITERS

Where were the police?

That was the question that many in Los Angeles, including members of the city's Police Department, were asking Thursday in the aftermath of widespread beatings, burning and looting that raged for hours in South Los Angeles before officers made any attempt to step it.

Even Chief Daryl F. Gates, who insisted beforehand that the LAPD was ready for "any emergency situation," conceded that his officers were overwhelmed by how quickly the crisis developed and were "much too slow" to respond.

"I asked the same question: Where were the police?" Gates told reporters. "We moved in with

NEWS ANALYSIS

his actions, the crisis demonstrated the grave difficulties encountered by the Police Department in the first hours of the worst urban turmoil in Los Angeles since the 1965 Watts riots.

Please see RESPONSE, A11

Jurors Rattled by Aftermath; Defend Verdicts

By PAUL LIEBERMAN
and STUART SILVERSTEIN
TIMES STAFF WRITERS

Some of the jurors fled their homes, fearful for their lives. Others retreated behind locked doors and struggled to comprehend the violent aftermath of their verdicts.

At least two, shaken to the edge of tears, wondered whether they could possibly be responsible for the rioting and fires that were spreading through Los Angeles.

"I've gotten some calls saying that I'll have to live with this for

Please see JURORS, A17

Beaten Driver a Searing Image of Mob Cruelty

By LAURIE BECKLUND
and STEPHANIE CHAVEZ
TIMES STAFF WRITERS

At every watershed through time, it seems a face emerges to brandish a moment in history. In Vietnam, a naked girl fled napalm. In Tian An Men Square, a single student stared down a line of Chinese tanks. In Los Angeles last year, Rodney G. King lay prone and beaten.

Now, a white gravel truck driver beaten nearly into oblivion in South Los Angeles has become the face on the flip side of the Rodney King case, the unofficial black-on-white response to the official white-on-black beating.

His name is Reginald Oliver Denny. He is 36. He is alive because four strangers—four black strangers who saw him dragged from his truck and beaten nearly to death—emerged from the crowd to drive his unwieldy 18-wheeler out of pandemonium to safety.

The rescuer were two women and two men: a young nutrition consultant, a laid-off data control worker, an unemployed aerospace worker and a still-unidentified young man in black whose fellow rescuers first feared was a gang-banger coming to finish Denny off.

Please see DRIVER, A14

■ Unrest: Troops begin deployment and a dusk-to-dawn curfew is clamped into place in the second day of violence.

By GREG BRAXTON
and JIM NEWTON
TIMES STAFF WRITERS

Thousands of looters ransacked stores and set fires Thursday in a chaotic rampage through the Los Angeles area as National Guard troops moved into the streets and a dusk-to-dawn curfew was clamped into force in numerous cities.

With the violence showing no sign of abating, Gov. Pete Wilson and Mayor Tom Bradley announced just before midnight that they have requested additional National Guard troops for a total of 6,000 in Los Angeles County. They said they have also asked federal authorities to place U.S. military forces on "standby alert" should greater troop strength become necessary.

"We are determined," Wilson said, "that this city is not going to suffer the kind of terrorizing that some people seem bent on inflicting upon it."

Triggered by Wednesday's not guilty verdicts of four Los Angeles police officers charged with beating black motorist Rodney G. King, the second day of mushrooming violence pushed the death toll to 25, including eight people shot by police. Another 572 injuries were reported, 100 of them critical.

In a period of a little more than 24 hours, about 1,000 structural fires were reported in Los Angeles County. It seemed as though, with each passing moment, fresh flames rose from new locations, sending ripples of fear through neighborhoods close to and miles away from the mayhem. Preliminary damage figures were being put at $200 million. Authorities have made more than 700 arrests.

As dusk approached, Police Commission President Stanley K. Sheinbaum said even the National Guard and the California Highway Patrol will not be enough to quiet the spreading unrest.

"The problem is widening, intensifying," Sheinbaum said. "You have a whole social upheaval."

Unlike the Watts riots of 1965, the violence this time has not been confined to an isolated area. Looters pilfered merchandise from mini-malls and swap meets throughout a combat zone that stretched from near downtown into South Los Angeles, through the heart of Hollywood and toward the Westside.

In incidents reminiscent of what happened in Los Angeles on Wednesday night, some whites in Long Beach were attacked by angry black demonstrators, who reportedly killed one man and injured at least 15 people, according to police and hospital officials.

A mob of about 15 rioters attacked two men on a motorcycle as they drove near Lemon Avenue and 20th Street, killing one of the men when he was shot in the back

Please see RIOT, A10

RISING FROM THE ASHES

IN MEMORIAM

Los Angeles, 1992: The Toll

12,111 people arrested.

2,383 people injured.

10,072 National Guard and 5,000 federal troops deployed.

3,600 fires.

1,100 buildings burned to the ground.

2,300 Korean-owned businesses destroyed.

$1 billion dollars in damage.

63 dead.

Of the 63 people who died, 56 were men and 7 were women. They included 28 Black, 19 Latino, 14 white, and 2 Asian American community members, and no law enforcement officials.

Twenty-three of these deaths are still unsolved.

Following are the people who died during the 1992 Los Angeles uprising and their ages. (An asterisk indicates an unsolved death.)

• • •

In Korean culture, for the tragic and untimely death of a person, it is customary to say: 부디 고통 없는 곳에서 편히 쉬시길 빕니다.

May your soul rest in peace in a place where there shall be no more pain.

April 29, 1992

Jimmie Harris, 38

Arturo C. Miranda, 23*

Dwight Taylor, 42*

Edward Anthony Travens, 15

Eduardo C. Vela, 33*

Louis A. Watson, 18*

John H. Willers, 37*

Willie Bernard Williams, 29

April 30, 1992

Cesar A. Aguilar, 18

Brian E. Andrew, 30

Franklin Benavidez, 27

Patrick Bettan, 30

Hector Castro, 49*

Jerel L. Channell, 26

Gregory Davis Jr., 15*

Kevin J. Edwards, 35

Howard Epstein, 45*

Jose L. Garcia, 15

Mark Garcia, 15

Andreas Garnica, 36

Matthew D. Haines, 32

DeAndre Harrison, 17

Dennis Ray Jackson, 38

Thanh Lam, 25*

Edward Jae Song Lee, 18

Frank D. Lopez, 36*

Darnell R. Mallory, 18

Ira F. McCurry, 45*

Ernest Neal Jr., 27*

Anthony Netherly, 21*

Juanita Pettaway, 37

Juan A. Pineda, 20

George A. Sosa, 20*

Anthony J. Taylor, 31

James L. Taylor, 26

Elbert O. Wilkins, 33*

May 1, 1992

George Alvarez, 42

Harry Doller, 56

Kevin A. Evanahen, 24*

Meeker Gibson, 35*

Paul D. Horace, 38

Betty Jackson, 56

Lucie R. Maronian, 51

Alfred V. Miller, 32

Suzanne R. Morgan, 24

Charles W. Orebo, 21

Aaron Ratinoff, 68

William Ross, 33*

Jose Solorzano, 25

May 2, 1992

Carol Benson, 42

Juana Espinosa, 65

Miguel Armando Quiroz Ortiz (formerly John Doe #80), 18
(in 2017, Ortiz was the last victim of the 1992 L.A. uprising
to be identified from a fire. The LAPD consider his death
a homicide. As of this writing, his case remains unsolved.)

Fredrick Ward, 20*

May 3, 1992

Vivian Austin, 87

Howard Eugene Martin, 22

Hugo G. Ramirez, 23

Victor R. Rivas, 26

Imad Sharaf, 31

May 20, 1992

Juan V. Salgado, 20 (Salgado's body was found on this date)

May 23, 1992

Wilson Alvarez, 40 (Alvarez died on this date from head
injuries after being assaulted on May 1, 1992)

August 12, 1992

Nissar Mustafa, 20 (Mustafa's body was found on this date)

December 16, 1992

Elias Garcia Rivera, 32 (Rivera died on this date after eight months in critical condition with a fractured skull after being attacked on April 29, 1992)

November 24, 1993

Wallace Tope, 54 (Tope died on this date after being in a coma for eighteen months after he was assaulted on April 30, 1992)

NOTES

Prologue: "Los Angeles Is Still on Edge"

1 **"How can you sit there":** Michele L. Norris, Avis Thomas-Lester, and David Von Drehle, "Sad roll call of riot victims: Death was random, not proud," *Orlando Sentinel*, May 17, 1992.

1 **Los Angeles County boasted:** Anne Kim-Dannibale, "In L.A.'s Koreatown, travelers find a 'second Seoul,'" *National Geographic*, November 8, 2021.

1 *Oh my God, that's my store!*: Live call recordings, Radio Korea, April–May 1992, provided by Jin Ho Lee of Radio Korea, January 28, 2022, transcribed in Korean and translated in English by Aerin Park; and Tim Loc, "How a radio station became Koreatown's lifeline during the '92 unrest," *LAist*, April 28, 2017.

2 **a jury had acquitted:** Independent Commission on the Los Angeles Police Department, "Report of the Independent Commission on the Los Angeles Police Department (Christopher Commission Report)," archive.org, 1991, https://archive.org/details/ChristopherCommissionLAPD.

2 **eight people:** *Los Angeles Times* Staff, "A *Los Angeles Times* special report: Understanding the riots: Part 3—Witness to rage," *Los Angeles Times*, May 13, 1992.

2 **including Fairfax High School:** Jenny Lee, interview with author, June 28, 2021, and July 3, 2021. All quotes from Jenny Lee are from author interviews unless otherwise noted.

2 **Mayor Tom Bradley declared:** *LA Times* Staff, "Witness to rage."

2 **"And the agony continued":** *Burn Motherf*cker, Burn!* directed by Sacha Jenkins (New York: Showtime Documentary Films, 2017).

2 **"Everything we have worked for":** *Sa I Gu*, directed by Dai Sul Kim-Gibson (San Francisco: Center for Asian American Media, 1993), DVD.

3 **"This is for Latasha!":** Itaberi Njeri, *The Last Plantation: Color, Conflict, and Identity—Reflection of a New World Black* (Boston: Houghton Mifflin Harcourt, 1997), 13.

3 **store owner Soon Ja Du:** Pyong Gap Min, *Caught in the Middle: Korean*

Communities in New York and Los Angeles (Berkeley: University of California Press, 1996), 84.

3 **Du was found guilty:** *The People of the State of California, Plaintiff, v. Soon Ja Du, Defendant*, No. BA 037738, D.N., p. 44 (November 15, 1991).

Chapter 1: Eddie

6 **"I think he grabbed":** Jung Hui Lee, interview with author, July 3, 2021, and January 22, 2022; Korean translated into English by Aerin Park. All quotes from Jung Hui Lee are from author interviews unless otherwise noted.

8 **"Mornings I worked":** Kim-Gibson, *Sa I Gu.*

9 **"We all loved him":** K. W. Lee, "In death, Eddie Lee left an undying legacy," *Korea Times English Edition*, March 29, 2001.

10 **"It didn't make me":** Young Hi Lee, interview with author, January 22, 2022; Korean translated into English by Aerin Park. All quotes from Young Hi Lee are from author interviews unless otherwise noted.

10 **"We came to America":** Kim-Gibson, *Sa I Gu.*

12 **"first Koreatown in America":** Frank Shyong, "The first Koreatown in America, and Riverside's role in South Korean democracy," *Los Angeles Times*, October 9, 2021; and Sakshi Venkatraman, "The story of the first Koreatown was lost to history," NBC News, October 15, 2021.

12 **In 1945, shortly after gaining its independence:** All Korean War and Three Waves information taken from various sources, including Bruce Cumings, *The Korean War: A History* (New York: Modern Library, 2010); David Halberstam, *The Coldest Winter: America and the Korean War* (New York: Hyperion Books, 2007); Max Hastings, *The Korean War* (New York: Simon & Schuster, 1988); and Katherine Yungmee Kim, *Images of America: Los Angeles's Koreatown* (Charleston, SC: Arcadia Publishing, 2011).

14 **In 1960, 84 percent:** Abby Budiman, Christine Tamir, Lauren Mora, and Luis Noe-Bustamante, "Facts on U.S. immigrants, 2018: Statistical portrait of the foreign-born population in the United States," Pew Research Center, August 20, 2020, https://www.pewresearch.org/hispanic/2020/08/20/facts-on-u-s-immigrants/.

15 **The Immigration and Nationality Act:** Hon. Emanuel Seller of New York, "National origin system in immigration law must be abolished," *Congressional Record—House*, January 29, 1964, pp. 1389–90, https://www.govinfo.gov/content/pkg/GPO-CRECB-1964-pt1/pdf/GPO-CRECB-1964-pt1-15-3.pdf.

15 **annual immigration increased:** "Immigration and Nationality Act of 1965," H.R. 2580, 82nd Congress, 1st sess., History, Art & Archives: United States House of Representatives, https://history.house.gov/Historical-Highlights/1951-2000/Immigration-and-Nationality-Act-of-1965/.

15 **By 1970:** Katherine Yungmee Kim, *Images of America: Los Angeles's Koreatown* (Charleston, SC: Arcadia Publishing, 2011), 9; and Joann Im, "The

History of Koreatown: A Heartbeat of Los Angeles," LAPL Blog, May 27, 2022.

15 **"He loved fishing":** Jung Hui Lee, "Reflection on the death of my beloved son, Jae Song Lee," *Chronicles of Koreatown Sa I Gu LA Riot: Honoring the Memory of Jae Song Lee, the Martyr and the Star of Koreatown* (Los Angeles: Edward Lee Memorial Scholarship Foundation, 1993), 121. Korean translated into English by Aerin Park.

16 **"We were very close":** Jenny Lee, interview with author.

Chapter 2: Glen

19 **as the Clippers . . . beat:** "Clippers @ Timberwolves," March 2, 1991, Target Center, Minneapolis, MN, NBA.com, https://www.nba.com/game/lac-vs-min-0029000759.

19 **Glen, who dreamed:** Soren Baker, "Rodney King turns music entrepreneur," *Chicago Tribune*, February 24, 1998.

19 **freestyle rapped along:** Rodney King, with Lawrence J. Spagnola, *The Riot Within: My Journey from Rebellion to Redemption* (San Francisco: HarperOne, 2012), 41.

19 **The music reminded:** Ashley Dunn and Andrea Ford, "The man swept up in the furor: Friends, family say King was sometimes lost but never violent," *Los Angeles Times*, March 22, 1991.

19 **As a child:** King and Spagnola, *Riot Within*, 1, 3.

20 **loved skiing:** Ed Leibowitz, "Rodney's rap," *Los Angeles Times*, March 28, 1999.

20 **"We had no definite":** King and Spagnola, *Riot Within*, 41.

20 **Helms sat in the front:** Joel Anderson, Jayson De Leon, and Chau Tu, "The tape," in *Slow Burn: The L.A. Riots* (podcast), season 6, episode 1, November 3, 2021, https://slate.com/podcasts/slow-burn/s6/the-la-riots/e1/george-hollidays-video-of-the-rodney-king-beating-changed-everything.

20 **"Trouble is":** King and Spagnola, *Riot Within*, 41.

20 **515 miles of freeway:** "Miles of public roads: Los Angeles County," *Los Angeles Almanac* (1998–2022), https://www.laalmanac.com/transport/tr01.php.

20 **Each colored grid:** Steven Kilgore, "Los Angeles land covenants, redlining: Creation and effects," *LAPL Blog*, June 22, 2020, https://lapl.org/collections-resources/blogs/lapl/los-angeles-land-covenants-redlining-creation-and-effects.

21 **From 1910 to 1970:** Kelly Simpson, "The Great Migration: Creating a new Black identity in Los Angeles," KCET, February 15, 2012; and "African American Heritage: The Great Migration (1910–1970)," National Archives, June 28, 2021, https://www.archives.gov/research/african-americans/migrations/great-migration.

21 **California's steel:** Richard Rothstein, "Why Los Angeles is still a segregated city after all these years," *Los Angeles Times*, August 20, 2017.

21 **L.A.'s Black population:** Simpson, "Great Migration."

22 **one street there:** Conan Nolan, "The rich history of West Adams, once a predominantly Black suburb," NBC 4 Los Angeles, February 12, 2016.

22 **In 1945:** Hadley Meares, "The LA lawyer who won housing rights for all Americans: Loren Miller was the go-to lawyer for Black homeowners fighting discrimination," *LA Curbed*, April 18, 2018.

23 **officials claimed this decision:** Matthew Fleisher, "Want to tear down insidious monuments to racism and segregation? Bulldoze L.A. freeways," *Los Angeles Times*, June 24, 2020; Carolina A. Miranda, " 'The prettiest park in Los Angeles' and why a freeway runs through it," *Los Angeles Times*, August 12, 2015; and Hadley Meares, "Why L.A.'s freeways are symbolic sites of protest," *LA Curbed*, June 11, 2020.

23 **Officer Melanie Singer spotted:** Anderson, De Leon, and Tu, "The tape."

23 **But Glen and Allen:** Leibowitz, "Rodney's rap."

24 **"Rodney, why don't you pull over?":** Lou Cannon, *Official Negligence: How Rodney King and the Riots Changed Los Angeles and the LAPD* (New York: Times Books/Random House, 1997), 200.

24 **"He was unemployed":** Dunn and Ford, "The man swept up."

24 **"They seen three":** David Freed, "Passenger with King on night of beating is killed in car crash," *Los Angeles Times*, June 30, 1991.

24 **"I was scared":** Cannon, *Official Negligence*, 43.

25 **"crooked rats":** Cannon, *Official Negligence*, 58, 60, 61.

25 **In January 1960:** United States Commission on Civil Rights, "Hearings before the US Commission on Civil Rights, hearings held in Los Angeles," January 25, 1960 (Washington, DC: US Government Printing Office, 1960); Online Books Page, University of Pennsylvania Library, https://onlinebooks.library.upenn.edu/webbin/book/lookupid?key=ha102835885 and https://catalog.hathitrust.org/Record/102835885; and Cannon, *Official Negligence*, 62.

26 **in 1959, a judge:** Cannon, *Official Negligence*, 67.

26 **The department's biggest:** Edward K. Escobar, "Bloody Christmas and the irony of police professionalism: The Los Angeles Police Department, Mexican Americans, and police reform in the 1950s," *Pacific Historical Review* 72:2 (May 1, 2003), 183–84.

26 **They suffered broken bones:** Cannon, *Official Negligence*, 65.

26 **multiple officers were criminally:** Cecilia Rasmussen, "The 'Bloody Christmas' of 1952," *Los Angeles Times*, December 21, 1997.

26 **Eight were indicted:** Escobar, "Bloody Christmas."

26 **He reminded the commission:** U.S. Commission on Civil Rights, "Hearings," 334; and Escobar, "Bloody Christmas."

26 **"There is no segregation":** U.S. Commission on Civil Rights, "Hearings," 327–28.

27 **Dull LAPD annual statistics reports:** Cannon, *Official Negligence*, 60.

27 **Fashion shows promoted:** Mike Davis and Jon Wiener, "How LAPD

Chief William H. Parker Influenced the Depiction of Policing on the TV Show *Dragnet*," *Verso*, June 16, 2020, https://www.versobooks.com/blogs/news/4756-how-lapd-chief-william-h-parker-influenced-the-depiction-of-policing-on-the-tv-show-dragnet.

27 **He invited the press:** Cannon, *Official Negligence*, 60.

27 **But Parker's biggest influence:** William Overhand, "Fighting crime and writing: Novel combination for L.A. cops—Police find fame and fortune with literary moonlighting," *Los Angeles Times*, April 15, 1984.

27 *Dragnet* **reenacted:** Cannon, *Official Negligence*, 61.

27 **"Ladies and gentlemen":** TeeVees Greatest, "Dragnet opening and closing theme, 1951–1959 and 1967–1970," March 5, 2016, https://youtu.be/o1hgGchn8p8.

27 **Roddenberry modeled:** Overhand, "Fighting crime and writing."

27 **"Most people think":** *Uprising: Hip Hop and the L.A. Riots* (documentary), directed by Mark Ford (Los Angeles: Creature Films, 2012), https://youtu.be/bcfvzrn_uJA.

28 **President Richard Nixon had first:** Benjamin T. Smith, "New documents reveal the bloody origins of America's long war on drugs," *Time*, August 24, 2021; and Richard Nixon, "Special message to the Congress on drug abuse prevention and control," American Presidency Project, June 17, 1971, https://www.presidency.ucsb.edu/documents/special-message-the-congress-drug-abuse-prevention-and-control.

28 **Black suspects were arrested at twice:** "Punishment and prejudice: Racial disparities in the War on Drugs," *Human Rights Watch*, vol. 12, no. 2 (G), May 2000, https://www.hrw.org/reports/2000/usa/index.htm#TopOfPage, https://www.hrw.org/reports/2000/usa/Rcedrg00-04.htm#P284_59547, and https://www.hrw.org/reports/2000/usa/Rcedrg00-05.htm#TopOfPage; and Robert A. Johnson and Cindy Larison, "Prevalence of substance use among racial and ethnic subgroups in the United States, 1991–1993," U.S. Department of Health and Human Services, Substance Abuse and Mental Health Services Administration (SAMHSA), Washington, DC, 1998, https://www.ojp.gov/ncjrs/virtual-library/abstracts/prevalence-substance-use-among-racial-and-ethnic-subgroups-united.

28 **By 1991, Black suspects:** Substance Abuse and Mental Health Services Administration, "National household survey on drug use, population estimates 1998 (U.S. Department of Health and Human Services, 1999)," *Human Rights Watch*, https://www.hrw.org/reports/2000/usa/Table1718.pdf.

28 **crack cocaine's roots:** Donovan X. Ramsey, *When Crack Was King: A People's History of a Misunderstood Era* (New York: One World, 2023), 99; Jesse Katz, "Tracking the genesis of the crack trade," *Los Angeles Times*, October 20, 1996; and Isidoro Rodriguez, "Rocks and riches: How crack cocaine affected America," *Crime Report*, February 4, 2020.

28 **Instead of inhaling:** Editorial Board, "Slandering the unborn: How bad

science and a moral panic, fueled in part by the news media, demonized mothers and defamed a generation," *New York Times*, December 28, 2018.

29 **Crack turned out:** Brenda Stevenson, *The Contested Murder of Latasha Harlins: Justice, Gender, and the Origins of the LA Riots* (Oxford: Oxford University Press, 2013), 38; and Editorial Board, "Slandering the unborn."

29 **crack's dangerous side effects:** "Effects of crack cocaine," Foundation for a Drug-Free World International, 2006–2022, https://www.drugfreeworld .org/drugfacts/crackcocaine/effects-of-crack-cocaine.html.

29 **And crack was cheap:** Stevenson, *Contested Murder*, 38.

29 **"It is as though McDonald's":** Gary Webb, "'Crack' plague's roots are in Nicaragua War," *San Jose Mercury News*, August 18, 1996.

29 **Competition to sell crack:** Kyeyoung Park, *LA Rising: Korean Relations with Blacks and Latinos after Civil Unrest* (Lexington: Lexington Books, 2019), 41.

29 **By 1984, five:** Mike Sager, "Say hello to Rick Ross," *Esquire*, September 25, 2013.

29 **"crack capital of the world":** Webb, "'Crack' plague's roots."

29 **President Reagan signed the 1986:** Deborah J. Vagins and Jesselyn McCurdy, "Cracks in the system: Twenty years of the unjust federal crack cocaine law," American Civil Liberties Union (ACLU), October 2006, https://www.aclu.org/documents/cracks-system-20-years-unjust-federal -crack-cocaine-law?redirect=cpredirect/27181.

29 **the average federal drug:** Vagins and McCurdy, "Cracks in the system."

29 **"gravest domestic threat,":** Ramsey, *When Crack Was King*, 243.

30 **He established Operation Hammer:** David Whitman, "The untold story of the L.A. riot," *U.S. News & World Report,* May 23, 1993.

30 **LAPD helicopters hovered:** Ben Westhoff, *Original Gangstas: The Untold Story of Dr. Dre, Eazy-E, Ice Cube, Tupac Shaker, and the Birth of West Coast Rap* (New York: Hachette Books, 2016), 12–14.

30 **The LAPD also offered:** Editorial Staff, "History of crack cocaine," *American Addiction Centers: National Rehab Directory,* October 6, 2022, https://rehabs.com/blog/a-complete-history-of-crack-cocaine/.

30 **"because I was an African American":** John L. Mitchell, "Ex-Laker's detainment by L.A. police criticized," *Los Angeles Times*, February 28, 1991.

30 **Even though 66 percent:** Vagins and McCurdy, "Cracks in the system."

30 **"People ask why":** Aaron Morrison, "50-year war on drugs imprisoned millions of Black Americans," *Associated Press*, July 23, 2021.

31 **For that night's session:** Sgt. Stacey C. Koon, L.A.P.D., with Robert Deitz, *Presumed Guilty: The Tragedy of the Rodney King Affair* (Washington, DC: Regency Gateway, 1992), 25.

31 **Koon preferred walking:** Koon, *Presumed Guilty*, 26.

31 **"My real love was working":** Koon, *Presumed Guilty*, 67.

31 **Koon graduated:** Koon, *Presumed Guilty*, 65–67.

31 **He entered the LAPD:** Koon, *Presumed Guilty*, 65–66.

31 **"Ninety-five percent":** Koon, *Presumed Guilty*, 65–66.

31 **As Koon finished:** Anderson, De Leon, and Tu, "The tape"; and Koon, *Presumed Guilty*, 26.

32 **Koon knew by their confused:** Koon, *Presumed Guilty*, 26.

32 **"By now the chase":** Koon, *Presumed Guilty*, 27–29.

32 **Glen raced through:** Cannon, *Official Negligence*, 25, 26, 30, 31, 435.

33 **Koon's was the third:** Cannon, *Official Negligence*, 26.

33 **It was now 12:50 a.m.:** Independent Commission on the Los Angeles Police Department, "Report," 4–5.

33 **Marquette Frye swerved:** Darrell Dawsey, "To CHP officer who sparked riots, it was just another arrest," *Los Angeles Times*, August 19, 1990.

33 **Around 7:00 p.m.:** "Watts rebellion," History.com, September 28, 2017, https://www.history.com/topics/1960s/watts-riots.

33 **Marquette, twenty-one:** John A. McCone, Warren M. Christopher, et al., "Violence in the city: An end or a beginning?" *A Report by the Governor's Commission on the Los Angeles Riots,* December 2, 1965, https://archive.org/details/ViolenceInCity and https://ia801401.us.archive.org/0/items/ViolenceInCity/violence%20in%20city.pdf.

33 **But California Highway Patrol:** Cannon, *Official Negligence*, 69.

33 **"I was just doing":** Dawsey, "To CHP officer."

33 **Marquette, still in a good mood:** Burt A. Folkart, "Marquette Frye, whose arrest ignited the Watts Riots in 1965, dies at age 42," *Los Angeles Times*, December 25, 1986.

33 **Officer Minikus laughed:** Dawsey, "To CHP officer."

33 **He allowed Ronald:** James Queally, "Watts riots: Traffic stop was the spark that ignited days of destruction in L.A.," *Los Angeles Times*, July 29, 2015.

34 **Rena berated her son:** Douglas Martin, "Rena Price is dead at 97: Catalyst for the Watts riots," *New York Times*, June 29, 2013.

34 **As the crowd doubled:** Dawsey, "To CHP officer."

34 **Ronald rushed over:** Arun Rath, "Out of long-gone rubble of the Watts Riots, scars and signs of healing," NPR, August 8, 2015, https://www.npr.org/transcripts/430753725.

35 **It was only 7:45 p.m.:** Arun Rath, "Out of long-gone rubble of the Watts riots, scars and signs of healing," NPR, August 8, 2015; and "Watts rebellion."

35 **As the night progressed:** Queally, "Watts riots."

35 **Black store owners placed:** Lyn Goldfarb and Alison Sotomayor, "Bridging the divide: Tom Bradley and the politics of race" (video), February 1, 2016, https://www.pbs.org/video/bridging-divide-tom-bradley-and-politics-race-full-episode/.

35 **"Burn baby burn!":** Martin, "Rena Price."

35 **He booked Marquette Frye:** Martin, "Rena Price."

35 **As Minikus headed to:** Dawsey, "To CHP officer."

36 **The civil unrest in Watts:** Queally, "Watts riots."

36   **On August 17, 1965:** UCLA Film & Television Archive, "Martin Luther King Jr. arrives in Los Angeles (Los Angeles, CA, 8/17/1965)," *YouTube,* May 6, 2013, https://youtu.be/diLC4hbJVF4.

36   **Although Dr. King believed:** UCLA Film & Television Archive, "Martin Luther King Jr."

36   **arresting him more than thirty times:** UPI, "Deaths: Marquette Frye, arrest led to Watts riots," *Miami Herald,* December 25, 1986.

36   **"You're the guy":** UPI, "Deaths: Marquette Frye."

36   **Seeking privacy and peace:** Thandisizwe Chimurenga, "The Watts uprising after 50 years," *Los Angeles Sentinel,* August 12, 2015; and UPI, "Deaths: Marquette Frye."

37   **"I'm no villain":** UPI, "Deaths: Marquette Frye."

37   **"I could see the smoke":** "Marquette Frye dead; 'Man who began riot,'" *New York Times,* December 25, 1986.

37   **"Get out of the vehicle!":** Koon, *Presumed Guilty,* 29.

37   **Glen was struggling:** Cannon, *Official Negligence,* 26; and Seth Abramovitch, "Flashback: How a plumber altered history by taping the attack on Rodney King," *Hollywood Reporter,* March 3, 2021.

38   **Eleven additional LAPD units:** Cannon, *Official Negligence,* 618.

38   **"Put your hands up":** Richard A. Serrano, "King tells of beating, racial taunts by police," *Los Angeles Times,* January 16, 1992.

38   **King later admitted:** Cannon, *Official Negligence,* 43.

38   **A high school track star:** Mike de la Cruz, "Witness for the prosecution: CHP officer Singer a former Mariposa standout," *Merced Sun-Star,* March 12, 1992.

38   **Later in court:** Linda Deutsch, "Policewoman: Officer severely beat motorist," *Standard-Speaker* (Hazleton, PA), March 7, 1992.

38   **"Knock it off!":** Deutsch, "Policewoman."

38   **"By drawing her gun":** Koon, *Presumed Guilty,* 34.

38   **"When I seen the stripes":** Serrano, "King tells of beating."

39   **But Koon claimed:** Whitman, "Untold story."

39   **"dusted suspect,":** Koon, *Presumed Guilty,* 32.

39   **Glen had no PCP:** Independent Commission on the Los Angeles Police Department, "Report," 8.

40   **"I can't sleep":** Cannon, *Official Negligence,* 30.

40   **Glen easily pushed:** Independent Commission on the Los Angeles Police Department, "Report," 6.

40   **"An exceptionally dangerous":** Koon, *Presumed Guilty,* 30.

40   **The sergeant ordered his officers:** Koon, *Presumed Guilty,* 35.

40   **"I felt a blow":** Serrano, "King tells of beating."

40   **On the other side:** Jim Newton, "Prosecutor says officers hit passenger in King's car," *Los Angeles Times,* March 6, 1993.

40   **"I just heard Rodney":** David Treadwell, "Passenger feels King beating was pre-meditated," *Los Angeles Times,* April 19, 1991.

40 **"Get down!":** Koon, *Presumed Guilty*, 38.

40 **But Glen didn't hear:** Serrano, "King tells of beating."

41 **He pulled the trigger:** Eric H. Holder Jr., with Laurie O. Robinson and John H. Laub, "National Institute of Justice research in brief: Police use of force, tasers and other less-lethal weapons," U.S. Department of Justice, July 2010, p. 2, https://www.ojp.gov/pdffiles1/nij/232215.pdf.

41 **"I felt a little string":** Serrano, "King tells of beating."

41 **He tased Glen again:** Anderson, De Leon, and Tu, "The tape."

41 **"No pain":** Serrano, "King tells of beating."

41 **the taser wires trailing:** Independent Commission on the Los Angeles Police Department, "Report," 6.

41 **Koon commanded his officers:** Koon, *Presumed Guilty*, 44.

41 **Officers Powell, Briseno, and Wind:** Professor Douglas O. Linder, "The Holliday videotape," Famous Trials, 1995–2022, https://www.famous-trials.com/lapd/586-videotape; and Romy Massarotta, "Rodney King beating full video," YouTube, March 12, 2015, https://youtu.be/sb1WywIpUtY.

41 **the officers struck Glen:** Linder, "Holliday videotape."

42 **"I looked around":** Serrano, "King tells of beating."

42 **"My dad and I":** Cannon, *Official Negligence*, 41, 43.

42 **"Who wants to go fishing?":** King and Spagnola, *Riot Within*, 1.

43 **Ronald King grew up:** Cannon, *Official Negligence*, 40, 41.

43 **He started his own business:** Leibowitz, "Rodney's rap."

43 **"Daddy would have us":** King and Spagnola, *Riot Within*, 10–11.

43 **Glen's fatigue and inability:** King and Spagnola, *Riot Within*, 12–13.

43 **"Baseball saved me":** Cannon, *Official Negligence*, 40; and King and Spagnola, *Riot Within*, 13.

43 **"The first time I drank":** King and Spagnola, *Riot Within*, 22.

44 **Glen drank to cope:** King and Spagnola, *Riot Within*, 9–10.

44 **"Every baton blow":** King and Spagnola, *Riot Within*, 46–47.

44 **"Glen, you got to live":** King and Spagnola, *Riot Within*, 47.

Chapter 3: The Videotape

45 **The thirty-one-year-old plumber:** Ali Paybarah, "He videotaped the Rodney King beating: Now, he is auctioning the camera," *New York Times,* July 29, 2021.

45 **They lived in a modest:** Gerrick D. Kennedy, "Ice Cube reflects on the 25 years since the release of 'Death Certificate,'" *Los Angeles Times,* June 30, 2017.

45 **"When you have the new camera":** Seth Abramovitch, "Flashback: How a plumber altered history by taping the attack on Rodney King," *Hollywood Reporter*, March 3, 2021.

45 **"I actually have footage":** Abramovitch, "How a plumber."

46 **At 12:45 a.m.:** Clay Risen, "Those we've lost: George Holliday, who taped

police beating of Rodney King, dies at 61," *New York Times*, September 22, 2021.

46 **"Oh my God!"**: Risen, "Those we've lost."

46 **"The rest is history"**: Abramovitch, "How a plumber."

46 **Holliday's video is seven minutes:** Linder, "Holliday videotape"; and Massarotta, "Rodney King beating."

46 **The remaining footage:** Massarotta, "Rodney King beating."

46 **"What did we just see?"**: Abramovitch, "How a plumber."

47 **Holliday moved to Los Angeles:** Risen, "Those we've lost."

47 **"There must be something"**: Abramovitch, "How a plumber."

47 **On Monday, March 4:** Cannon, *Official Negligence*, 22.

48 **"That's when everything"**: Abramovitch, "How a plumber."

48 **The next morning:** Abramovitch, "How a plumber"; and Risen, "Those we've lost."

48 **"When the officers saw"**: Cannon, *Official Negligence*, 24.

48 **"Many of us who had"**: Eric Spillman, Samantha Cortese, Andy Riesmeyer, and Bobby Gonzalez, "30 years later: Rodney King beating video still a painful memory for L.A.," KTLA 5 Live, March 3, 2021, https://ktla.com/5-live/30-years-later-rodney-king-lapd-beating-video -still-a-painful-memory-for-la/.

48 **"This was a lynching"**: Ford, *Uprising*.

49 **"It ain't nothing"**: Ford, *Uprising*.

49 **"Is this gonna be enough"**: Ford, *Uprising*.

49 **On March 7:** Cannon, *Official Negligence*, 49.

49 **The LAPD's Internal Affairs:** Richard A. Serrano, "3 in King beating say they feared for their lives," *Los Angeles Times*, May 21, 1991.

50 **"Wait, what?"**: Gretchen Voss, "Rodney King's daughters: The world watched as their father was beaten," *Glamour,* January 11, 2011.

50 **"As soon as I looked"**: Dennetta Lyles King, interview with author, September 26, 2022. All quotes from Dennetta Lyles King are from author interviews unless otherwise noted.

50 **"super daddy's girl"**: Voss, "Rodney King's daughters."

50 **"I was extremely shy"**: Lora King, interview with author, May 9, 2022. All quotes from Lora Dene King are from author interviews unless otherwise noted.

53 **Rodney Glen King was released:** Tracy Wood and Faye Fiore, "Rodney King says he obeyed police," *Los Angeles Times*, March 7, 1991.

53 **"I was scared for my life"**: Wood and Fiore, "Rodney King says he obeyed."

54 **"I was struck all over"**: Serrano, "King tells of beating."

55 **"He's depressed"**: Leslie Berger, "King fights emotional and physical scars," *Los Angeles Times,* April 14, 1991.

55 **During the beating:** Berger, "King fights."

55 **"used to get on"**: Berger, "King fights."

55 **Five doctors tended:** Berger, "King fights."

56 **These injuries did not match:** Serrano, "King tells of beating."

56 **"It is a horrible":** Associated Press, "Los Angeles jury widens inquiry in police beating," *New York Times,* March 19, 1991.

57 **"The Man Swept Up":** Dunn and Ford, "The man swept up."

58 **"A 15-year-old girl":** "Girl, 15, shot to death over orange juice," *Los Angeles Times*, March 17, 1991.

Chapter 4: Tasha

59 **"I would see her":** Dr. Christina Rogers, interview with author, May 26, 2022. All quotes from Christina Rogers are from author interviews unless otherwise noted.

59 **Tasha's sister, Christina:** Shinese Harlins, interview with author, May 23, 2022. All quotes from Shinese Harlins are from author interviews unless otherwise noted.

62 **"She was a caretaker":** Kamilah Kashanie, producer, "She had dreams in life: A remembrance of Latasha Harlins," StoryCorps, 2022, https://storycorps.org/stories/she-had-dreams-in-life-a-remembrance-of-latasha-harlins/.

62 **Their grandmother:** Njeri, *Last Plantation*, 88.

62 **Born in 1941:** Stevenson, *Contested Murder*, 8.

63 **Like Los Angeles:** Stevenson, *Contested Murder*, 18–20.

63 **In 1980, Ruth decided:** Stevenson, *Contested Murder*, 39.

63 **She found a job:** Jesse Katz and John H. Lee, "Bullet ends one life, kills two dreams," *Los Angeles Times*, April 8, 1991.

63 **The apartment was near:** Koon, *Presumed Guilty*, 87.

64 **On the night before Thanksgiving:** Katz and Lee, "Bullet ends."

64 **The woman who shot:** Cannon, *Official Negligence*, 115.

64 **"My daughter was a kind":** Stevenson, *Contested Murder*, 46.

65 **"Our favorite song":** *A Love Song for Latasha*, directed by Sophia Nahli Allison (Los Gatos, CA: Netflix, 2020).

65 **"She just didn't want to end":** Allison, *Love Song*.

65 **"The most important thing":** Cannon, *Official Negligence*, 116.

66 **Shinese loved her:** Njeri, *Last Plantation*, 140; Stevenson, *Contested Murder*, 4; and Harlins, interview with author.

66 **"Time is the most important":** Cillea Houghton, "The tasteful meaning behind the name Flavor Flav," *American Songwriter*, July 2023.

66 **On Friday, March 15:** Stevenson, *Contested Murder*, 57; and Harlins, interview with author.

67 **Coincidentally, Tasha's uncle:** Stevenson, *Contested Murder*, 70.

67 **she impulsively popped:** Harlins, interview with author; and author visit to Empire Liquor (now Numero Uno Market) and to the Harlins's former residence.

68 **The area was considered:** "Homelessness and food deserts in Los

Angeles," Poverty USA, 2022, https://www.povertyusa.org/stories/homelessness-food-deserts-los-angeles.

68 **In 1963, there were:** Kyeyoung Park, *LA Rising: Korean Relations with Blacks and Latinos after Civil Unrest* (Lanham, MD: Lexington Books, 2019), 58.

68 **Even in 2020:** Shawn Donnan, Ann Choi, Hannah Levitt, and Christopher Cannon, "Wells Fargo rejected half its Black applicants in mortgage refinancing boom," *Bloomberg*, March 10, 2022.

68 **So they used a traditional:** Joel Garreau, "For Koreans, 'keh' is key to success," *Washington Post,* November 3, 1991.

68 **Similar versions of this system:** Dakota Kim, "The radical economics of lending your friends money," *Vice*, May 30, 2018.

69 **Within just fourteen years:** Park, *LA Rising*, 43.

69 **By 1991, 80 percent:** Park, *LA Rising*, 43; and Min, *Caught in the Middle*, 43, 66–67.

69 **Because 1.2 million people:** Calvin Sims, "Vons opens store in city torn by riots," *New York Times*, January 13, 1994.

69 **Korean-owned stores:** Nancy Ablemann and John Lie, *Blue Dreams: Korean Americans and the Los Angeles Riots* (Cambridge, MA: Harvard University Press, 1995), 139.

69 **And because they were small:** Sims, "Vons opens"; and Ablemann and Lie, *Blue Dreams*, 139.

69 **Soon Ja Du was late:** *The People of the State of California v. Soon Ja Du,* No. BA 037738, Billy H. Du witness testimony, p. 221 (Superior Court of the State of California for the County of Los Angeles, October 1, 1991), transcript, Stanley Mosk Courthouse, Archives and Records Center.

70 **Soon Ja suffered:** Stevenson, *Contested Murder*, 67.

70 **her village in the mountainous:** Stevenson, *Contested Murder*, 61.

70 **After the war:** Stevenson, *Contested Murder*, 61.

70 **He also served:** *People of the State of California v. Soon Ja Du,* p. 216, October 1, 1991.

70 **"She had a good life":** Katz and Lee, "Bullet ends."

70 **In December 1976:** *People of the State of California v. Soon Ja Du,* p. 216, October 1, 1991.

70 **Soon Ja worked various:** Joel Anderson, Jayson De Leon, and Chau Tu, "No justice," in *Slow Burn: The L.A. Riots* (podcast), season 6, episode 2, Slate, February 5, 2022, https://slate.com/podcasts/slow-burn/s6/the-la-riots/e2/slow-burn-latasha-harlins-soon-ja-du-la-riots.

71 **"It was his":** Katz and Lee, "Bullet ends."

71 **"As a parent":** Katz and Lee, "Bullet ends."

71 **In 1990:** Katz and Lee, "Bullet ends."

71 **"I see it":** *People of the State of California v. Soon Ja Du,* p. 300, October 2, 1991.

71 **Rival gangs trafficking:** Edward T. Chang and Jeannette Diaz-Veizades,

Ethnic Peace in the American City: Building Community in Los Angeles and Beyond (New York: New York University Press, 1999), 16–17.

72 **In 1969:** Celeste Fremon, "Behind the Crips mythos," *Los Angeles Times*, November 20, 2007.

72 **"We started the Crips":** Greg Lefevre, "Death row inmate nominated for Nobel Peace Prize," CNN, December 4, 2000.

72 **Both gangs became involved:** Herbert C. Covey, *Crips and Bloods: A Guide to an American Subculture* (Santa Barbara, CA: Greenwood, 2015), 8–9, 132.

72 **In 1981, Williams was:** Lefevre, "Death row inmate"; and Leslie Fulbright, "Measure of a man's life: Questions of redemption, atonement and clemency swirl as Stanley Tookie Williams' execution date approaches," *San Francisco Gate*, December 4, 2005.

72 **By 1990, six hundred gangs:** Seth Mydans, "Life in girls' gang," *New York Times*, January 29, 1990.

72 **Korean American gangs:** Katherine Yungmee Kim, *Images of America: Los Angeles's Koreatown* (Charleston, SC: Arcadia Publishing, 2011), 93; and "Extradited Korean faces 271 years in U.S.," UPI, October 31, 2001.

73 **Main Street Crips:** *People of the State of California v. Soon Ja Du*, pp. 298, 300, October 2, 1991; and Anderson, De Leon, and Tu, "No justice."

73 **She longed to escape:** Katz and Lee, "Bullet ends."

73 **"We made every possible":** *People of the State of California v. Soon Ja Du*, pp. 224–25, October 1, 1991.

73 **Fearing for their safety:** Katz and Lee, "Bullet ends."

73 **Ten years earlier:** *People of the State of California v. Soon Ja Du*, p. 152, October 1, 1991; and Katz and Lee, "Bullet ends."

73 **"The gangsters had come":** *People of the State of California v. Soon Ja Du*, pp. 264–65, October 1, 1991.

73 **Meanwhile, the family:** Katz and Lee, "Bullet ends."

73 **When the store reopened:** *People of the State of California v. Soon Ja Du*, p. 322, October 2, 1991.

74 **But he advised her:** *People of the State of California v. Soon Ja Du*, pp. 350–51, October 2, 1991.

74 **But on Saturday:** *People of the State of California v. Soon Ja Du*, p. 323, October 2, 1991.

74 **Billy went to their van:** Andrea Ford and John H. Lee, "Slain girl was not stealing juice, police say," *Los Angeles Times*, March 19, 1991.

74 **Soon Ja was the only:** *People of the State of California v. Soon Ja Du*, p. 323, October 2, 1991.

74 **Around 9:45 a.m.:** *People of the State of California v. Soon Ja Du*, pp. 3–5, September 30, 1991.

74 **Lakeshia Combs:** *People of the State of California v. Soon Ja Du*, p. 27, September 30, 1991.

74 **Her brother, Ismail Ali:** *People of the State of California v. Soon Ja Du*, p. 3, September 30, 1991.

74   **Soon Ja went behind:** *People of the State of California v. Soon Ja Du,* p. 29, September 30, 1991.

75   **As Lakeshia paid:** *People of the State of California v. Soon Ja Du,* p. 30, September 30, 1991.

75   **"When I was working":** *People of the State of California v. Soon Ja Du,* pp. 326–27, October 2, 1991.

75   **"Please pay":** *People of the State of California v. Soon Ja Du,* pp. 327–28, 351, October 2, 1991.

75   **"She said, 'Bitch, are you'":** *People of the State of California v. Soon Ja Du,* pp. 32–34, September 30, 1991.

75   **Soon Ja denied:** *People of the State of California v. Soon Ja Du,* p. 329, October 2, 1991.

75   **Soon Ja tried to take:** *People of the State of California v. Soon Ja Du,* pp. 327–28, October 2, 1991.

75   **Soon Ja was two inches:** Njeri, *Last Plantation,* 157.

76   **she grabbed her sleeve:** *Clash of Colors: LA Riots of 1992,* produced, written, and directed by David D. Kim (Los Angeles: DDK Productions, 2012), YouTube, 2012, https://youtu.be/aOx7xYI9lBU; and *People of the State of California v. Soon Ja Du,* p. 328, October 2, 1991.

76   **"That's my orange juice!":** *People of the State of California v. Soon Ja Du,* p. 5, September 30, 1991.

76   **She had promised:** Stevenson, *Contested Murder,* 57.

76   **"Let me go!":** *People of the State of California v. Soon Ja Du,* p. 5, September 30, 1991.

76   **Soon Ja clutched:** Kim, *Clash of Colors.*

76   **"All of a sudden":** *People of the State of California v. Soon Ja Du,* p. 328, October 2, 1991.

76   **Tasha adjusted:** Kim, *Clash of Colors.*

76   **"After she hit me":** *People of the State of California v. Soon Ja Du,* p. 351, October 2, 1991.

77   **Soon Ja fumbled:** Kim, *Clash of Colors.*

77   **"And as she was walking":** *People of the State of California v. Soon Ja Du,* p. 6, September 30, 1991.

77   **her blue and gold:** *People of the State of California v. Soon Ja Du,* pp. 123–24, September 30, 1991; Stevenson, *Contested Murder,* 3; and Njeri, *Last Plantation,* 140.

77   **two crumpled dollar bills:** *People of the State of California v. Soon Ja Du,* p. 6, September 30, 1991; and Ford and Lee, "Slain girl."

77   **filled with her overnight items:** *People of the State of California v. Soon Ja Du,* pp. 111–12, September 30, 1991; and Stevenson, *Contested Murder,* 4.

77   **Tasha's notebook:** Dr. Christina Rogers and Shinese Harlins, interview with author, November 11, 2022.

77   **Billy Du woke up:** *People of the State of California v. Soon Ja Du,* pp. 231–32, October 1, 1991.

77 **"Where is she?":** *People of the State of California v. Soon Ja Du,* pp. 335–36, October 2, 1991.

77 **"We got a holdup!":** *People of the State of California v. Soon Ja Du,* pp. 233, 246, October 1, 1991.

78 **The first police officer:** *People of the State of California v. Soon Ja Du*, pp. 76, 96, 100, September 30, 1991.

78 **The paramedics arrived:** Ford and Lee, "Slain girl."

78 **Meanwhile, Billy remained:** *People of the State of California v. Soon Ja Du,* pp. 88–89, September 30, 1991.

Chapter 5: "Black Korea"

79 **On Saturday, March 23:** George Ramos and John H. Lee, "Demonstrators demand that Korean market never reopen," *Los Angeles Times,* March 22, 1991.

79 **a blush pink coffin:** Shinese Harlins and Dr. Christina Rogers, interview with author, October 2, 2022. All quotes from Shinese Harlins and Dr. Christina Rogers are from author interviews unless otherwise noted.

79 **"Another teenager":** "Letters to the *Times*: Slaying of Black in Korean market," *Los Angeles Times*, March 29, 1991.

80 **"My grandmother asked me":** Allison, *Love Song.*

80 **"I do remember being sad":** Rogers, interview with author, May 26, 2022.

80 **"I stopped going to":** Harlins, interview with author, May 23, 2022.

81 **Shinese's mother, Denise Harlins:** Penelope McMillan, "'I'll never quit': The slaying of Latasha Harlins impels her aunt on a crusade," *Los Angeles Times*, January 1, 1993.

81 **On Thursday, March 21:** Hon. Melvyn M. Dymally of California in the House of Representatives, "In loving memory of Sabriya Ihsan Bakewell," May 7, 1992, pp. 10828–29, https://www.govinfo.gov/content/pkg/GPO -CRECB-1992-pt8/pdf/GPO-CRECB-1992-pt8-5-3.pdf.

82 **"We are declaring":** Ramos and Lee, "Demonstrators demand."

82 **Closed for Murder:** Ramos and Lee, "Demonstrators demand."

82 **"It's a matter of who":** Edward Taehan Chang, interview with author, November 5, 2021. All quotes from Edward Taehan Chang are from author interviews unless otherwise noted.

82 **This group was created:** Sophia Kyung Kim, "Mass media, agitators fan violence against KA merchants," *Korea Times English Edition*, April 3, 1991.

83 **"godfather of South Central":** Gale Holland, "Larry Aubry, black activist icon and 'godfather of South Central Los Angeles,' dies," *Los Angeles Times,* May 20, 2020.

83 **"He was a conscience":** Steve Chiotakis, "Remembering LA black rights activist Larry Aubry" (podcast), KCRW, May 27, 2020, https://www.kcrw .com/news/shows/greater-la/us-federal-prison-systems-worst-covid-19 -outbreak/larry-aubry-south-la.

83 **BKA members held:** Sandy Banks, "Korean merchants, black customers—tensions grow," *Los Angeles Times*, April 15, 1985.

83 **They arranged diplomatic trips:** Min, *Caught in the Middle*, 135–39.

83 **"We, Korean American":** "Statement of Korean American community leaders on the death of Latasha Harlins," *Korea Times English Edition*, March 27, 1991.

84 *Los Angeles Times* **headline:** Andrea Ford and John H. Lee, "Racial tensions blamed in girl's death," *Los Angeles Times*, March 20, 1991.

84 **"See, the lede says":** Kim, *Clash of Colors*.

84 **Born Lee Kyung Won in 1928:** K. W. Lee, interview with author, December 21, 2021. All quotes from K. W. Lee are from author interviews unless otherwise noted.

85 **A spokesperson for the:** Sophia Kyung Kim, "The ethnic media's role in the L.A. riots," *Korea Times English Edition*, August 10, 1992.

85 **headlines across the country:** Examples include the *New York Times*, *Fort Worth Star-Telegram*, *Tampa Tribune*, and other sources.

85 **A Senseless and Tragic Killing:** Editorial Board, "A senseless and tragic killing," *Los Angeles Times*, March 20, 1991.

86 **Friction, Tempers Worsen:** "Friction, tempers worsen between Korean, Blacks in L.A.," *Tampa Tribune*, October 6, 1991.

86 **A Sad Tale:** Halford H. Fairchild, "A sad tale of persecuted minorities," *Los Angeles Times*, March 24, 1991.

86 **"media-fanned bogus":** Jake Stump, "Truth, justice and karma: The life of the godfather of Asian American journalism," *West Virginia University Magazine*, July 18, 2017.

86 **"When a Black gangster":** Kim, *Clash of Colors*.

86 **"middleman minority":** Park, *LA Rising*, 7–8.

87 **Korean American store owners reported:** "Merchant kills robber during hold-up attempt," *Los Angeles Times*, June 6, 1991; and "Molotov cocktail tossed onto boycotted store," *Los Angeles Times*, June 19, 1991.

87 **"You had a group":** Jenkins, *Burn, Motherf*cker, Burn!*

87 **"One day I came up":** Ford and Lee, "Racial tensions blamed."

87 **the 1990 year-long boycott:** Min, *Caught in the Middle*, 77–78.

87 **to picketing over accusations:** Marja Mills, "Racial lines erased inside church doors," *Chicago Tribune*, December 13, 1990.

88 **"There is consistent":** Seth Mydans, "Shooting puts focus on Korean-Black frictions in Los Angeles," *New York Times*, October 6, 1991.

88 **"I ain't tryin' to":** Ice Cube, "Black Korea," track 15 on *Death Certificate*, Lench Mob Records/Priority Records, October 29, 1991.

88 **"The song is meant":** Richard Harrington, "War of songs escalates," *Washington Post*, November 13, 1991.

88 **"Nobody is safe":** Kennedy, "Ice Cube reflects."

89 **"So an African American":** Anderson, De Leon, and Tu, "No justice."

89 **"The African American community"**: Eric Malnic, "Blacks vow to purchase Korean market," *Los Angeles Times*, March 28, 1991.

89 **That fall, a nine-year-old:** Hyungwon Kang, "Los Angeles: Home sweet home," *Reuters*, May 4, 2012; and author's informal discussion with Juri Kang, March 23, 2022.

89 **"Stand up once and for all":** Jesse Katz, "Girl shot in market holdup makes a 'miracle' recovery," *Los Angeles Times*, October 23, 1991.

89 **"We are here today":** Katz, "Girl shot."

90 **"reflects the kind of vicious":** "Violence Condemned," *Los Angeles Times*, October 24, 1991.

90 **"It's a miracle":** Katz, "Girl shot."

90 **"It's a terrible tragedy":** Jesse Katz, "Anguished father goes back to work: Crime—The Korean operator of a mini-mart in a Black area feared looting if he closed his store to be with his daughter, 9, critically shot by a robber," *Los Angeles Times*, October 21, 1991.

90 **"Brother Lee":** Sophia Kim, "Korean throws shindig in Watts: Shopkeeper thanks Black friends, neighbors for support," *Los Angeles Times*, November 19, 1982.

91 **He gave candy:** Sophia Kim, "Seeking a dialogue by Koreans, Blacks: Workshop aims for reduced tensions with an increase in understanding," *Los Angeles Times*, June 8, 1984.

91 **He hired Black employees:** Kim, "Seeking a dialogue."

91 **Because welfare checks:** Kim, "Korean throws shindig."

91 **"There are good people":** Kim, "Korean throws shindig."

91 **To celebrate the eighth anniversary:** Kim, "Korean throws shindig."

91 **"Pay me next time":** Don Terry, "A multiracial farewell to 'Mama,'" *New York Times*, February 12, 1999.

91 **Chung-Bok Hong:** C. M. Rhyu, "Dear Mama: Only after she was shot down in cold blood does our community know her name," *KoreAm Journal*, April 1999, https://edition.pagesuite.com/html5/reader/production/default .aspx?pubname=&edid=72b40a1b-f4e9-4d63-bdcf-40623618d930.

92 **"How's your brother's leg?":** Rhyu, "Dear Mama."

92 **Born in northern Korea:** Scott Martelle, "A portrait of loss," *Los Angeles Times*, February 21, 1999.

92 **Mama hit it off:** Rhyu, "Dear Mama."

92 **Wan Joon Kim ran:** Sam Quiñones, "Wan Joon Kim of Cycadelic Records helped gangsta rappers start," *Los Angeles Times*, July 28, 2012.

93 **Compton Fashion Center:** Quiñones, "Wan Joon Kim."

93 **It became one of the largest:** Sam Quiñones, "As a legend passes, a Walmart in Compton?" *NewsTaco*, January 12, 2015.

93 **"My dad saw an":** Karen Grigsby Bates, "Gangsta rap swap meet proprietor Wan Joon Kim has died," All Things Considered, NPR, March 14, 2013.

93   **"My father knew":** Kyoung Min Lee, "A Korean American has cultivated a 'mecca' for Black hip hop and continued its legacy for the last thirty years as the second generation," *Korea Daily*, August 19, 2015. Translated by Aerin Park, July 6, 2022.

93   **"Oh, I like this":** Bates, "Gangsta rap swap meet."

93   **"This music I don't":** Quiñones, "Wan Joon Kim."

93   **Wan Joon Kim was born:** Kirk Kim, interview with author, May 28, 2022; and Quiñones, "Wan Joon Kim." All quotes from Kirk Kim are from author interviews unless otherwise noted.

93   **His children suggested:** Quiñones, "Wan Joon Kim."

94   **Rap music had originated:** David Dye, "The birth of rap," NPR, February 22, 2007, https://www.npr.org/2007/02/22/7550286/the-birth-of-rap-a -look-back; and Westhoff, *Original Gangstas*, 21–22.

94   **"We're telling the real story":** Westhoff, *Original Gangstas*, 80.

94   **But many major music retailers:** Westhoff, *Original Gangstas*, 92.

94   **So Wan Joon Kim filled:** Kirk Kim, interview with author; and Quiñones, "Wan Joon Kim."

95   **Wan Joon Kim supported struggling:** Kirk Kim, interview with author; and Quiñones, "Wan Joon Kim."

96   **"He gave me my shot":** Quiñones, "Wan Joon Kim."

96   **Instead of getting angry:** Kyoung Min Lee, "Korean American has cultivated."

97   **sonamu, the red pine tree:** "Visual history of Korea: 'Sehando,' painting by a literati," *Korea Herald*, September 17, 2022.

97   **Soon Ja slumped:** Katz and Lee, "Bullet ends."

97   **Grandma Ruth, Aunt Denise:** Katz and Lee, "Bullet ends."

97   **the Dus' defense attorney:** Katz and Lee, "Bullet ends."

98   **"You can't use deadly force":** *Wet Sand: Voices from LA*, directed by Dai Sul Kim-Gibson (New York: Silence Broken Foundation, 2003), DVD.

Chapter 6: The People of the State of California v. Soon Ja Du

100   **"Buddha head":** Cannon, *Official Negligence*, 151; Sheryl Stolberg, "Karlin called independent, caring," *Los Angeles Times*, December 9, 1991; and Andrea Ford and Tracy Wilkinson, "Grocer convicted in slaying of teenager," *Los Angeles Times*, October 13, 1991.

100   **"I'm not going to talk":** Njeri, *Last Plantation,* 106; and Stevenson, *Contested Murder*, 60.

100   **"My mother is made":** Njeri, *Last Plantation*, 106; and Stevenson, *Contested Murder,* 151.

100   **Out of the 135:** Stevenson, *Contested Murder*, 138.

100   **"We can relate to":** Ford and Wilkinson, "Grocer convicted."

100   **The first day of the trial:** Andrea Ford, "Videotape shows teen being shot after fight," *Los Angeles Times*, October 1, 1991.

101   **"This is not television":** Ford, "Videotape shows teen."

101 **Jurors and spectators gasped:** Njeri, *Last Plantation*, 155.

101 **"That's me!":** *People of the State of California v. Soon Ja Du*, p. 10, September 30, 1991.

101 **Defense attorney Charles Lloyd:** Ford, "Videotape shows teen."

102 **On October 2:** *People of the State of California v. Soon Ja Du,* Soon Ja Du witness testimony, pp. 155 and various pages, October 2, 1991.

102 **"When you grabbed":** *People of the State of California v. Soon Ja Du,* pp. 334–35, October 2, 1991.

102 **Carvajal handed the gun:** *People of the State of California v. Soon Ja Du,* pp. 343–45, October 2, 1991.

102 **The store owner testified:** *People of the State of California v. Soon Ja Du,* pp. 378–79, October 2, 1991.

103 **"Do the People rest?":** *People of the State of California v. Soon Ja Du*, p. 383, October 2, 1991.

103 **Karlin believed Soon Ja Du:** Associated Press, "Judge reduces charge against Korean merchant," *Californian*, October 4, 1991.

104 **"Deliberation and premeditation":** Andrea Ford, "1st degree murder ruled out in grocer trial," *Los Angeles Times*, October 4, 1991.

104 **The Harlins family denounced:** Ford, "1st degree murder."

104 **"It's the kind of thing":** Ford, "1st degree murder."

104 **On October 7, 1991:** Associated Press, "Korean shopkeeper's killing of Black teen goes to L.A. jury," *Sacramento Bee*, October 8, 1991.

104 **"She doesn't know how":** Andrea Ford, "Closing arguments presented in grocer's trial for shooting," *Los Angeles Times*, October 8, 1991.

104 **"You have to consider":** Ford, "Closing arguments."

105 **But instead of being guilty:** "Penal Code 192 PC—Voluntary Manslaughter—California Law," *Shouse California Law Group*, 2022, https://www.shouselaw.com/ca/defense/penal-code/192/; and "Imperfect self-defense in criminal law cases," *Justia*, October 2022, https://www.justia.com/criminal/defenses/imperfect-self-defense/.

105 **Soon Ja Du lowered her head:** Ford and Wilkinson, "Grocer convicted."

105 **"She got away":** Ford and Wilkinson, "Grocer convicted."

105 **Several security guards:** Ford and Wilkinson, "Grocer convicted."

105 **"There's no victory":** Ford and Wilkinson, "Grocer convicted."

106 **They placed a giant poster:** Ford and Wilkinson, "Grocer convicted."

106 **Prosecutor Roxane Carvajal:** Richard Reyes Fruto, "Soon Ja Du sentencing: Outcry over no jail term," *Korea Times English Edition*, November 25, 1991.

106 **"If Mrs. Du is not":** *People of the State of California v. Soon Ja Du*, p. 16, November 15, 1991.

106 **"This is not a time":** People of the State of California v. Soon Ja Du, pp. 37–38, November 15, 1991.

106 **a "beautiful 15-year-old":** *People of the State of California v. Soon Ja Du*, pp. 19, 24, November 15, 1991.

107   **"People have tried to"**: *People of the State of California v. Soon Ja Du,* p. 5, November 15, 1991.

107   **He said in his twenty-nine-year career:** *People of the State of California v. Soon Ja Du,* pp. 4–5, November 15, 1991.

107   **"I feel like I am suffering"**: Cannon, *Official Negligence,* 164–65; and *People of the State of California v. Soon Ja Du,* pp. 10, 33, November 15, 1991.

107   **Although Carvajal acknowledged:** *People of the State of California v. Soon Ja Du,* p. 27, November 15, 1991.

107   **"Any other sentence"**: *People of the State of California v. Soon Ja Du,* p. 32, November 15, 1991.

108   **"My family and I"**: *People of the State of California v. Soon Ja Du,* pp. 35–36, November 15, 1991.

108   **"I would be very disappointed"**: *People of the State of California v. Soon Ja Du,* p. 36, November 15, 1991.

108   **"There's never been any"**: Sam Stanton, "Killing, trial add to bitterness in L.A. area," *Sacramento Bee,* November 11, 1991.

108   **She accused supporters:** *People of the State of California v. Soon Ja Du,* p. 37, November 15, 1991.

109   **"Although Latasha Harlins"**: *People of the State of California v. Soon Ja Du,* pp. 40–41, November 15, 1991.

109   **Although Judge Karlin:** *People of the State of California v. Soon Ja Du,* pp. 39–40, November 15, 1991.

109   **"It is my opinion"**: *People of the State of California v. Soon Ja Du,* pp. 42–43, November 15, 1991.

109   **The judge then sentenced:** *People of the State of California v. Soon Ja Du,* p. 44, November 15, 1991.

109   **"Is the defendant"**: *People of the State of California v. Soon Ja Du,* pp. 38–39, November 15, 1991.

109   **Judge Karlin then addressed:** *People of the State of California v. Soon Ja Du,* p. 45, November 15, 1991.

110   **"Murderer!"**: Tracy Wilkinson and Frank Clifford, "Korean grocer who killed Black teen gets probation," *Los Angeles Times,* November 16, 1991.

110   **"Thank you, God"**: Wilkinson and Clifford, "Korean grocer."

110   **"I was stunned"**: Najee Ali, interview with author, June 8, 2022. All quotes from Najee Ali are from author interviews unless otherwise noted.

111   **"I think it was an injustice"**: "Footage throughout the Rodney King trial and subsequent 1992 LA Riots," NBCLA, April 29, 2020, https://youtu .be/sl8fFV5LNUY.

111   **"I'm not mad"**: Wilkinson and Clifford, "Korean grocer."

111   **Danny Bakewell and:** Gerald Faris and Ashley Dunn, "Anti-Karlin protesters enter courthouse," *Los Angeles Times,* December 13, 1991; and "Footage throughout the Rodney King trial," NBCLA.

111   **"I don't believe"**: Fruto, "Soon Ja Du sentencing."

112   **"It's going to make"**: Fruto, "Soon Ja Du sentencing."

112 **"At one point":** Kim-Gibson, *Wet Sand*.

112 **In a searing editorial:** K. W. Lee, "An American passage: Latasha becomes part of our collective conscience," *Korea Times English Edition*, November 25, 1991.

113 **"I think Koreans":** Kay Hwangbo, "Fifth grocery store firebombed in 6 months in South Central," *Korea Times English Edition*, December 9, 1991.

Chapter 7: The People of the State of California v. Laurence Powell, Timothy E. Wind, Theodore Briseno, and Stacey Koon

116 **"I just thought the whole thing":** "Peers 'out of control' in beating of motorist, L.A. officer testifies," *Washington Post*, April 4, 1992.

117 **Defense attorneys believed:** Andrea Ford and Daryl Kelley, "King case to be tried in Ventura County," *Los Angeles Times,* November 27, 1991.

117 **So the trial was moved:** Ford and Kelley, "King case to be tried."

117 **Only 2 percent:** Jane Gross, "In Simi Valley, Defense of a Shared Way of Life," *New York Times*, May 4, 1992.

117 **And Simi Valley:** Jim Newton, "ACLU says 83% of police live outside L.A.," *Los Angeles Times*, March 29, 1994.

117 **The jury was mostly white:** Professor Douglas O. Linder, "LAPD (King Beating) Trials (1992–1993)," Famous Trials, 1995–2022, https://www.famous-trials.com/lapd; and "The LAPD Officers' Trials: A Chronology," University of Missouri, Kansas City, Law School, http://law2.umkc.edu/faculty/projects/ftrials/lapd/kingchronology.html.

117 **In 2012, one of the:** Melia Patria and Enjoli Francis, " 'Let it fall': Rodney King juror in his own words," ABC News, April 28, 2017, https://abcnews.go.com/Entertainment/fall-rodney-king-juror-words/story?id=46712060.

117 **Dozens of sheriff's deputies:** Richard A. Serrano, "2 views of King drawn by lawyers," *Los Angeles Times*, March 6, 1992.

117 **Was this a case:** Kim, *Clash of Colors*.

117 **"Whatever Rodney King was":** Serrano, "2 views."

118 **"You have a videotape":** Associated Press, "Prosecutor: Without videotape, Rodney King would be on trial," *St. Joseph News Press*, April 21, 2022.

119 **"I was as (repulsed)":** Eric Malnic, "Foreman in Simi Valley trial says riots, 'national hate' stressed jury," *Los Angeles Times*, March 9, 1993.

119 **"What it shows is":** Kim, *Clash of Colors*.

119 **George Holliday was the first:** Associated Press, "Patrol officer testifies in King assault trial," *Marion Star* (Marion, OH), March 7, 1992.

119 **Because Holliday missed:** Clay Risen, "George Holliday, who taped police beating of Rodney King, dies at 61," *New York Times*, September 22, 2021.

119 **Once the video:** Linder, "LAPD (King Beating) Trials."

120 **"I was completely":** Associated Press, "Officer 'feared for his life' in King beating," *San Bernardino County Sun*, April 1, 1992.

120 **In his testimony:** Christine Pelisek, "Stacey Koon's disturbing testimony," *Daily Beast,* April 28, 2012.

120 **The four LAPD police:** Deirdre Edgar, "Latino, and white too," *Los Angeles Times*, April 23, 2010; and Lou Cannon, "One stop on policeman's beat sent officer's life off course," *Washington Post*, February 28, 1993.

121 **One officer compared:** Richard A. Serrano, "Staggering King scared him, officer says," *Los Angeles Times,* March 11, 1992.

121 **"Oops, I haven't beaten":** Richard A. Serrano, "Police joked about King, nurses say," *Los Angeles Times*, March 14, 1992.

121 **One nurse said:** Serrano, "Police joked."

121 **"It was right out of":** Tracy Wood and Sheryl Stolberg, "Patrol car log in beating is released," *Los Angeles Times*, March 19, 1991.

121 **"bigoted remarks":** Wood and Stolberg, "Patrol car."

122 **Officer Powell testified:** Associated Press, "Officer 'feared for his life."

122 **"At any time":** Cannon, *Official Negligence*, 224.

123 **In his closing arguments:** Richard A. Serrano, "Jury told video proves case against officers," *Los Angeles Times*, April 21, 1992.

123 **"When you make a decision":** Richard A. Serrano, "Tape is not the full story, jurors are told," *Los Angeles Times*, April 22, 1992.

124 **Like prosecutor Terry White:** Serrano, "Tape is not."

124 **Attorney John Barnett:** Richard A. Serrano, "Courtroom tensions high as King case goes to jury," *Los Angeles Times*, April 23, 1992.

124 **"Sgt. Koon was making":** Serrano, "Courtroom tensions."

125 **"All Tim Wind did":** Serrano, "Courtroom tensions."

125 **On April 22:** Serrano, "Courtroom tensions."

125 **White saved his harshest:** Cannon, *Official Negligence*, 250.

126 **"Those jurors needed":** King and Spagnola, *Riot Within*, 60.

126 **"Reach a just verdict":** Cannon, *Official Negligence*, 250–51.

126 **The jurors were sequestered:** Associated Press, "Jurors retire after 5th day of deliberations," *San Bernardino County Sun*, April 28, 1992; and Richard Serrano and Tracy Wilkinson, "All 4 in King beating acquitted," *Los Angeles Times*, April 30, 1992.

127 **Public-opinion polls:** Cannon, *Official Negligence*, 251.

127 **The church, founded in 1872:** First AME Church official website, https://www.famechurchla.org/ministries/.

127 **"faith in action":** "Reverend Cecil L. 'Chip' Murray, biography," History Makers, https://www.thehistorymakers.org/biography/reverend-cecil-l-chip-murray; and Cora Jackson-Fossett, "Community pays tribute to Rev. Dr. Cecil Murray on his 90th birthday," *Los Angeles Sentinel*, October 2, 2019.

127 **"Be cool":** Sheryl Stolberg, "Leaders appeal for calm after King verdict," *Los Angeles Times*, April 27, 1992.

127 **"We should not repeat":** Shawn Hubler, "Black leaders accuse Gates of inflaming racial tensions," *Los Angeles Times*, April 29, 1992.

128 **"We're not going to overreact":** Hubler, "Black leaders."

128 **"Do what you have to do":** Associated Press, "After the riots: A juror describes the ordeal of deliberations," *New York Times*, May 6, 1992.

128 **CHP Officers Melanie:** Richard A. Serrano, "CHP Officer describes chase, beating of King," *Los Angeles Times*, March 7, 1992; and Richard A. Serrano, "CHP officer's testimony, memo on beating differ," *Los Angeles Times*, March 10, 1992.

128 **"We could not prove":** Malnic, "Foreman."

129 **"a vague, nagging feeling":** Malnic, "Foreman."

129 **"You cannot convict a man":** Malnic, "Foreman."

129 **the jury finally agreed:** Associated Press, "After the riots."

129 **"It was highly":** Paul Lieberman and Stuart Silverstein, "Jurors rattled by aftermath; defend verdicts," *Los Angeles Times*, May 1, 1992.

129 **"We the jury":** "L.A. officer to be retried in beating," *Tampa Bay Tribune*, May 16, 1992.

130 **"Ladies and gentlemen":** "7 key moments from 1992 L.A. riots," ABC 7 News, April 28, 2017, https://abc7.com/los-angeles-riots-la-1992-rodney - king/1921781/.

Chapter 8: Flashpoint—Florence and Normandie

131 **Strangers called their homes:** Voss, "Rodney King's daughters."

132 **"King's reaction was":** Cannon, *Official Negligence*, 261.

133 **"I just wanted to close":** King and Spagnola, *Riot Within*, 60.

133 **"Today, the jury":** Lou Cannon, "Worlds collide at Florence and Normandie," *Washington Post*, January 26, 1998.

134 **Reverend Dr. Cecil Murray:** Daniel Lindsay and T. J. Martin, "LA 92," *National Geographic*, 2017, https://youtu.be/uaotkHlHJwo.

134 **"If something in you":** Amy Wallace and David Ferrell, "Verdicts greeted with outrage and disbelief," *Los Angeles Times*, April 30, 1992.

134 **"Now I can breathe":** Héctor Tobar and Leslie Berger, "Verdict greeted with relief and elation among LAPD officers," *Los Angeles Times*, April 30, 1992.

135 **Neighbors had nicknamed:** Whitman, "Untold story"; and Cannon, "Worlds collide."

135 **"Man, you should be":** Paul Taylor, "Tape shows L.A. police abandoning area where riot began," *Washington Post*, May 6, 1992.

135 **"It got ugly":** Cannon, *Official Negligence*, 283.

136 **"All of a sudden":** John Blackstone, "Two brothers recall LA riots 20 years later," CBS News, April 27, 2012; and CBS This Morning, "20 years after LA riots, brothers reflect," https://youtu.be/9OcesHkaAiI?si=aj5pSAGS EmaseXQt.

136 **"Be cool, it's not":** Penelope McMillan, "Riot aftermath: After first moments, cameraman lost empathy with rioters," *Los Angeles Times*, May 6, 1992.

136 **"I might as well":** Blackstone, "Two brothers recall"; and CBS This Morning, "20 years after LA riots."

137 **But after high school:** Blackstone, "Two brothers recall."

137 **Goldman had moved:** McMillan, "Riot aftermath."

137 **"I didn't know it would":** McMillan, "Riot aftermath."

137 **there were only:** Cannon, *Official Negligence*, 265.

137 **In a city of over:** "Historical general population: City and County of Los Angeles, 1850 to 2020," *Los Angeles Almanac since 1998*, https://www.laalmanac.com/population/po02.php.

137 **Barely two-and-a-half hours:** Cannon, *Official Negligence*, 286.

138 **"When I heard":** Hyungwon Kang, interview with author, October 1, 2023.

138 **"Anarchy was occurring":** Whitman, "Untold story."

138 **"The officers were being":** Cannon, *Official Negligence*, 287.

139 **"We could have a massacre":** Cannon, *Official Negligence*, 287.

139 **"I want everybody out":** Cannon, *Official Negligence*, 287.

139 **"Bullshit":** Whitman, "Untold story."

139 **"Everybody out of here":** Lindsay and Martin, "LA 92."

139 **"There was no correct":** Associated Press, "Mike Moulin, key police figure during L.A. riots, dies at 70," *Los Angeles Times*, August 5, 2019.

139 **Meanwhile, Police Chief Daryl F. Gates:** Lou Cannon, "When thin blue line retreated, L.A. riot went out of control," *Washington Post,* May 10, 1992.

139 **"There are going to be":** Cannon, "When thin blue line."

139 **Back at Florence:** Paul Taylor, "Tape shows L.A. police abandoning area where riot began," *Washington Post*, May 6, 1992.

140 **One of their gas station's:** Allan Lengel, "A rose with another name: Crack pipe," *Washington Post*, April 5, 2006.

140 **Carol later learned:** Carol K. Park, interview with author, November 22, 2021. All quotes from Carol K. Park are from author interviews unless otherwise noted.

140 **Life was dangerous:** Park, interview with author, January 8, 2022.

141 **"She ate like nothing":** Park, interview with author, January 8, 2022; and Carol Park, *Memoir of a Cashier: Korean Americans, Racism, and Riots* (Riverside, CA: Young Oak Kim Center for Korean American Studies, 2017), 68, 72.

141 **"It was mass chaos":** Voss, "Rodney King's daughters."

142 **Wade told Swerdlow:** Yael Swerdlow, interview with author, October 1, 2023.

142 **"That's when I realized":** Sandhya Dirks, "The L.A. riots, 30 years later," NPR, April 29, 2022.

142 **"I heard that":** Hyungwon Kang, interview with author, January 22, 2022, and February 9, 2023. All quotes from Hyungwon Kang are from author interviews unless otherwise noted.

143 **"He lay there defenseless":** Kirk McKoy and Brian Chan, "Photographer Kirk McKoy recounts covering the 1992 Los Angeles riots," Vimeo, 2014, https://vimeo.com/107280146.

143 **Earlier, Timothy Goldman:** Cannon, *Official Negligence*, 288; Ford, *Uprising*; Whitman, "Untold story"; and John Rogers, "How the L.A. riots changed those who were caught in them," *Las Vegas Review-Journal*, April 29, 2017.

144 **Another family rescued:** Jim Dwyer, "He will not forget: Hands that saved him were black," *Newsday*, May 1, 1992; and James Rainey, "Freelance reporter shot four times but family in South L.A. saves him," *Los Angeles Times*, May 1, 1992.

144 **"It definitely protected me":** Kirk McKoy, interview with author, December 7, 2022. All quotes from Kirk McKoy are from author interviews unless otherwise noted.

145 **Around 6:00 p.m.:** Nita Lelyveld, "Caught up in a violence of L.A. riots, victim has lasting empathy," *Los Angeles Times*, April 30, 2021.

146 **"I'm an Asian face":** Jason McGaham, "25 years after the riots: A photographer recounts a dangerous day on the job," *L.A. Weekly*, March 23, 2017.

146 **"If you were just going":** Lelyveld, "Caught up."

147 **While Fujii recovered:** Rhiannon Walker, "When the Dodgers, Lakers and Clippers postponed their games because of the Rodney King riots," *Andscape*, May 2, 2018.

147 **Ten minutes after Fujii's attack:** Cannon, *Official Negligence*, 304.

147 **Just a month away:** Jim Newton, "Denny suspects are thugs to some, heroes to others," *Los Angeles Times*, May 25, 1992.

147 **recovered from substance use:** Edward J. Boyer, "Defendant in Denny case gets probation," *Los Angeles Times*, November 10, 1993.

147 **Around age twelve:** Newton, "Denny suspects."

147 **Before Denny could react:** Newton, "Denny suspects."

148 **"I'm not your typical":** Madison Gray, "The L.A. riots: 15 years after Rodney King—Rodney King," *Time*, April 2007.

148 **"It was rage":** Gray, "L.A. riots: Rodney King."

148 **While Denny struggled:** Fatima Curry and Enjoli Francis, " 'Let it fall': 'L.A. Four' members speak about life lessons, 25 years after riots," ABC News, April 28, 2017.

149 **Just ten minutes before:** Jesse Singal, "The L.A. riots: 15 years after Rodney King—Damian Williams," *Time*, April 2007.

149 **After Williams struck:** Cannon, "Worlds collide."

149 **Gary Williams . . . rummaged:** Newton, "Denny suspects."

150 **"That is enough":** Stephanie Chavez, "A rescuer's tale: Fight, then flight," *Los Angeles Times,* April 22, 2022.

150 **Yuille, Murphy, and Barnett:** Carla Hall, "Rescue makes strangers friends," *Los Angeles Times*, October 20, 1993; and Chavez, "A rescuer's tale."

150 **The closest hospital:** Cannon, *Official Negligence*, 309.

150 **Bobby Green was:** Chavez, "A rescuer's tale."

151 **"Blood was shooting":** Dave Gardena, "20 years after: The good Samaritan—Titus Murphy was changed forever by the riots," *Los Angeles Magazine*, April 1, 2012; and Cannon, *Official Negligence*, 309.

151 **"if we had been":** Staff, "The Good Samaritan: Titus Murphy saved Reginald Denny from the worst riot in this century," *Black History Magazine*, March 16, 2013.

151 **Doctors immediately performed:** Gray, "L.A. riots: Rodney King."

151 **Green knew exactly:** Chavez, "A rescuer's tale."

152 **Around 6:30 p.m.:** Cannon, *Official Negligence*, 314.

152 **The crowd chanted:** "Rodney King riots in Los Angeles: Live KABC reports from 25 years ago," ABC News, 2017, https://youtu.be/bSeCpFCS32M; and Wallace and Ferrell, "Verdicts greeted."

152 **Protesters rushed toward:** Cannon, *Official Negligence*, 314.

153 **"As you can see right now":** ABC News, "Rodney King riots."

153 **James Henry, a supervisor:** Robin Greene, "Riot victim pushes for monument to good samaritans," *Los Angeles Times*, May 26, 1993.

154 **The thirty-six-year-old:** Patrick Healy, "GregAlan Williams tried to be 'voice of reason' in riots," NBC News Los Angeles, April 29, 2012.

154 *Los Angeles Times* **reporter:** John L. Mitchell, "Understanding the riots—six months later," *Los Angeles Times*, November 19, 1992.

155 **"Kill him, and you":** Steve Lopez, "The forgotten victim from Florence and Normandie," *Los Angeles Times*, May 6, 2012.

155 **"Last year, this good man":** Sonia Nazario, "Mourners say farewell to one of riots' heroes," *Los Angeles Times*, May 2, 1993.

156 **several demonstrators stopped:** Lopez, "The forgotten."

156 **Someone had set:** Patt Morrison, "Symbol of pain survives flames," *Los Angeles Times*, May 7, 1992.

156 **"I remember her going":** Dirks, "L.A. riots, 30 years."

157 **At 11:00 p.m., Mayor Tom Bradley:** Marc Lacey and Shawn Hubler, "Riots set fires, loot stores; 4 reported dead," *Los Angeles Times*, April 30, 1992.

Chapter 9: 화 Hwa

159 **"Nobody showed up":** Seth Mydans, "Riot in Los Angeles: Pocket of tension, a target of rioters, Koreatown is bitter, armed and determined," *New York Times*, May 3, 1992.

160 **"If any urgent news":** Richard Choi, "Legacy project: SaIGu LA riots," YouTube, April 24, 2017, https://youtu.be/Cuzh0_UxxD8.

160 **"Ladies and gentlemen":** Choi, "Legacy project"; and Jin Ho Lee, interview with author, January 28, 2022. All quotes from Jin Ho Lee are from author interviews unless otherwise noted.

161 **On the morning of:** Kye Hong Ko, "After I met the parents of Jae Song," *Chronicles of Koreatown*, 32–33.

161 **"He sat there":** Norris, Thomas-Lester, and Von Drehle, "Sad roll call."

161 **"Everything we have worked for":** Kim-Gibson, *Sa I Gu.*

162 **"Since childhood":** Melia Patria and Enjoli Francis, "'Let it fall': Jung Hui Lee, whose son was killed during the LA uprising, in her own words," *Los Angeles Times*, April 28, 2017.

162 **"I pleaded with him":** Kim-Gibson, *Sa I Gu.*

162 **Shortly after the not-guilty:** Han Sung Chang, "Legacy project: SaIGu LA riots," YouTube, April 27, 2017, https://www.youtube.com/watch?v=TPtOP8g-OaA.

162 **"Let's protect Koreatown!":** Chang, "Legacy project."

162 **Many of them belonged:** Jenkins, *Burn Motherf*cker, Burn!*

162 **"The young kids":** Jenkins, *Burn Motherf*cker, Burn!*

163 **The Korean Young Adult Team:** Chang, "Legacy project."

163 **"All this was being looted":** Anthony Bourdain, "Exploring Koreatown in Los Angeles," *Parts Unknown* (transcript), April 21, 2013, https://transcripts.cnn.com/show/abpu/date/2013-04-21/segment/01.

164 **"A lot of people":** Jong Min Kang, "In their own words: 'My brother's business burned,'" *Los Angeles Times*, April 28, 2002.

164 **At 3:47 a.m.:** Bénédicte Dousset, Pierre Flament, and Robert Bernstein, "Los Angeles fires seen from space," *Eos* 74:3 (January 19, 1993), 33; and Min Young Song, *Strange Future: Pessimism and the 1992 Los Angeles Riots* (Durham, NC: Duke University Press, 2005), 27.

164 **Bus service was canceled:** Los Angeles Times Staff, "The L.A. Riots: 25 years later," *Los Angeles Times*, April 26, 2017.

164 **On April 29:** Douglas Shur, interview with author, May 8 and September 22, 2022. All quotes from Douglas Shur are from author interviews unless otherwise noted.

165 **Like Douglas Shur:** Ben Lee, interview with author, May 8 and September 29, 2022. All quotes from Ben Lee are from author interviews unless otherwise noted.

167 **The Dodgers would lose:** Benjamin Oreskes, "Former Dodgers officials recall the night in 1992 when riots erupted in Los Angeles," *Los Angeles Times*, April 29, 2017.

167 **"Do you want":** Blake Chow, "Legacy project: SaIGu LA riots," YouTube, April 20, 2017, https://youtu.be/m6_3oACB_-4.

167 **"This is what doomsday":** Chow, "Legacy project."

168 **"Around noon":** Chow, "Legacy project."

168 **When Chow started working:** Blake Chow, interview with author, January 26, 2022. All quotes from Blake Chow are from author interviews unless otherwise noted.

170 **"I think the worst thing":** Chow, interview with author.

171 **"All the Koreans":** Howard Choy, interview with author, May 10, 2022. All quotes from Howard Choy are from author interviews unless otherwise noted.

172 **"We're going to get"**: Emile Mack, interview with author, February 9, 2022. All quotes from Emile Mack are from author interviews unless otherwise noted.

172 **"Here you had"**: "Bridging the divide: Tom Bradley and the politics of race," KCET: PBS, February 1, 2016, https://www.ket.org/program/ bridging-the-divide-tom-bradley-and-the-politics-of-race-15187/bradley -s-la-becomes-polarized-and-erupts-into-civil-unrest/.

174 **"My two cultures"**: Interview with Emile Mack, *Nightline*, April 28, 2017, https://www.facebook.com/watch/?v=10155244527372801.

176 **"Okay, I guess I'm not going to be a doctor"**: Mack, interview with author.

176 **RADIO KOREA HOST:** Live call recordings, Radio Korea, April–May 1992, provided by Jin Ho Lee of Radio Korea, January 28, 2022, transcribed in Korean and translated in English by Aerin Park.

177 **In February 1989:** 2022 RadioKorea.com Media Kit, Radio Korea Media, Los Angeles, https://rk-asset.s3.us-west-2.amazonaws.com/ pdf/2022_Mediakit.pdf.

177 **"Every other month"**: Jin Ho Lee, interview with author; and Jin Ho Lee, "Legacy project: SaIGu LA riots," YouTube, April 19, 2017, https://youtu .be/bCyMFbay4wo.

177 **"The police weren't"**: Jin Ho Lee, interview with author.

178 **Over seventy-two hours:** Jin Ho Lee, interview with author.

179 **The Pacific Bell company:** Choi, "Legacy project."

179 **Radio Korea also set:** Choi, "Legacy project."

179 **"My brother and I"**: Live call recordings, Radio Korea, April–May 1992.

179 **"A community radio station"**: Lee, "Legacy project."

179 **"I don't see any police"**: Michael Martin, "Korean store owner on arming himself for riots," *Tell Me More*, NPR, April 27, 2012.

180 **"I was standing"**: Martin, "Korean store owner."

180 **It took six hours:** Jim Crogan, "The fire last time: The L.A. 53," *Los Angeles Weekly*, April 26, 2002, https://www.lafire.com/famous_fires/1992 -0429_LA-Riots/LAWEEKLY-2002-0426/2002-0426_laweekly_ TheLA53_Crogan.htm.

180 **"It's very painful"**: Josie Huang, "30 years ago, he talked Koreatown through the unrest of '92," *LAist,* April 29, 2022; and Martin, "Korean store owner."

180 **"The police have abandoned"**: Choi, "Legacy project."

182 **The radio reporter:** Song, *Strange Future*, 162.

182 **Jung Hui told her son:** "Haengjuchima," *Encyclopedia of Korean Folk Culture*, https://folkency.nfm.go.kr/en/topic/detail/7257.

182 **"How can you sit"**: Kim-Gibson, *Sa I Gu.*

182 **"You cannot go"**: Jung Hui Lee, "Personal essay of a mother of Jae Song Lee who was shot and killed while defending Koreatown during L.A. riot," *Chronicles of Koreatown*, 123.

182   **"He wanted to help"**: Steve Lopez, "Slain Korean youth just wanted to defend his own," *Philadelphia Inquirer,* May 3, 1992.

182   **"They were breaking"**: Ashley Dunn, "The riot's enduring wounds," *Los Angeles Times*, August 18, 1992.

183   **"Do not go"**: Jung Hui Lee, "Personal essay of a mother of Jae Song Lee," 123.

183   **"This isn't fair"**: *Let It Fall: Los Angeles 1982–1992*, directed by John Ridley (Los Angeles: ABC Studios, 2017).

183   **On Thursday, April 30:** Mydans, "Pocket of tension."

184   **"Pack up some guns"**: David Joo, interview with author, September 28, 2022. All quotes from David Joo are from author interviews unless otherwise noted.

185   **"Just a few minutes"**: "Korean store owners defend their property with firearms during Rodney King riots," YouTube, April 26, 2015, https://www.youtube.com/watch?v=Py4AMYebHGI; and One9 and Erik Parker, *L.A. Burning: The Riots 25 Years Later,* 2017.

185   **"The mainstream media depicted"**: Peter Pak, interview with author, January 28, 2022. All quotes from Peter Pak are from author interviews unless otherwise noted.

185   **"They were standing up"**: Andy Campbell and Matt Ferner, "What photographers of the LA riots really saw behind the lens," *Huffington Post*, April 28, 2017.

185   **"They said they were fed up"**: "Korean store owners defend."

186   **"I want to make it clear"**: Mydans, "Pocket of tension."

186   **"I love this country"**: Mydans, "Pocket of tension."

187   **"When law and order"**: Vin Suprynowicz, "Commentary: Media picky when it comes to covering gun stories," *Daily Press* (Victorville, CA), July 30, 1995; and David Joo testimony, "Gun Laws Part 1," C-SPAN, March 31, 1995, https://www.c-span.org/video/?64298-1/gun-laws-part-1.

188   **"I was ready"**: Karen Koh Gersten and Soo Myung Koh, interview with author, June 11, 2021. All quotes from Karen Koh Gersten and Soo Myung Koh are from author interviews unless otherwise noted.

188   **John Denver's "Country Roads"**: Bill Danoff, Taffy Nivert, and John Denver, "Country Roads," side 2, track 1, *Poems, Prayers and Promises* (New York: RCA Records, 1971).

191   **As night fell:** Norris, Thomas-Lester, and Von Drehle, "Sad roll call."

191   **"the superheroes"**: "Korean Young Adult Team of L.A.," *Chronicles of Koreatown,* 105.

192   **Police later described:** Norris, Thomas-Lester, and Von Drehle, "Sad roll call."

192   **"There was a lot"**: Richard Reyes Fruto, "Mistaken identity cause in Edward Lee death," *Korea Times English Edition*, May 18, 1992.

193   **"James, start the car!"**: John Kim, interview with author, August 20, 2021. All quotes from John Kim are from author interviews unless otherwise noted.

193   **The police joined:** Fruto, "Mistaken identity."

193   **"Eddie was alive":** Dunn, "The riot's enduring wounds."

193   **Police confiscated about:** Richard Reyes Fruto, "KA fatality during four-day riot: Community mourns for Edward Lee," *Korea Times English Edition*, May 11, 1992.

194   **"He was alive":** K. W. Lee, "In death, Eddie Lee left an undying legacy," *Korea Times English Edition*, March 29, 2001.

195   **"You're going to be okay":** Lopez, "Slain Korean."

195   **Their driver told:** "Photojournalist gives first-hand account of photographing the '92 LA riots," PetaPixel, July 3, 2013, https://petapixel.com/2013/07/03/photojournalist-gives-first-hand-account-of-photographing-the-92-la-riots/.

195   **"Eddie Lee was already":** Hyungwon Kang, "Korean American photojournalist describes living through LA riots," ABC News, April 26, 2017, https://abcnews.go.com/Nightline/video/korean-american-photojournalist-describes-living-la-riots-horrific-47033939; and Gracie Zheng, "L.A. riots: Former *L.A. Times* photojournalist remembers Koreatown," Annenberg Media Center, April 20, 2012, http://www.neontommy.com/news/2012/04/la-riots-former-la-times-photojournalist-remembers-covering-koreatown.html.

195   **At 10:30 p.m.:** Lopez, "Slain Korean."

196   **"He was not shot":** Fruto, "KA fatality."

196   **The district attorney's office:** Fruto, "Mistaken identity."

197   **"According to our source":** Ridley, *Let It Fall*.

197   **"Mom, something has":** Kim-Gibson, *Sa I Gu*.

197   **"My heart was beating":** Jung Hui Lee, "Reflection on the death of my beloved son," *Chronicles of Koreatown*, 121.

197   **Jung Hui called:** Jung Hui Lee, "Reflection on the death of my beloved son," 123.

197   **"This couldn't be":** Kim-Gibson, *Sa I Gu*.

198   **"You've got to say":** Anderson, De Leon, and Tu, "The tape."

198   **"I felt very sorry":** King and Spagnola, *Riot Within*, 79.

198   **President George H. W. Bush:** President George H. W. Bush, "Address to the nation on the civil disturbances in Los Angeles, California," *Public Papers of the Presidents of the United States: George H. W. Bush* (1992, Book 1), May 1, 1992, 685–87.

198   **Instead, the L.A. civil unrest:** Cannon, *Official Negligence*, 349.

198   **"I could barely breathe":** King and Spagnola, *Riot Within*, 80–81.

198   **At 2:45 p.m.:** *LA Times* Staff, "The L.A. riots."

199   **"I was going to speak":** King and Spagnola, *Riot Within*, 81.

199   **"People, I just want to say":** "Rodney G. King's Statement," *Washington Post*, May 1, 1992.

200   **"I was holding the last":** Jung Hui Lee, "Reflection on the death of my beloved son," 123.

200 **"I cried out aloud"**: Jung Hui Lee, "Reflection on the death of my beloved son," 123; and autopsy report from the Los Angeles County Department of Medical Examiner, May 1, 1992.

200 **"Slain sentry"**: "Arms, and the Agony," *Los Angeles Times*, May 2, 1992.

201 **"About that black T-shirt"**: Kim-Gibson, *Sa I Gu*.

Chapter 10: 한 Han

203 **"LOOK WHAT"**: David K. Yoo and Darnell Hunt, eds., "Los Angeles since 1992: Commemorating the 20th anniversary of the uprisings" (special issue), *Amerasia Journal* 38:1 (Spring 2012), 51.

204 **"In truth"**: Chang, "Legacy project."

204 **During the Joseon Dynasty**: "Manggeon," *Encyclopedia of Korean Folk Culture*, https://folkency.nfm.go.kr/en/topic/detail/6977.

204 **In modern times**: "망건 쓰자 파장된다," Korean Wiki Project, https://www.koreanwikiproject.com/wiki/망건_쓰자_파장된다; and Hyungwon Kang, interview with author, December 20, 2022.

204 **"Since then, we promised"**: Chang, "Legacy project."

204 **"I feel so lonely"**: Jung Hui Lee, "Reflection on the death of my beloved son," 120.

205 **"He always took care"**: Jung Hui Lee, "Reflection on the death of my beloved son," 120.

205 **"Right now, it doesn't"**: Patricia Smith, Diego Ribadeneira, Lynda Gorov, and Tom Mashberg, "A city mourns: Profiles of four killed by riots," *Boston Globe*, May 5, 1992; and John Ridley, *Let It Fall*.

205 **"One of the pivotal"**: John H. Lee, interview with author, May 2, 2022. All quotes from John H. Lee are from author interviews unless otherwise noted.

206 **"We reporters of color"**: Grace Lee, "K-Town '92: Los Angeles 1992—Who gets to tell the story?" (video), 2017, https://ktown92.com.

207 **"You have to explain"**: Lee, "K-Town '92."

207 **Edward "Eddie" Travens**: Judy Pasternak and Nora Zamichow, "After the riots: The search for answers—sad task of burying the dead begins," *Los Angeles Times*, May 7, 1992.

208 **Eddie Travens died**: Pasternak and Zamichow, "After the riots."

208 **Travens, whose father**: *Los Angeles Times* Graphics Staff, "L.A. riots by the numbers," *Los Angeles Times*, April 26, 2017.

208 **"Héctor, you go"**: Lee, "K-Town '92."

208 **During the L.A. uprising**: Maria Newman, "After the riots: Riots put focus on Hispanic growth and problems in South Central area," *New York Times*, May 11, 1992; and Ryan Reft, "Policing a global city: Multiculturalism, immigration and the 1992 uprising," KCET, June 2, 2020, https://www.kcet.org/shows/lost-la/policing-a-global-city-multiculturalism-immigration-and-the-1992-uprising.

209 **more than five hundred newsstands**: George Ramos and Tracy

Wilkinson, "Unrest widens rifts in diverse Latino population," *Los Angeles Times*, May 8, 1992; and Newman, "After the riots."

209   **In 1990:** Newman, "After the riots."

210   **"I saw a lot":** Angela Eunjin Oh, interview with author, July 23, 2022. All quotes from Angela Eunjin Oh are from author interviews unless otherwise noted.

210   **Many in the Latino community:** Cora Cervantes and Edwin Flores, "Latinos recall L.A. riots' 30th anniversary and a 'levantamiento,'" NBC News, April 29, 2022.

210   **"Latinos were a very important":** Gustavo Arellano, "He was murdered during the L.A. riots: We can't forget Latinos like him," *Los Angeles Times*, April 27, 2022.

210   **"The number-one":** Daniel B. Wood, "L.A.'s darkest days: Ten years ago today, the worst race riot in US history erupted in Los Angeles. Here, the story is told in three diverse lives," *Christian Science Monitor*, April 29, 2022; and Najee Ali, interview with author, June 8, 2022.

211   **"Did I really":** Eric Manic, "Foreman in Simi Valley trial says riots, 'national hate' stressed jury," *Los Angeles Times*, March 9, 1993.

212   **"This is the worst":** Paul Lieberman and Stuart Silverstein, "Jurors rattled by aftermath; defend verdicts," *Los Angeles Times*, May 1, 1992.

212   **"I've gotten some calls":** Lieberman and Silverstein, "Jurors rattled."

212   **When Radio Korea broadcast:** Min, *Caught in the Middle*, 155.

212   **Protesters carried signs:** Steve Lopez, "Slain Korean"; and Brenda Paik Sunoo, "Out of ashes, solidarity: 30,000 KAs march for peace through K-town," *Korea Times English Edition*, May 11, 1992.

212   **"We don't know how":** Lee, "K-Town '92."

213   영정 사진 **youngjeong sajin:** "Korean funerals," Daily Dose of Korea, https://dailydoseofkorea.tumblr.com/post/180753977154/orean-funerals; and other Korean culture sources.

213   **Marchers carried brooms:** Lee, "K-Town '92"; and Sunoo, "Out of ashes."

213   **Black and Latino marchers:** Irene Chang and Greg Krikorian, "30,000 show support in Koreatown march,'" *Los Angeles Times*, May 3, 1992; and Tracy Wilkinson, "Street drama: Actor Edward James Olmos plays leading role in cleanup effort," *Los Angeles Times*, May 5, 1992.

213   **A group of elderly:** Chang and Krikorian, "30,000 show."

214   **"We want justice!":** Sunoo, "Out of ashes."

214   **"I'm like, 'Oh, this is so beautiful'":** T.C. Kim, interview with author, December 4, 2021. All quotes from T.C. Kim are from author interviews unless otherwise noted.

214   **"God wants people":** David Lin, interview with author, September 15, 2022. All quotes from David Lin are from author interviews unless otherwise noted.

216   **"All my groomsmen":** Mack, interview with author.

216 **"I'm watching all these"**: Carol Kim, interview with author, December 13, 2021. All quotes from Carol Kim are from author interviews unless otherwise noted.

217 **"The Koreans were being"**: Carol Kim, "Legacy project: SaIGu LA riots," YouTube, April 21, 2017, https://www.youtube.com/watch?v=UUxrzHeqPKQ.

218 **"In the aftermath"**: Ted Koppel, *Nightline*, ABC, May 6, 1992, Vanderbilt Television News Archive, https://tvnews.vanderbilt.edu/broadcasts/647291.

219 **"You must have heard"**: Koppel, *Nightline*.

219 **"To which I say"**: Koppel, *Nightline*.

219 **"I'm a die-hard optimist"**: Garry Abrams, "Out of chaos, a new voice: Angela Oh is emerging as a spokeswoman for Korean Americans," *Los Angeles Times*, July 20, 1992.

220 **"She expressed the Korean"**: Abrams, "Out of chaos"; and Rose Kim, "Fighting to end a Korean stereotype," *Los Angeles Times*, July 20, 1992.

220 **"I want to make a statement"**: Koppel, *Nightline*.

220 **U.S. Representative Maxine Waters**: Abrams, "Out of chaos."

221 **someone had spray-painted**: Pasternak and Zamichow, "After the riots."

221 **Five thousand people attended**: Pasternak and Zamichow, "After the riots."

221 **"It didn't need"**: Dunn, "The riot's enduring wounds."

221 **Giant wreaths**: Fruto, "KA fatality."

222 **Mourners held up**: Mee Sook Lee, "Jae Song is gone: What do we have to do now?" *Chronicles of Koreatown*, 126; and Pasternak and Zamichow, "After the riots."

222 **Eddie's friends**: Jung Hui Lee, "Reflection on the death of my beloved son," 120.

223 **"He is gone"**: Jung Hui Lee, "Reflection on the death of my beloved son," 106, 127.

223 **"I keep looking"**: Jung Hui Lee, "Reflection on the death of my beloved son," 119.

223 **An old kimchi jar**: Jung Hui Lee, "Reflection on the death of my beloved son," 120–21.

224 **"Jae Song was reading"**: Jung Hui Lee, "Reflection on the death of my beloved son," 120.

224 **She then found**: Jung Hui Lee, "Reflection on the death of my beloved son," 121.

224 **"I felt like something"**: Jung Hui Lee, "Reflection on the death of my beloved son," 121.

224 ***"Don't say goodbye"***: Lee Seungchul and Kim Feel, "Don't Say Goodbye" (Immortal Songs 2), YouTube, July 6, 2016, https://youtu.be/61Rmbtwoj3E. Lyrics translated by Aerin Park.

224 **"Who can mend"**: Shawn Hubler and John L. Mitchell, "A legacy as complex as the '92 riots," *Los Angeles Times*, April 20, 1997.

Chapter 11: Out of the Ashes

225   **On Monday, May 4:** Dean E. Murphy and Jim Newton, "Bradley lifts curfew tonight," *Los Angeles Times,* May 4, 1992.

225   **"All signs of normalcy":** Eric Brazil, Charles C. Hardy, and Steven Chin, "L.A. breathes a little easier, but peace still held at gunpoint," *San Francisco Examiner,* May 4, 1992.

225   **army troops slept:** "Photos: Scenes from the 1992 L.A. riots," NBC Los Angeles, April 29, 2022, https://www.nbclosangeles.com/news/local/photos-scenes-from-the-1992-la-riots/2880574/.

225   **More than half:** Stuart Silverstein and Ron Russell, "Rampage in L.A. disrupts everyday routine nationwide," *Los Angeles Times*, May 2, 1992; and Maura Dolan and Judy Pasternak, "Riot aftermath: Experts warn of dangers that might be in rubble," *Los Angeles Times*, May 6, 1992.

226   **Koreatown had suffered:** Frank Shyong, "What we got wrong about Black and Korean communities after the L.A. riots," *Los Angeles Times*, April 27, 2022.

226   **More than two-thirds:** Sandy Banks, "The damage went deep: Koreans call the upheaval sa-i-gu, or 4/29—shorthand like 9/11," *Los Angeles Times*, May 1, 2012.

226   **Many people lost their life savings:** Stephen Braun and Sheryl Stolberg, "City returns to work, school," *Los Angeles Times*, May 5, 1992; and *LA Times* Staff, "The L.A. riots."

226   **Their children helped:** Kay Hwangbo, "Relief checks on the way for KA riot victims," *Korea Times English Edition*, May 18, 1992.

227   **More than $2.5 million:** Hwangbo, "Relief checks."

227   **Many store owners, employees:** Sophia Kyung Kim, "KA victims seeking professional help: Post-riot depression," *Korea Times English Edition*, June 8, 1992.

227   **But language barriers:** Grace Galletti, "How the mental health system fails Asian Americans—and how to help," California Health Report, February 2, 2022, https://www.calhealthreport.org/2022/02/02/heres-why -many-asian-americans-dont-get-mental-health-care-and-how-to-help/.

227   **one of the highest suicide rates:** Sam Kim, "Korea's suicide rate rises, remains highest in developed world," *Bloomberg*, September 26, 2022.

228   **"The whole perception":** T.C. Kim, interview with author.

229   **"The roofs are wood":** Pettus, interview with author.

229   **"It was overwhelming":** Cornelius Pettus, interview with author, December 14, 2021. All quotes from Cornelius Pettus are from author interviews.

230   **During the next:** Lajja Mistry, Sam Schwartz, and Randy Vazquez, "Reflections of the L.A. uprising: Scars left behind," *Los Angeles Times*, August 26, 2022.

230   **James Fugate was working:** Livia Albreck-Ripka, "A beloved Black-run bookstore in Los Angeles is closing," *New York Times*, July 1, 2022.

230 **"He looked around"**: James Fugate, interview with author, December 3, 2021. All quotes from James Fugate are from author interviews unless otherwise noted.

230 **The Aquarian Book Shop**: Seth Mydans, "Los Angeles journal: Riot leveled a font of Black culture," *New York Times,* August 5, 1992.

230 **The Aquarian and**: Edward J. Boyer and Andrea Ford, "Black-owned businesses pay a heavy price," *Los Angeles Times*, May 8, 1992; and "History lost," *LA Weekly*, May 14, 1992.

231 **On November 17**: Sophia Kyung Kim, "BKA ends six years in urban trenches," *Korea Times English Edition*, December 9, 1992.

231 **They were a volunteer**: Kim, "BKA ends."

231 **"We need people"**: Jake Doherty, "Black-Korean Alliance says talk not enough, disbands," *Los Angeles Times*, December 24, 1992.

231 **"My dad was trying"**: Erin Aubry Kaplan, interview with author, July 22, 2022. All quotes from Erin Aubry Kaplan are from author interviews unless otherwise noted.

231 **"There are tensions"**: Doherty, "Black-Korean Alliance."

232 **"I met a lot of people"**: Kim, "BKA ends."

232 **The owner of Farm Fresh**: Sophia Kim, "Seeking a dialogue by Koreans, Blacks: Workshop aims for reduced tensions," *Los Angeles Times*, June 8, 1984.

232 **"I worked hard"**: Richard Reyes Fruto, "1 killed, 50 injured and 250 stores looted," *Korea Times English Edition*, May 4, 1992.

232 **A sign on the property**: Penelope McMillan, "Making a grateful pay-back: Watts Market customers pitch in to help out Korean American merchant," *Los Angeles Times*, July 11, 1992.

233 **"We were trying"**: McMillan, "Making a grateful pay-back."

234 **"Mama contradicts"**: Terry, "A multiracial farewell to 'Mama.'"

235 **"We will always love"**: Rhyu, "Dear Mama"; and Terry, "A multiracial farewell to 'Mama.'"

235 **"failed to provide"**: Elaine Woo and Eric Manic, "Daryl F. Gates dies at 83; innovative but controversial chief of the LAPD," *Los Angeles Times*, March 8, 2014.

235 **"Amnesty International's findings"**: "United States of America: Torture, ill-treatment and excessive force by police in Los Angeles, California: Index Number: AMR 51/076/1992," Amnesty International, May 31, 1992, https://www.amnesty.org/en/documents/amr51/076/1992/en/.

235 **"The record on police"**: Lou Cannon, "Gates bids farewell to LADP, leaving legacy of controversy," *Washington Post*, June 27, 1992.

235 **"It was a terrible"**: Richard A. Serrano, "Williams takes oath as new police chief," *Los Angeles Times*, June 27, 1992.

237 **"We love you, Chief!"**: Serrano, "Williams takes oath."

237 **"We will be addressing"**: Serrano, "Williams takes oath."

237 **"I was just trying":** Seth Mydans, "Rodney King testifies on beating: 'I was just trying to stay alive,'" *New York Times*, March 10, 1993.

237 **People lined the block:** Cannon, *Official Negligence*, 423.

237 **"willfully and intentionally":** Dollie F. Ryan, "Four officers face federal charges in King beating," UPI, August 5, 1992, https://www.upi.com/Archives/1992/08/05/Four-officers-face-federal-charges-in-King-beating/3841712987200/.

237 **The jury consisted:** Jim Newton, "Racially mixed jury selected for King trial," *Los Angeles Times*, February 23, 1993.

238 **"I'm not actually sure":** Mydans, "Rodney King testifies."

238 **"I was finally able":** King and Spagnola, *Riot Within*, 101–2.

239 **Gun sales had doubled:** Jessica Cross, "Around L.A., the laying in of arms," *Washington Post*, April 4, 1993.

239 **David Joo, the manager:** Dexter H. Kim, "Gun sales shoot up after riots," *Korea Times English Edition*, May 26, 1992.

239 **The new LAPD:** Cross, "Around L.A."

239 **On April 17:** Jim Newton, "Federal jury finds that Stacey Koon and Laurence Powell violated beating victim's civil rights," *Los Angeles Times*, April 18, 1993.

239 **Koon and Powell:** Jim Newton, "Koon, Powell get two and half years in prison," *Los Angeles Times*, August 5, 1993.

239 **Koon, released in 1995:** John Rogers, "A look at prominent figures in 1992 riot, where they are now," *Associated Press News*, April 27, 2017.

239 **Although they had been acquitted:** Jean-Paul Renaud, "Timothy Wind, jobless and lonely in Indiana, can't move beyond his role in the Rodney King beating," *Los Angeles Times*, July 12, 2004; and Rogers, "A look at prominent figures."

239 **"But I was at peace":** King and Spagnola, *Riot Within*, 103.

240 **On Monday, August 23:** Edward J. Boyer, "Diverse jury chosen for Denny trial," *Los Angeles Times*, August 13, 1993; and "Robbed driver tells of riot melee," *Los Angeles Times*, August 24, 1993.

240 **"I get incredibly":** Craig Fujii, interview by author, December 15, 2021. All quotes from Craig Fujii are from author interviews unless otherwise noted.

240 **"I couldn't tell you":** Edward J. Boyer, "Denny testifies, hugs mothers of defendants," *Los Angeles Times*, August 26, 1993.

241 **"I couldn't quite figure":** Boyer, "Denny testifies."

241 **Three months later:** Jane Hall, "Watson apologizes for Denny assault," *Los Angeles Times*, November 9, 1993.

241 **After five weeks:** Edward J. Boyer and Jesse Katz, "Jury convicts Denny defendants on reduced charges, acquits others," *Los Angeles Times*, October 19, 1993.

242 **"I had a choice":** Curry and Francis, "'Let it fall'"; and Jesse Singal,

"Damian Williams," *Time*, 2007, https://content.time.com/time/specials/2007/la_riot/article/0,28804,1614117_1614084_1614510,00.html.

242   **"I believe in myself"**: Curry and Francis, "'Let it fall.'"

242   **In 1997**: Lelyveld, "Caught up."

243   **a civil suit against**: John L. Mitchell and Shawn Hubler, "Rodney King gets award of $3.8 million," *Los Angeles Times*, April 20, 1994.

243   **The final amount**: King and Spagnola, *Riot Within*, 119, 127.

Chapter 12: 사이구 Sa I Gu

244   **"A riot is the language"**: Martin Luther King Jr., "The Other America," Grosse Pointe Historical Society, March 14, 1968, https://www.gphistorical.org/mlk/mlkspeech/.

244   **newspapers describing**: Daniel King, "The reliably racist cherry-picking of the word 'riot,'" *Mother Jones*, June 1, 2020.

244   **former President Donald**: Katy Steinmetz, "'A war of words': Why describing the George Floyd protests as 'riots' is so loaded," *Time*, June 8, 2020.

245   **Sa I Gu "played"**: Josie Huang, "30 years ago, he talked Koreatown through the unrest of '92," *LAist*, April 29, 2022.

246   **"After January 6th"**: Rep. Andy Kim (D-NJ), interview with author, June 10, 2022. All quotes from Andy Kim are from author interviews unless otherwise noted.

246   **"Admittedly there is prejudice"**: Rep. Marilyn Strickland (D-WA), interview with author, July 15, 2022. All quotes from Marilyn Strickland are from author interviews unless otherwise noted.

246   **"Korean immigrants realized"**: Edward Taehan Chang, interview with author.

246   **"That's when I was reborn"**: *Chosen*, directed by Joseph Juhn (New York: Diaspora Film Production, 2022).

247   **"When you have thirty thousand demonstrators"**: Juhn, *Chosen*.

248   **"We know Mrs. Park"**: Hany Elyamany, interview with author, January 8, 2022. All quotes from Hany Elyamany are from author interviews unless otherwise noted.

249   **"child of Sa I Gu"**: K. W. Lee, qtd. in Carol Park, *Memoir of a Cashier: Korean Americans, Racism, and Riots* (Riverside, CA: Young Oak Kim Center for Korean American Studies, University of California, Riverside): jacket.

249   **On January 15**: Sam Quiñones, "As a legend passes, a Walmart in Compton?" *NewsTaco*, January 12, 2015.

250   **"The genre often"**: Rhiannon Shepherd, "From Compton to Seoul: Cycadelic Records' Kirk Kim builds bridges through hip hop," *Seoul*, July 10, 2017.

253   **Koreatown has become**: Jeong Park and Andrew J. Campa, "Thirty years after it burned, Koreatown has transformed: But scars remain,"

Los Angeles Times, April 29, 2022; and Jay Park and Hit-Boy, "K-Town," track 3 on *This Wasn't Supposed to Happen*, 2019 (video, YouTube, https://youtu.be/8sZMrwM2Cec), and Allyson Tollett, "Top 5 music videos shot in Koreatown," *KTownly*, September 25, 2021, https://ktownly.com/top-music-videos-shot-in-koreatown/.

253   **When BTS played:** Ahh Sung-mi, "Highlights from BTS' 'Love Yourself: Speak Yourself' stadium tour," *Korea Herald*, October 25, 2019.

253   **In 2023, more than 50 percent:** Karla Tatiana Vasquez, "How a Salvadoran market became the soul of a community," *Los Angeles Times*, October 27, 2022.

253   **El Salvador Community Corridor:** Park and Campa, "Thirty years after."

254   **"It's much better":** Michael Martin, "Korean store owner on arming himself for riots," NPR, April 27, 2012, https://www.npr.org/2012/04/27/151526930/orean-store-owner-on-arming-himself-for-riots.

254   **In 1983, 75 percent of the LAPD:** LAPD diversity statistics provided by retired LAPD detective Ben Lee, September 22, 2022; Los Angeles Police Department, "Percentage of sworn officers by sex and race, 1983 to 2020," https://www.laalmanac.com/crime/cr70.php; and "Infographic: LAPD diversity over the years," *Los Angeles Times*, March 28, 2015.

254   **Asian American–Pacific Islander officers:** K. Connie Kang, "Showing the way: Paul Kim becomes LAPD's first Asian American captain," *Los Angeles Times*, January 24, 1996.

254   **"I hope that I":** Shur, interview with author, September 29, 2022.

255   **"One of the best things":** Blake Chow, interview with author.

255   **Ben Lee was promoted:** Ben Lee, interview with author; and Choy, interview with author.

255   **KALEO promotes advocacy:** Ben Pak, interview with author, May 3, 2022; and KALEO, "Homepage," https://kaleousa.org. All quotes from Ben Pak are from author interviews unless otherwise noted.

257   **"Our nation now faces":** *Los Angeles Times* Editorial Board, "An examination of the *Times'* failures on race, our apology and a path forward," *Los Angeles Times*, September 27, 2020.

258   **even though there were no:** Kenneth Reich, "Robert Richardson: Part of team reporting on Watts riots," *Los Angeles Times*, December 25, 2000.

258   **"balanced, comprehensive":** David Shaw, "Times wins a Pulitzer for coverage of riots," *Los Angeles Times*, April 14, 1993.

258   **The newspaper had to recruit:** Hyungwon Kang, interview with author; and Laura Newberry, "K. Connie Kang, pioneering Korean American journalist, dies at 76," *Los Angeles Times*, August 19, 2019.

259   **"[The *Times*] sensationalized":** All quotes from the *Times* Editorial Board, "An examination of the *Times'* failures."

260   **He died of cardiopulmonary:** Richard J. Oppel Jr. and Kim Barker, "New transcripts detail last moments for George Floyd," *New York Times*, July 8, 2020.

260 **a pop culture meme:** Technology and Social Change Research Project, "Memes as vigilantism: The multi-racial right and anti-Black racism," Medium.com, September 16, 2020, https://medium.com/memewarweekly/memes-as-vigilantism-the-multi-racial-right-and-anti-black-racism-f3709477c91a.

260 **"Bring back the #RooftopKorean":** Brittany Wong, "The real, tragic story behind that 'roof Korean' meme you may have seen," *Huffington Post*, June 11, 2020.

260 **"What we see here":** Wong, "Real, tragic story."

260 **"They were merely trying":** Andy Campbell and Matt Ferner, "What photographers of the LA riots really saw behind the lens," *Huffington Post*, April 30, 2017.

261 **So she created:** Hyepin Im, "FACE and civic leaders announce SAIGU 30 campaign at City Hall steps commemorating the 30th anniversary of the L.A. riots," Faith and Community Empowerment, April 5, 2022, https://files.constantcontact.com/00aab2b6001/1c4d1102-cfaa-4ee1-a948-38a57a6d8f57.pdf.

261 **But Im believed:** Hyepin Im, interview with author, March 3, 2022. All quotes from Hyepin Im are from author interviews unless otherwise noted.

261 **"The city has survived":** Brennon Dixson, "3 decades after L.A. riots' violence, leaders call for unity, healing," *Pasadena Star-News*, April 29, 2022.

261 **"At the end of the day":** Dixson, "3 decades."

262 **"Thirty years later":** CBS L.A. Staff, "Community leaders mark 30th anniversary of L.A. riots," CBS News, April 5, 2022, https://www.cbsnews.com/losangeles/news/community-leaders-mark-30th-anniversary-of-la-riots/?msclkid=152681f0b54111ec89c7bda1d049c04a.

263 **"My late father":** "How L.A. is marking 30 years since the 1992 Rodney King verdict," NBC Los Angeles, April 29, 2022.

264 **"You just saw a picture":** Jung Hui Lee, speech at *Korean Times* Sa I Gu conference, Los Angeles, April 20, 2022, recorded by author and translated by Aerin Park.

Chapter 13: 정 Jeong

265 **K. W. Lee once described:** K. W. Lee, "This thing called Jeong," *Korea Times English Edition*, June 21, 1996.

265 **"It is out of a sense":** John H. Lee, "Koreatown: Together, we suffer," *Los Angeles Times*, May 14, 1992.

266 **"Stop trying to parse":** Marcia Choo, interview with author, July 25, 2022. All quotes from Marcia Choo are from author interviews unless otherwise noted.

266 **So Koreans created:** Wilson Wong, "The story behind Sandra Oh's Black Lives Matter jacket and mask at the Emmys," NBC News, September

21, 2020, https://www.nbcnews.com/news/asian-america/story-behind
-sandra-oh-s-black-lives-matter-jacket-mask-n1240634; and Hayley
Maitland, "The delicate embroidery on Sandra Oh's laid-back Emmys
look carries a weighty message," *British Vogue*, September 21, 2020.

267 **the changing demographics:** Jackie Mansky, "How South (Central) L.A.
is forging its future," Zócalo Public Square, July 28, 2021, https://www
.zocalopublicsquare.org/2021/07/28/south-central-los-angeles-future/
events/the-takeaway/.

267 **In February 2021:** Kailyn Brown, "Latasha Harlins' name sparked an
L.A. movement," *Los Angeles Times*, February 1, 2021.

268 **"The people in [this] neighborhood":** Brown, "Latasha Harlins' name
sparked," *Los Angeles Times*, February 1, 2021.

268 **"Now, every time":** Taylor Torregano, "City dedicates South L.A.
park in honor of Latasha Harlins," Spectrum News 1, April 29, 2021,
https://spectrumnews1.com/ca/la-west/human-interest/2021/04/30/city
-dedicates-south-la-park-in-honor-of-latasha-harlins#.

268 **"Candles are my vibe":** Harlins, interview with author.

269 **Jane Oak, an attorney:** Convergence, "Homepage," https://www.tapestry
.la/convergence.

269 **"She's just very bubbly":** David Lin, interview with author.

269 **Paradise Memorial Park in:** Associated Press, "California graveyard in
grave trouble," *Deseret News*, June 21, 1995.

269 **In 1995, one of the largest:** Gary Libman, "Families grieve again after
graves disturbed: Families cope with renewed grief, pain," *Los Angeles
Times*, June 28, 1995; and Sandy Mazza, "A paradise lost," *Daily Breeze*,
October 10, 2005.

270 **For Tasha's forty-sixth birthday:** Paradise Memorial Park visit by
author, January 22, 2022.

270 **he died from:** Associated Press, "George Holliday, who shot the video
of officers beating Rodney King, has died," NPR, September 21, 2021,
https://www.npr.org/2021/09/21/1039236256/george-holliday-who-shot
-the-video-of-officers-beating-rodney-king-has-died.

270 **"I didn't recognize him":** Risen, "George Holliday."

271 **Rodney Glen King continued:** Cannon, *Official Negligence*, 41–42, 565,
567.

271 **"I need to forgive":** King and Spagnola, *Riot Within*, 209.

271 **Glen's death was ruled:** CNN Wire Staff, "Rodney King dead at 47,"
CNN, June 18, 2012, https://www.cnn.com/2012/06/17/us/obit-rodney
-king/index.html; and Dennis McDougal, "Legacy of a flawed martyr,"
Los Angeles Times, June 19, 2012.

272 **"We're all stuck here":** "Rodney G. King's Statement," *Washington Post*,
May 1, 1992.

272 **On March 1:** Janell Ross, "The families of George Floyd and Rodney King

didn't ask to be part of history, but they know they are," *Time*, March 1, 2022; and Faith Abubey, "Two women linked by difficult moments in US history meet for first time," ABC News, April 1, 2022, https://abcnews.go .com/GMA/GMA3/video/women-linked-difficult-moments-us-history -meet-time-83811452.

272   **"I'd say God":** Lora King and her daughter Jailyn, interview with author, May 9, 2022. All quotes from Lora King and her daughter are from author interviews unless otherwise noted.

273   **The Forest Lawn Memorial Park cemetery:** Minda Powers-Douglas, "List of 12 famous people buried at Forest Lawn Memorial Park," Cake, May 13, 2022, https://www.joincake.com/blog/famous-people-buried-at -forest-lawn/.

274   **On the night of April 30:** Author interview with Jung Hui Lee, November 13, 2023, and *Jung Hui Lee, Young Hi Lee, James Kang, Sang Youp Lee vs. City of Los Angeles,* No. BC 079848, pp. 6, 45–46, 50–51 (Superior Court of the State of California for the County of Los Angeles, August 11, 1992), transcript, Stanley Mosk Courthouse, Archives and Records Center.

274   **Edward Jae Song Lee is buried:** Jung Hui and Young Hi Lee, interview with author, July 25, 2022, at Forest Lawn Memorial Park. Korean translated into English by Aerin Park and Hyungwon Kang. All quotes from Jung Hui and Young Hi Lee are from author interviews unless otherwise noted.

276   **In high school:** Jung Hui Lee, "Reflection on the death of my beloved son," *Chronicles of Koreatown,* 122.

Author's Note

277   **Young Sik Yoo was twenty-one years old :** Ancestry, "Homepage," https://www.ancestry.com.

277   **My dad was one of only a handful:** Tennessee Tech University information and resources all from my interviews with Jennifer Dewar, archives assistant, Volpe Library-Archives and Special Collections, Tennessee Tech University, Cookeville, https://tntech.access.preservica.com.

278   **"Your father was gracious":** Kenneth Yoo (Paula Yoo's uncle), in discussion with the author, March 13, 2022. All quotes from Kenneth Yoo are from author interviews unless otherwise noted.

Rising from the Ashes: In Memoriam

291   **12,111 people:** Brentin Mock, "What was lost in the fires of the L.A. riots," *Bloomberg,* April 25, 2017.

291   **10,072 National Guard:** Elizabeth Hinton, "Los Angeles had a chance to build a better city after the Rodney King violence in 1992: Here's why it failed," *Time,* May 18, 2021; and *LA Times* Staff, "The L.A. riots."

291   **2,300 Korean-owned businesses:** Claire Wang, "30 years after 'Saigu':

Korean Americans reckon with L.A.'s past on anniversary of riots," NBC News, April 28, 2022.

291   **Twenty-three of these deaths:** *LA Times* Graphics Staff, "L.A. riots by the numbers."

291   **it is customary to say:** Aerin Park and Hyungwon Kang, interview with author, July 26, 2023. All quotes from Aerin Park and Hyungwon Kang are from author interviews unless otherwise noted.

294   **Ortiz was the last victim:** Christine Pelisek, "25 years later, cops ID the last homicide victim of the L.A. riots—as they now hunt for his killer," *People*, June 7, 2017.

BIBLIOGRAPHY

Abelmann, Nancy, and John Lie. *Blue Dreams: Korean Americans and the Los Angeles Riots*. Cambridge, MA: Harvard University Press, 1995.

Ali, Najee. *Raising Hell: A Life of Activism*. Detroit: Noble Trinity Media, 2021.

Bartoletti, Susan Campbell. *They Called Themselves the K.K.K.: The Birth of an American Terrorist Group*. Boston: Houghton Mifflin Harcourt, 2010.

Boggs, Grace Lee. *Living for Change: Grace Lee Boggs, An Autobiography*. Minneapolis: University of Minnesota Press, 1998.

Boggs, Grace Lee, with Scott Kurashige. *The Next American Revolution: Sustainable Activism for the Twenty-First Century*. Berkeley: University of California Press, 2011.

Buntin, John. *L.A. Noir*. New York: Broadway Books, 2009.

Cannon, Lou. *Official Negligence: How Rodney King and the Riots Changed Los Angeles and the LAPD*. New York: Random House Times Book, 1997.

Castuera, Ignacio. *Dreams on Fire: Embers of Hope—From the Pulpits of Los Angeles after the Riots*. St. Louis: Chalice Press, 1992.

Cha, Steph. *Your House Will Pay*. New York: HarperCollins Ecco, 2019.

Chang, Edward T. *Pachappa Camp: The First Koreatown in the United States*. Lanham, MD: Lexington Books, 2021.

Chang, Edward T., and Jeannette Diaz-Veizades. *Ethnic Peace in the American City: Building Community in Los Angeles and Beyond*. New York: New York University Press, 1999.

Chang, Edward T., and Russell C. Leong. *Los Angeles: Struggles toward Multiethnic Community (Asian American, African American and Latino Perspectives)*. Seattle: University of Washington Press, 1993.

Chang, Edward T., and Carol K. Park. *Korean Americans: A Concise History*. Riverside: Young Oak Kim Center for Korean American Studies at the University of California Riverside, 2019.

Chang, Leonard. *The Fruit 'N Food*. Seattle: Black Heron Press, 2010.

Choi, Roy, with Tien Nguyen and Natasha Phan. *L.A. Son: My Life, My City, My Food*. New York: HarperCollins, 2013.

Cho, John, and Sarah Suk. *Troublemaker*. New York: Little, Brown and Company, 2022.

Coates, Ta-Nehisi. *Between the World and Me*. New York: One World, 2015.

Colbert, Brandy. *Black Birds in the Sky: The Story and Legacy of the 1921 Tulsa Race Massacre*. New York: Balzer and Bray, 2021.

Covey, Herbert C. *Crips and Bloods: A Guide to American Subculture*. Santa Barbara, CA: Greenwood, 2015

Cumings, Bruce. *The Korean War: A History*. New York: Modern Library, 2010.

Davis, Mike. *City of Quartz: Excavating the Future in Los Angeles*. London: Verso, 1990.

Deggans, Eric. *Race-Baiter: How the Media Wields Dangerous Words to Divide a Nation*. New York: St. Martin's Press, 2012.

Dumas, Alexandre. *The Count of Monte Cristo*. New York: Modern Library, 1986.

Fujino, Diane C. *Heartbeat of Struggle: The Revolutionary Life of Yuri Kochiyama*. Minneapolis: University of Minnesota Press, 2005.

Gates, Daryl F., with Diane K. Shah. *Chief: My Life in the LAPD*. New York: Bantam Books, 1992.

George, Lynell. *No Crystal Stair: African-Americans in the City of Angels*. New York: Anchor Books, 1992.

Giangreco, D. M. *War in Korea, 1950–1953: A Pictorial History*. Novato: Presido Press, 2000.

Halberstam, David. *The Coldest Winter: American and the Korean War*. New York: Hyperion Books, 2007.

Han, Woo Sung. *Unsung Hero: The Col. Young O. Kim Story*. Translated by Edward T. Chang. Riverside, CA: Young Oak Kim Korean Center for Korean American Studies, 2011.

Hannah-Jones, Nikole. *The 1619 Project: A New Origin Story*. New York: One World, 2021.

Hartfield, Claire. *A Few Red Drops: The Chicago Race Riot of 1919*. Boston: Clarion Books, 2018.

Hastings, Max. *The Korean War*. New York: Simon & Schuster, 1988.

Hong, Cathy Park. *Minor Feelings: An Asian American Reckoning*. New York: One World, 2020.

Hunt, Darnell M. *Screening the Los Angeles "Riots": Race, Seeing, and Resistance*. Cambridge: Cambridge University Press, 1997.

Hunt, Darnell, and Ana-Christina Ramón. *Black Los Angeles: American Dreams and Racial Realities*. New York: New York University Press, 2010.

Johnson, Robert Lee. *Images of America: Compton*. Charleston, SC: Arcadia Publishing, 2012.

Joyce, Patrick D. *No Fire Next Time: Black-Korean Conflicts and the Future of American Cities*. Ithaca, NY: Cornell University Press, 2003.

Kang, Hyungwon. *Visual History of Korea*. Seoul: Random House Korea, 2022.

Kang, Jay Caspian. *The Loneliest Americans*. New York: Crown, 2021.

Kaplan, Erin Aubry. *Black Talk, Blue Thoughts, and Walking the Color Line: Dispatches from a Black Journalista*. Boston: Northeastern University Press, 2011.

Kendi, Ibram X. *How to Be an Antiracist*. New York: One World, 2019.

———. *Stamped from the Beginning: The Definitive History of Racist Ideas in America*. New York: Bold Type Books, 2016.

Kim, Eric. *Korean American: Food That Tastes Like Home*. New York: Clarkson Potter, 2022.

Kim, Katherine Yungmee. *Images of America: Los Angeles's Koreatown.* Charleston, SC: Arcadia Publishing, 2011.

King, Rodney, with Lawrence J. Spagnola. *The Riot Within: My Journey from Rebellion to Redemption.* New York: HarperCollins Harper One, 2012.

Kochiyama, Yuri. *Passing It On: A Memoir.* Los Angeles: UCLA Asian American Studies Center Press, 2004.

Koon, Sgt. Stacey C. with Robert Deitz. *Presumed Guilty: The Tragedy of the Rodney King Affair.* Washington, DC: Regnery Gateway, 1992.

Kurashige, Scott. *The Shifting Grounds of Race: Black and Japanese Americans in the Making of Multiethnic Los Angeles.* Princeton, NJ: Princeton University Press, 2008.

Lee, Chol Sul. *Freedom without Justice: The Prison Memoirs of Chol Sul Lee.* Edited by Richard S. Kim. Honolulu: University of Hawaii Press, 2017.

Lee, Erika. *The Making of Asian America: A History.* New York: Simon & Schuster, 2015.

Lee, James Kyung-Jin. *Urban Triage: Race and the Fictions of Multiculturalism.* Minneapolis: University of Minnesota Press, 2004.

Lee, Jennifer. *Civility in the City: Blacks, Jews, and Koreans in Urban America.* Cambridge, MA: Harvard University Press, 2002.

Lee, Jennifer, and Min Zhou. *The Asian American Achievement Paradox.* New York: Russell Sage Foundation, 2015.

Lee, Julia. *Biting the Hand: Growing Up Asian in Black and White America.* New York: Henry Holt, 2023.

Lee, Marie G. *Saying Goodbye.* Boston: Houghton Mifflin, 1994.

Lee, Shelley Sang-Her. *Koreatown, Los Angeles: Immigration, Race, and the "American Dream."* Stanford, CA: Stanford University Press, 2022.

Leong, Russell C., Karen Umemoto, and Soo Mee Kim, with Vince Leus. *Sa I Gu: Korean and Asian American Journalists Writing Truth to Power—Lessons from the 1992 Los Angeles Civil Unrest.* Stanford, CA: Stanford University Press, 2022.

Loh-Hagan, Virginia. *What Is Asian-Black Solidarity?* Ann Arbor, MI: Cherry Lake Press, 2022.

Los Angeles Times Staff. *Understanding the Riots: Los Angeles before and after the Rodney King Case.* Los Angeles: Los Angeles Times, 1992.

Magoon, Kekla. *Revolution in Our Time: The Black Panther Party's Promise to the People.* Somerville, MA: Candlewick Press, 2021.

Molinaro, Joanne Lee. *The Korean Vegan Cookbook: Reflection and Recipes from Omma's Kitchen.* New York: Avery/Random House, 2021.

Njeri, Itabari. *The Last Plantation: Color, Conflict, and Identity—Reflections of a New World Black.* Boston: Houghton Mifflin Harcourt, 1997.

Oh, Angela E. *Open: One Woman's Journey.* Los Angeles: UCLA Asian American Studies Center Press, 2002.

Park, Carol. *Memoir of a Cashier: Korean Americans, Racism, and Riots.* Riverside, CA: Young Oak Kim Center for Korean American Studies, 2017.

Park, Kyeyoung. *The Korean American Dream: Immigrants and Small Business in New York City*. Ithaca, NY: Cornell University Press, 1997.

———. *LA Rising: Korean Relations with Blacks and Latinos after Civil Unrest*. Lanham, MD: Lexington Books, 2019.

Peters, Richard. *Voices from the Korean War: Personal Stories of American, Korean, and Chinese Soldiers*. Lexington: University Press of Kentucky, 2004

Ramsey, Donovan X. *When Crack Was King: A People's History of a Misunderstood Era*. New York: One World, 2023.

Reed, Christina Hammonds. *The Black Kids*. New York: Simon & Schuster BFYA, 2020.

Rich, John. *Korean War in Color*. Seoul: Seoul Selection USA, Inc., 2011.

Richardson, Allissa V. *Bearing Witness While Black: African Americans, Smartphones, and the New Protest #Journalism*. Oxford: Oxford University Press, 2020.

Rogers, Dr. Christina S. *Success Comes from You: Success Comes from Creating the Best Life for Yourself*. Los Angeles: Latasha Harlins Foundation, 2021.

Rothstein, Richard. *The Color of Law: A Forgotten History of How Our Government Segregated America*. New York: Liveright Publishing, 2017.

Song, Min Young. *Strange Future: Pessimism and the 1992 Los Angeles Riots*. Durham, NC: Duke University Press, 2005.

Stanford, Karin L. *Images of America: African Americans in Los Angeles*. Charleston, SC: Arcadia Publishing, 2010.

Stevenson, Brenda. *The Contested Murder of Latasha Harlins: Justice, Gender, and the Origins of the LA Riots*. Oxford: Oxford University Press, 2013.

Various. *Chronicles of Koreatown Sa I Gu LA Riot: Honoring the Memory of Jae Song Lee, the Martyr and the Star of Koreatown*. Los Angeles: Edward Lee Memorial Scholarship Foundation, 1993.

West, Cornel. *Race Matters, with a New Introduction*. 25th anniversary ed. Boston: Beacon Press, 2017.

Westhoff, Ben. *Original Gangstas: The Untold Story of Dr. Dre, Eazy-E, Ice Cube, Tupac Shakur, and the Birth of West Coast Rap*. New York: Hachette Books, 2016.

Windom, Saundra Henderson née Chang Bang Sun. *Orchestration*. New York: Wordee, 2021.

Wong, Ryan Lee. *Which Side Are You On*. New York: Catapult, 2022.

Wu, Elle D. *The Color of Success: Asian Americans and the Origins of the Model Minority*. Princeton, NJ: Princeton University Press, 2014.

Wu, Frank H. *Yellow: Race in America beyond Black and White*. New York: Basic Books, 2002.

Yang, Jeff, Phil Yu, and Philip Wang. *Rise: A Pop History of Asian America from the Nineties to Now*. Boston: Mariner Books, 2022.

Yang, Wesley. *The Souls of Yellow Folk: Essays*. New York: W.W. Norton, 2018.

Yoo, David K. *Los Angeles since 1992: Commemorating the 20th Anniversary of the Uprisings*. Los Angeles: UCLA Asian American Studies Center Press, 2012.

Yoon, Africa Byongchan. *The Korean*. Black Yoonicorn Press, 2021.

Yu, Eui-Young. *Black-Korean Encounter: Toward Understanding and Alliance.* Los Angeles: Institute for Asian American and Pacific Asian Studies, 1994.

Zauner, Michelle. *Crying in H Mart: A Memoir.* New York: Alfred A. Knopf, 2021.

Audio/Video Resources

Boyz n the Hood. Directed by John Singleton. Los Angeles: Columbia Pictures, 1991.

Burn, Mother*cker, Burn! Directed by Sacha Jenkins. New York: Showtime Documentary Films, 2017.

Chosen. Directed by Joseph Juhn. New York: Diaspora Film Production, 2022.

Clash of Colors: LA Riots of 1992. Directed by David D. Kim. Los Angeles: DDK Productions, 2012.

Do the Right Thing. Directed by Spike Lee. Los Angeles: Universal Pictures, 1989.

Free Chol Soo Lee. Directed and produced by Julie Ha and Eugene Yi. Chol Soo Lee Documentary, LLC, ITVS, and Center for Asian American Media (CAAM), 2022.

Gook. Directed by Justin Chon. Los Angeles: Samuel Goldwyn Films, 2017.

K-Town 92: Reporters. Directed by Grace Lee. Los Angeles: Center for Asian American Media, 2017.

LA 92. Directed by Daniel Lindsay and T. J. Martin. Washington, DC: National Geographic Partners, 2017.

L.A. Burning: The Riots 25 Years Later. Directed by One9 and Erik Parker. Toronto: Entertainment One, 2017.

Let It Fall: Los Angeles 1982–1992. Directed by John Ridley. Los Angeles: ABC Studios, 2017.

Liquor Store Dreams. Directed and produced by So Yun Um, 2022.

The Lost Tapes: LA Riots. Directed by Tom Jennings. Los Angeles: 1895 Films, 2017.

A Love Song for Latasha. Directed by Sophia Nahli Allison. Los Gatos, CA: Netflix, 2020.

Menace II Society. Directed by the Hughes Brothers. Los Angeles: New Line Cinema, 1993.

Sa I Gu. Directed by Dai Sul Kim-Gibson. San Francisco: Center for Asian American Media, 1993.

Slow Burn: The L.A. Riots, Season 6 (Episodes 1–8). Podcasts. Slate, 2021.

Uprising: Hip Hop and the L.A. Riots. Directed by Mark Ford. Los Angeles: Creature Films, 2012.

Wet Sand: Voices from L.A. Directed by Dai Sul Kim-Gibson. New York: Silence Broken Foundation, 2004.

CREDITS

INDEX